ONE · TF

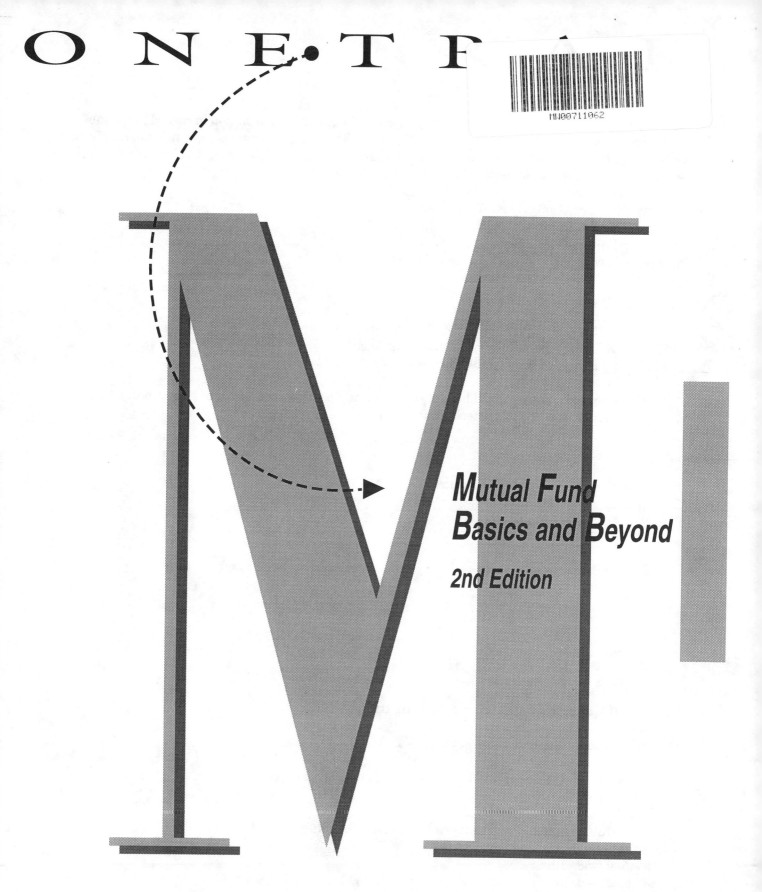

**Mutual Fund
Basics and Beyond**

2nd Edition

Dearborn
Financial Publishing, Inc.

This publication is designed to provide accurate and authoritative information in regard to the subject matter covered. It is sold with the understanding that the publisher is not engaged in rendering legal, accounting, or other professional service. If legal advice or other expert assistance is required, the services of a competent professional person should be sought.

Executive Editor: Kimberly K. Walker-Daniels
Senior Technical Editor: Kenneth R. Walker-Daniels
Managing Editor: Nicola Bell
Associate Development Editor: Laura Schlachtmeyer

Printed in the United States of America.

96　97　98　　10　9　8　7　6　5　4　3　2

Library of Congress Cataloging-in-Publication Data

OneTrak mutual fund basics and beyond. — 2nd ed.
　　　p.　cm.
　　Rev. ed. of: OnTrak mutual fund basics and beyond. c 1994.
　　Includes index.
　　ISBN 0-7931-2292-9 (pbk.)
　　1. Mutual funds.　　I. Dearborn Financial Publishing.　　II. OnTrak mutual fund basics and beyond.
HG4530.O58 1996
332.63'27—dc20　　　　　　　　　　　　　96-13978
　　　　　　　　　　　　　　　　　　　　　　CIP

Contents

Introduction

Welcome to *OneTrak Mutual Fund Basics and Beyond*. This book provides comprehensive mutual fund information for individuals both inside and outside the securities industry.

The popularity of mutual funds has been steadily increasing. One reason is that customers who typically put their savings into certificates of deposit or bank savings accounts are now searching for greater returns than those products currently offer. Simultaneously, an increasing number of banks are offering mutual funds to these same customers and helping them to understand the benefits. For these reasons alone, there are more mutual funds and more mutual fund investors than ever before.

OneTrak Mutual Fund Basics and Beyond presents the essential elements of mutual funds in a logical order to help potential investors feel comfortable investing in them. The text focuses on the characteristics, purchase plans, and risks and rewards of mutual funds. For people who have limited amounts of money to invest or who are learning about investing, mutual funds are often a good addition to a portfolio.

OneTrak Mutual Fund Basics and Beyond is a powerful tool for financial professionals who need to help customers understand the more technical facets of mutual funds. The rules and regulations that govern the investment companies that market mutual funds are complex. The text concentrates on the regulatory constraints of mutual funds, including suitability of recommendations, ethical treatment of customers, and customer accounts and taxation.

Each chapter in the book concludes with a set of questions to test your understanding of the material. Answers with their rationale are also included to strengthen your comprehension. The extensive glossary at the back of the book explains the terminology of investing and mutual funds.

OneTrak Mutual Fund Basics and Beyond may well be the key to making an informed decision about purchasing mutual funds.

1 Investment Company Products

Key Terms

ask price
asset allocation fund
balanced fund
bid price
bond fund
breakpoint
closed-end investment company
combination fund
diversified investment company
dual-purpose fund
expense ratio
face-amount certificate (FAC)
family of funds
growth fund - CAP gAins
income fund - dividends
index fund DoU JONE
Investment Company Act of 1940

investment policy
management company
money-market fund
mutual fund
nondiversified company
open-end investment company
portfolio intermediaries - mANAglmnt co
portfolio turnover
publicly traded fund - co. end fund
redeemable securities - mF
sales load
75-5-10 test
shares of beneficial interest
specialized (sector) fund
underwriting group
unit investment trust (UIT)
U.S. government fund
        L Bond

Overview

An investment company is a *corporation* or a *trust* through which individuals can invest in a large, diversified portfolio of securities by pooling their funds with other investors' funds. By investing through an investment company, individuals can gain some of the advantages large investors enjoy (diversification of investments, lower transaction costs, professional management and more) that the smaller investor might not otherwise be able to achieve.

This chapter describes the different types of investment companies and how they are structured. Areas that will be highlighted include how the companies are established, their distinguishing characteristics, and the risks and rewards they offer investors.

Investment Company Offerings

An investment company is in the business of pooling investors' money and investing in securities for them. The management of an investment company attempts to invest and manage funds for people more effectively than the individual investors could themselves (given the limited time, knowledge of various securities markets and resources that most investors have). Investment companies operate and invest these pooled funds as a single large account jointly owned by every shareholder in the company.

The Investment Company Act of 1940

During the early decades of this century, Congress directed the Securities and Exchange Commission (SEC) to study investment trusts and investment companies, their corporate structure, their investment policies and their influence on the companies in which they invest. This study led to the passage of the Investment Company Act of 1940, providing for SEC regulation of investment companies and their activities. In declaring the necessity for federal legislation, the act of 1940 states:

". . . investment companies are affected with a national public interest in that:

- the securities they issue constitute a significant percentage of all securities publicly offered;
- their process of issuing redeemable securities and their redemption of those securities is continuous; and
- the investing, reinvesting and trading by investment companies constitutes a significant percentage of all transactions in the securities markets of the nation."

The Investment Company Act of 1940 was designed to protect investors from unfair dealings, regulate borrowing by company management and provide investors with current information. The act does not regulate ethical sales practices; that is covered by the Securities Exchange Act of 1934 and the various rules and regulations put forth by the National Association of Securities Dealers, Inc. (NASD) and other self-regulatory organizations (SROs).

Investment Company Purpose

Like corporate issuers, investment companies raise capital by selling shares to the public. Investment companies must abide by the same registration and prospectus requirements imposed by the Securities Act of 1933 on every other issuer, plus more. Because of what investment companies do with the capital they raise, they are subject to stringent regulations regarding the manner, means, methods and conditions under which their shares are sold to the public, which is the subject of the Investment Company Act of 1940, as amended.

Investment companies have one thing in common: they are all *portfolio intermediaries* in the business of pooling the public's money and investing it for them. In the public's mind, an investment company's portfolio managers should be able to outperform the average investor in the market, which is one of the reasons people invest in these managed funds.

Types of Investment Companies

The Investment Company Act of 1940 classifies investment companies into three broad types: face-amount certificate companies (FACs); unit investment trusts (UITs); and management investment companies, which are the most common. The various classifications of investment companies are shown in Figure 1.

Face-amount Certificate Companies

A face-amount certificate is a contract between an investor and an issuer in which the issuer guarantees a payment of a **stated** (or *fixed)* sum to the investor at some set date in the future. In return for this future payment, the investor agrees to pay the issuer a set amount of money either as a lump sum or in periodic installments. If the investor chooses to pay for the certificate in a lump sum, the investment is known as a **fully paid face-amount certificate**. Issuers of these investments are called, naturally enough, face-amount certificate companies.

Face-amount certificates may be backed by specific assets, such as U.S. government issues, VA and FHA mortgages, corporate debt issues or preferred stock. Usually, however, they are backed by bonds that mature when the certificates mature. In either case, principal and interest are guaranteed. When the value of the certificates is paid to the investor at maturity, the investment fund is exhausted.

Face-amount certificate companies continuously offer their shares (or investment contracts). A typical face-amount certificate contract will require the investor to make 20 semiannual payments of $1,000 each over a period of ten years (for a total investment of $20,000). In return, the company will guarantee that, at the end of ten years, it will return to the investor $25,000. Very few face-amount certificate companies operate today because of tax code changes.

Figure 1   Classifications of Investment Companies

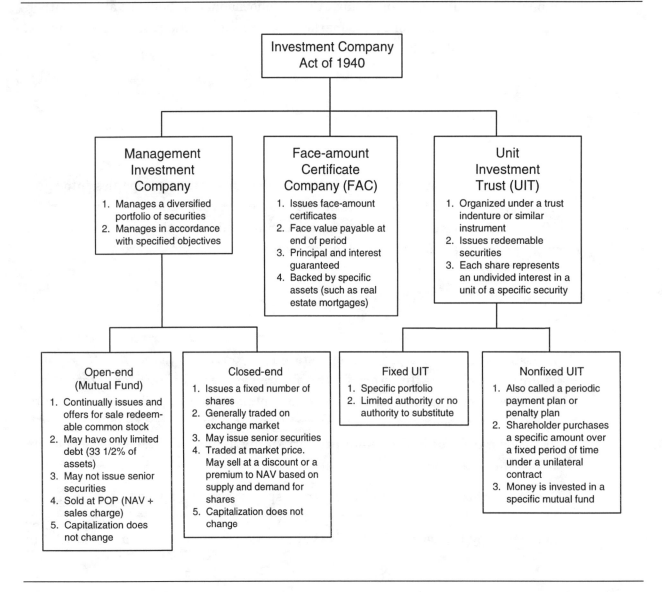

Unit Investment Trusts

A unit investment trust (UIT) is an investment company organized under a trust indenture. The primary characteristics that set UITs apart from other types of investment companies are that UITs:

- do not have a board of directors
- do not employ an investment adviser
- do not actively manage their own portfolios (trade securities)

A UIT functions basically as a holding company for its investors. The managers of a UIT typically purchase an investment portfolio, consisting of other investment company shares or of fixed-income securities (such as government or municipal bonds). They then sell redeemable shares (also known as *units of beneficial interest* or *shares of beneficial interest)* in this portfolio of securities. Each share represents the ownership of an *undivided interest* in the underlying portfolio. Since UITs are not managed, once any of the securities in the portfolio are sold, mature, or are otherwise liquidated, the proceeds must be distributed. Remember, UITs are organized without boards of directors and investment advisers; therefore, they are not able to reinvest proceeds or otherwise manage the trust's portfolio.

A UIT may be fixed or nonfixed. A typical fixed UIT may purchase a portfolio of bonds. When the bonds in the portfolio have matured, the trust is terminated. The nonfixed UIT is often used by investors interested in purchasing units on a contractual basis (a *contractual plan)*. The trust may purchase shares of an underlying mutual fund for the nonfixed UIT portfolio.

Under the act of 1940, the trustee of a UIT is required to maintain a secondary market in the units, thus guaranteeing a measure of liquidity to the shareholders.

Management Investment Companies

The most familiar type of investment company, to most people, is the **management investment company**. These companies actively *manage* a portfolio of securities in accordance with the investment objectives stated in their prospectuses. The single most important distinction between different types of management investment companies is their status as either *closed-end* or *open-end*. Both closed- and open-end companies sell shares to the public; the difference between them lies in the type of securities they sell and where investors buy and sell their shares.

Closed-end Investment Companies

As with many corporations, when a closed-end investment company wants to raise capital for investments, it conducts a stock offering. For the initial offering, the company registers a fixed number of shares with the SEC and makes these shares available to the public for a limited time through an **underwriting group** (the broker-dealers chosen to handle the distribution). When all of the shares that the investment company has registered to sell have been distributed by the under-writers, the public offering period comes to a close. The fund's capitalization is basically fixed (unless an additional issue public offering is made).

Closed-end investment companies are more commonly known as **publicly traded funds**. After the stock is distributed, anyone who wants to buy or sell shares does so in the secondary market (either on an exchange or over-the-counter). Supply and demand determine the price the investor will receive or will have to pay for shares. The **bid** price (or price at which an investor can sell) and the **ask** price (or price at which an investor can buy) for the shares of many larger investment companies are published daily in the financial pages of most major newspapers; these bid and ask prices reflect the open market's current valuation of their shares.

Open-end Investment Companies

An **open-end** investment company (or **mutual fund**), unlike the closed-end com-pany, does not specify the exact number of shares it intends to sell; rather, it registers an open offering with the SEC. With this type of registration, the open-end invest-ment company can raise an unlimited amount of investment capital by continuously selling new shares in its portfolio of investments. By the same token, when investors liquidate their holdings in a mutual fund, the fund's capital shrinks. Because the number of shares the company can offer is not limited, the offering in effect never "closes." Any person who wants to make an investment in—or increase his holdings in—the company buys shares directly from the company or its underwriters at the public offering price (net asset value plus a sales charge, if any).

The shares that an open-end investment company sells fall into a special category known as **redeemable securities**. Instead of buying and selling shares on the open market (like the investors in a closed-end company), investors place both their buy orders and their sell orders directly with the investment company's underwriters. When investors choose to sell their shares, the company itself redeems them at their **net asset value** (**NAV**). For each share an investor sells back (or redeems) the company will send the investor her proportionate share of the company's net assets.

Figure 2 provides a comparison of open-end and closed-end investment companies.

Figure 2   Open-end and Closed-end Investment Companies

Characteristic	Open-end	Closed-end
Capitalization	Unlimited; continuous offering of shares.	Fixed; single offering of shares.
Issues	Common stock only; no debt securities; permitted to borrow.	May issue common, preferred and debt securities.
Shares	Full or fractional shares.	Full shares only.
Offerings and trading	Sold and redeemed by the fund only. Continuous primary offering. Must redeem shares.	Initial primary offering. Secondary trading OTC or on an exchange. Does not redeem shares.
Pricing	NAV plus sales charge. Selling price is determined by a formula found in the prospectus.	Current market value plus commission. Price is determined by supply and demand.
Shareholder rights	Dividends (when declared), voting.	Dividends (when declared), voting, preemptive.

Diversified and Nondiversified

Diversified. In the mutual fund business, advertising the fact that the fund is an open-end diversified investment company is an important selling point. Diversification is a combination risk management technique and investment approach that makes mutual funds popular with many investors. But not all investment companies feature diversified portfolios.

Under the Investment Company Act of 1940, an investment company will qualify as a diversified investment company if it meets the following **75-5-10** test:

- *75%* of total assets must be invested in securities issued by companies *other than the investment company itself* or its affiliates. Cash on hand and cash equivalent investments (short-term government and money market securities) are counted as part of the 75% required investment in outside companies.
- No more than *5%* of total assets can be invested *in any one corporation's* securities.
- No more than *10%* of an outside corporation's *voting class securities* (common stock) can be owned by the investment company.

An example follows of the 75-5-10 diversification test being applied. Assume an investment company (in this case, a mutual fund) has $100 million in assets.

- To qualify as a diversified investment company, the fund must keep at least 75% ($75 million) of the $100 million invested in publicly held securities.
- To ensure adequate diversification, not more than 5% of the $100 million in total assets may be invested in any one publicly held corporation. The maximum investment allowed, in this case, is $5 million (5% of the fund's $100 million in total assets).
- The fund must not own more than 10% of any one company's voting-class common stock. If it is assumed that the total common stock outstanding for a particular company amounts to $40 million, the maximum investment the fund is allowed to make in the company's common stock is $4 million (10% of $40 million).

Nondiversified. A nondiversified investment company, on the other hand, is any company that fails to meet one or more of these criteria. Some investment companies choose to invest their assets so as to concentrate (or specialize) in a geographic area or industry. Investors may be familiar with investment companies specializing in natural resources, precious metals or gold mining stocks, to name a few specialties.

The fact that an investment company chooses to specialize in an industry does not make it a nondiversified company. Even if an investment company has made all of its investments in a single industry, it can still be considered diversified as long as it meets the 75-5-10 test. Figure 3 illustrates the asset distribution requirements that must be met in order to qualify as a diversified investment company.

Figure 3   Diversified Investment Company 75-5-10 Requirement

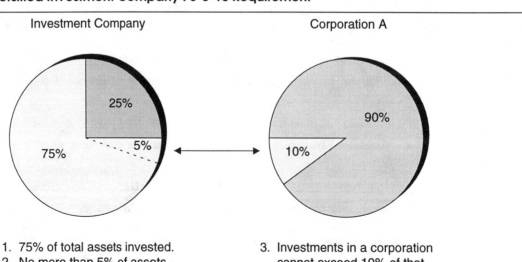

Investment Company   Corporation A

25%   75%   5%   10%   90%

1. 75% of total assets invested.
2. No more than 5% of assets invested in one corporation.

3. Investments in a corporation cannot exceed 10% of that corporation's outstanding stock.

Characteristics of Mutual Funds

A mutual fund pools investors' money and invests it in various securities, as determined by the fund's objective. When an individual invests in a mutual fund, the money is used to purchase more securities for the portfolio.

Each investor in the mutual fund's portfolio owns an *undivided interest* in the portfolio. All investors in the open-end fund are *mutual* participants; no one investor has a preferred status over any other investor. In other words, mutual funds issue only one class of common share; no preferred class of shares or debt can be issued. Each investor shares mutually with other investors in gains and distributions derived from the investment company portfolio.

Each investor's share in the performance of the fund's portfolio is based solely on the number of shares owned. These shares may be purchased in either full or fractional units, unlike corporate stock, which may be purchased in full units only. Because mutual fund shares can be fractional, the investor can think in terms of dollars rather than number of shares owned. For example, if ArGood Mutual Fund shares are $15 per share, a $100 investment will purchase 6.666 shares.

An investment company portfolio is elastic; that is, money is constantly being invested to purchase shares or paid out from the fund when shares are redeemed. The value of the mutual fund portfolio fluctuates as money is invested or redeemed and as the value of the securities held by the portfolio rises and falls. The investor's account value will fluctuate proportionately with the value of the mutual fund portfolio.

Advantages to Investors

Mutual funds (open-end investment companies) offer the investor several advantages. Of primary importance to fund investors is a mutual fund's *guaranteed marketability*. Guaranteed marketability is the ability to sell out of an investment. An open-end mutual fund must redeem shares presented to it by investors at the NAV within seven days (although the company may require a written request for redemption). A redemption transaction executed through a broker-dealer, however, is subject to the SEC's three-business-day settlement rule.

A second advantage offered to investors in mutual funds is *professional portfolio management*. Investment decisions for the funds are made by full-time professional advisers, a luxury few investors can afford when investing independently.

Finally, mutual fund shares offer *diversification*. Mutual funds provide a greater degree of diversification than most private investors are able to achieve independently. Other investor advantages include the following:

- A mutual fund's shares are held by a custodian, which ensures safekeeping.
- The investor has the ability to invest almost any sum at any time he wants because investment companies continuously offer full and fractional shares.
- Most funds allow a minimum investment, often $500 or less, to open an account, which is substantially less than the investment required by most other types of individual securities. Also, once an account is open, many funds allow additional investment for as little as $25.
- The investment company may allow investments at reduced sales charges by offering *breakpoints*. The investor may also qualify for breakpoints through a statement of intention or rights of accumulation.
- The fund may provide for reinstatement of investment. This privilege allows an investor to remove money from an account for emergencies and redeposit the money without paying a second sales charge. Certain rules apply:
  - Reinstatement must be provided for in the prospectus.
  - The investor has only 30 days to reinvest the money.
  - The investor cannot reinstate more than the amount withdrawn.
  - Reinstatement can be used only during the life of the investment.
- The investor retains voting rights similar to those rights extended to common stockholders, such as the right to vote for changes in the board of directors and management functions, including approval of the investment adviser, changes in the fund's investment objective, certain sales charges (12b-1 plans), liquidation of the fund and so on.
- Many funds offer automatic reinvestment of capital gains distributions and dividend distributions without a sales charge.
- The investor is able to liquidate a portion of his holding without disturbing the balance or diversification of the investment. To do so, he submits a written request with a signature guarantee.
- Tax liabilities for the investor are greatly simplified. Each year the fund must distribute to the investor a Form 1099B explaining taxability of distributions.
- The fund may offer various withdrawal plans allowing the investor choices of payment methods upon withdrawal from the fund.

Figure 4 compares common stock and mutual fund shares.

Figure 4   Comparison of Common Stock and Mutual Fund Shares

Common Stock	*Mutual Fund Shares*
Form of ownership in a corporation	Form of ownership in an investment company
Unsecured	Unsecured
Dividends when declared	Dividends when declared
Dividends from corporate profits	Dividends from net investment income
Price of stock determined by supply and demand	Price of share determined by forward pricing—that is, the next price calculated as determined by the fund's pricing policy
Traded on an exchange or the over-the-counter market	Purchased from and redeemed with the investment company; no secondary trading
Sold in full units only	Can purchase full or fractional shares
First security issued by a public corporation	Only security issued by an investment company
High degree of financial risk	Lower degree of financial risk due to diversification of portfolio holdings
Carries voting rights	Carries voting rights
May carry preemptive rights	Does not carry preemptive rights
Gives holders residual rights to assets	Gives holders residual rights to portfolio assets
Not callable	Not callable
Ex-dividend: 2 business days prior to record date	Ex-dividend: typically the day after record date

Investment Objectives

Because the fund is operating with a pool of cash supplied by the shareholders, it is able to diversify to a greater extent than any individual could. The portfolio of a mutual fund may be invested in stocks, bonds or other investment securities. The investments can be diversified by company, industry or investment vehicle.

Once an open-end investment company has decided on an objective, the portfolio can be invested to match the objective. The objective must be clearly stated in the investment company's *prospectus* and can be changed only by a majority vote of the fund's outstanding shares. The potential investor can then shop around to find a mutual fund with an objective similar to the investor's own. With more than 5,000 mutual funds to choose from, finding a match is not difficult.

Diversified Common Stock Funds

Diversified common stock funds are probably the most typical of all investment companies. The portfolio will be made up of a wide range of common stocks.

Asset Allocation Funds

These funds use the techniques of asset allocation in an attempt to provide a consistent return for the investor. These funds will split investments between stocks, bonds and money-market instruments or cash. The advisers of the funds will switch the percentage holdings in each asset category according to the performance, or expected performance, of that group.

For example, the fund may have 60% of its investments in stock, 20% in bonds and the remaining 20% in cash. If the stock market is expected to do well, the adviser may switch from cash and bonds into stock. The result may be a portfolio of 80% in stock, 10% in bonds and 10% in cash. On the other hand, if the stock market is in turmoil or there is uncertainty concerning the market, the fund may invest more heavily in cash, thus reducing its investments in stock.

Balanced Funds

Many funds attempt to combine the objectives of growth and income by investing in different vehicles. Balanced funds invest in stocks for appreciation and bonds for income payments. Some funds take an even more conservative approach by balancing their investments between preferred stock and bonds. In a balanced fund, different types of securities are purchased according to a preset formula designed to be balanced. For example, a balanced fund's portfolio might contain 60% equity securities and 40% debt securities.

Bond and Preferred Stock Funds

If income is a primary investment objective, it is often obtained by investing in bonds. Bond funds may also vary in their approach. Some funds invest solely in corporate bonds. Others, seeking enhanced safety, invest in government issues only. Still others seek capital appreciation by investing in lower rated issues (junk bonds) at high interest rates.

Combination Funds

A combination fund may attempt to combine the objectives of growth and current yield by diversifying its portfolio among companies showing long-term growth potential and companies currently paying high dividends.

Dual-purpose Funds

Dual-purpose funds are closed-end funds that meet two objectives. Investors seeking income purchase income shares and receive all the interest and dividends earned by the fund's portfolio. Other investors interested in capital gains purchase the gains shares and receive all gains on portfolio holdings. The two types of shares in a dual fund are listed separately in the financial pages.

Growth Funds

Growth funds and emerging growth funds invest in equity securities of companies expected to increase in value more rapidly than the overall market. Growth companies tend to retain all or most of their earnings for research and development and reinvest profits in the company rather than pay out dividends. The objective may be long-term capital appreciation, by investing in firmly established growth companies, or aggressive growth, by investing in newly emerging companies and technologies.

Income Funds

An income fund stresses current yield, or income. The fund's objective may be accomplished by investing in equities of companies with long histories of dividend payments (utility companies, blue chip stocks and so on) or in investment-quality bonds. Such funds may sacrifice safety of principal for increased potential income (investing in lower grade corporate bonds, for example). The investor who selects income funds is more interested in current income than in potential growth.

Index Funds

Index funds are invested in a portfolio of securities that is selected to mirror a broad-based market index, such as the S&P 500. An index fund will buy and sell the securities in its portfolio in such a way that the portfolio maintains the same type and weightings of stock as the selected index. Index funds do not attempt to beat the performance of the underlying index by actively managing the portfolio. The fund's performance will track the underlying index's performance, and will rise and fall according to the movement of the market the index tracks.

Turnover of securities in an index fund's portfolio is kept to a minimum. As a result, a portfolio based on an index (a passive management strategy) generally has lower fund management costs than other types of funds.

Specialized (Sector) Funds

Many funds attempt to specialize in particular sectors of the economy or in specific industries. Usually, the funds have a minimum of 25% of their assets invested in their specialties. Examples include mutual funds investing in gold mining stock (gold funds), public utilities funds and portfolios that might be invested in nothing but low-grade (noninvestment-grade) bonds.

Other special situation funds buy for their portfolios securities of companies that may benefit from a change within the company or in the economy. Securities of takeover candidates and other special situations are common investments. Sector funds offer high appreciation potential, but may also offer higher risks to the investor.

Tax-exempt Bond Funds

Tax-exempt funds contain instruments such as municipal bonds or notes that produce income exempt from federal income tax. Municipal bond funds and tax-exempt money-market funds are common types of tax-exempt funds.

U.S. Government and Agency Security Funds

U.S. government funds purchase securities backed by the U.S. Treasury or issued by an agency of the U.S. government, such as Sallie Mae or Ginnie Mae. Investors in these funds seek current income and maximum safety.

Money-market Funds

Money-market funds are usually no-load, open-ended mutual funds, which means there are no sales charges to customers buying shares nor are there liquidation charges for customers selling shares. The management invests the fund's capital in money-market instruments that have high interest rates and short maturities, such as Treasury bills, Treasury bonds with a short time to maturity, commercial paper, bankers' acceptances and certificates of deposit (CDs). The interest rates on money-market funds are not fixed or guaranteed and change as frequently as daily. Interest earned by these funds is computed daily and credited to customers' accounts monthly. Many funds offer draft- (check-) writing privileges; however, checks must normally be written for amounts of $500 or more. The largest expense to investors is the management fee, which is usually around .5%.

The net asset value of money-market funds is set at $1.00 per share. Although this price is not guaranteed, the fund is managed so as to maintain it regardless of market changes. Thus, the price of money-market shares does not fluctuate in response to changing market conditions—that is, the NAV of these funds is not volatile.

Restrictions on money-market fund investments. SEC rules limit certain investments that can be made by money-market funds, and require certain disclosures to investors. These restrictions are:

- The front cover of the prospectus must prominently disclose that an investment in a money-market fund is neither insured nor guaranteed by the U.S. government and there is no assurance that the fund will be able to maintain a stable NAV. This statement must also appear in all literature used to market the fund.
- No more than 5% of the fund's assets may be invested in the securities of any one issuer.
- Investments are limited to securities with remaining maturities of not more than 13 months, with the average portfolio maturity not exceeding 90 days.
- Investments are limited to eligible securities determined to have minimal risk. *Eligible* securities are defined as securities rated by nationally recognized rating organizations (Standard & Poor's, Moody's, Fitch and so on) in one of the top two categories (no more than 5% of the portfolio in the second tier of ratings). Comparable unrated securities must adhere to the definition of "safety" as provided by the rating organizations. (Tax-exempt money-market funds are exempt from certain parts of the requirement to invest only in rated securities.)

Comparing Mutual Funds

The funds described previously by no means should be taken to represent the only types of funds available. Objectives will vary according to each fund. With the selection available, the investor should be careful to scrutinize each fund before making an investment.

When comparing funds, the investor should start by defining a personal investment objective. Once an objective has been determined, the investor can select from those funds that most closely parallel that objective. The investor will probably find that there are many investment companies with similar objectives; consequently, a further narrowing of the field will be required.

When comparing funds with similar objectives, the investor should scrutinize the information contained in the fund's prospectus. Items to compare include:

- performance
- costs
- portfolio turnover
- taxation
- services provided

Performance

The investor will want to review the performance of the fund over a period of time, as well as review how well the management of the fund has met the objectives set forth in the fund's prospectus. The Securities Act of 1933 requires that each fund list a history of its performance over the lesser of ten years or the fund's life. These histories are an invaluable source of information because they show the fund's performance in good years and in bad. The ten-year history must show what an investment made at the beginning of the period would have returned if held until the reporting date, which serves as a useful comparison between similar funds.

Naturally, the investor will also want to see how well the management of the fund has met the objectives set forth in the fund's prospectus. For example, a growth fund with a high dividend payout is a fund which has failed to follow through with its investment policy.

Costs

The cost of investing is a critical comparison to make. Sales loads, management fees and operating expenses reduce the return an investor can expect from the investment. Management fees and operating expenses are summarized in the fund's expense ratio.

Expense Ratio

The expense ratio of a fund relates the expenses of operating the fund, such as costs of administration and fees paid to the custodian, adviser or transfer agent, to the net assets of the fund (that is, *the expenses of the fund divided by its average net assets*). Typically, the more aggressive a fund, the higher its expense ratio. For example, an aggressive growth fund's expense ratio is expected to be higher than a AAA bond fund's expense ratio as a result of more frequent trading in the growth fund's portfolio.

Generally for stock funds, the expense ratio is between 1% and 1.5% of a fund's average net assets, for bond funds, the ratio is typically between 0.5% and 1.0%. Funds with expense ratios exceeding these norms are expensive to own. Unless the fund shows superior performance as a direct result of higher management fees, an individual investor is better off in a fund with a lower expense ratio. You will see that the cost of operating a fund reduces the money available to be distributed to shareholders.

Sales Loads

Historically, mutual funds have charged front-end loads of up to 8.5% of the money invested. This charge reduces the amount of money actually invested and "working" in the fund. Not all funds charge the maximum allowable. Many "low-load" funds are available charging between 2% and 5%. Additionally, funds may charge a load on the "back-end" upon withdrawal. Recently, funds have started charging an ongoing fee under section 12b-1 of the Investment Company Act of 1940. These funds deduct a fee to pay for marketing and distribution costs from the assets managed annually.

Regardless of the method used, the sales charge is a cost and reduces the potential return to the investor. However, the charge pays for the services rendered by the offering company. The investor must decide if the cost is worth the service and performance provided.

Portfolio Turnover

Investors pay for the costs of the adviser buying and selling portfolio securities. These costs include commissions or markups (or markdowns) when a security is bought (or sold). The measure used to identify these costs is the portfolio turnover rate. It is not uncommon for an aggressive growth fund to reflect a turnover rate of 100% or greater. In other words, the fund replaces its portfolio annually. If superior returns are achieved, the strategy is working—if not, the strategy is subjecting the investor to undue costs.

Portfolio turnover rates reflect a fund's holding period. If a fund has a turnover rate of 100%, it has held its securities, on average, for less than one year. All gains are therefore likely to be short term and subject to the maximum tax rate. On the other hand, a portfolio with a turnover rate of 25%, has an average holding period of four years and gains will likely be taxed at the long-term rate.

Taxation

Investors in mutual funds pay taxes on gains received by the fund based upon the holding period of the security owned by the fund. Until recently, it did not matter whether a gain was long term or short term—it was taxed at the same rate. Now, however, there is a cap on tax rates for long-term gains. As a result, it is better to receive a long-term gain than a short-term gain.

Services Offered

Mutual funds today make investing simple. The services that funds offer to investors include retirement accounts, investment plans, check-writing privileges, telephone transfers, conversion privileges, combination investment plans, withdrawal plans and others. However, these services cost money; the cost of the services provided should always be weighed against the cost of the services used.

When comparing mutual funds, the goal is to find a fund that is easy to invest in, that matches the investor's objective, and that provides service and performance exceeding those of similar funds and at a lower cost than its competitors.

Review Questions

1. All of the following are purposes of the Investment Company Act of 1940 EXCEPT to

   A. ensure that sponsors and managers of investment companies deal fairly with the public

   B. restrict borrowing by persons in management positions

   C. ensure that investors are provided with current information

   D. promote ethical sales practices in the investment company industry

   L NASD

2. Face-amount certificate companies can include any or all of the following conditions in their contracts EXCEPT

   A. require the payment of a stated sum of money on a fixed date by the issuer

   B. require the payment of stated sums by the purchaser at fixed intervals

   C. provide a return that varies daily based on market fluctuation

   D. provide a fixed rate of return during periods of prolonged market decline

3. A unit investment trust is an

   A. investment contract that represents an obligation on the part of the issuer to pay a determinable sum at a fixed date more than 24 months after the date of issue

   B. investment company that issues redeemable securities, each of which represents an undivided interest in a portfolio's securities, which are professionally selected

   C. issuer who acquires investment securities exceeding 40% of the value of the issuer's total assets

   D. account established and managed by an insurance company under which income, gains and losses (whether or not realized) are credited to or charged against such account

4. An investment company that is not classified as either a unit investment trust or a face-amount certificate company would be classified as a(n)

    A. mutual fund
    B. management company
    C. open-end company
    D. closed-end company

5. All of the following statements are true of a closed-end investment company EXCEPT that it

    A. can redeem its own shares
    B. is a type of management company
    C. sells at the market price plus a commission
    D. may be referred to as a mutual fund

6. Which of the following statements describe(s) an open-end investment company?

    A. It can sell new shares in any quantity at any time.
    B. It must redeem shares in any quantity within seven days of request.
    C. It provides for mutual ownership of portfolio assets by shareholders.
    D. All of the above describe an open-end company.

7. A diversified investment company must invest at least ____ of its assets such that no more than ____ of its assets are in any one company and each investment may represent no more than ____ of the voting securities of the target company.

    A. 50%—10%—5%
    B. 75%—5%—10%
    C. 75%—10%—5%
    D. 100%—5%—15%

8. The portfolio of a diversified common stock fund would MOST likely consist of

    A. all growth stocks within one particular industry
    B. stocks of many companies in many different industries
    C. convertible bonds and other debt instruments
    D. bargain stocks

9.   All of the following statements are true of money-market funds EXCEPT that

    A.   investors pay a management fee
    B.   interest is computed daily and credited to the investor's account monthly
    C.   investors can buy and sell shares quickly and easily
√D.   high interest rates are guaranteed

10.   Your client asks whether he should invest in a particular investment company. You should tell him to check the investment company's

    I.   investment policy
  II.   track record
III.   portfolio
 IV.   sales load

    A.   I, II and III only
    B.   I and IV only
    C.   III only
√D.   I, II, III and IV

Answers & Rationale

1.   **D.**   The Investment Company Act of 1940 was designed to protect investors from unfair dealings, regulate borrowing by company management and provide investors with current information. The act does not regulate ethical sales practices; that is covered by the Securities Exchange Act of 1934 and various rules and regulations put forth by the NASD and other self-regulatory organizations.

(Page 2)

2.   **C.**   Face-amount certificate companies pay a fixed return.   (Page 3)

3.   **B.**   A unit investment trust issues redeemable securities representing an undivided interest in a portfolio of securities that have been professionally selected. A UIT does not actively manage its portfolio. Answer A refers to face-amount certificate companies (FACs). Answer C defines investment companies in general. Answer D describes a separate account but, because the portfolio is managed, the account is set up as a management investment company, not as a UIT.   (Page 5)

4.   **B.**   Management companies are the third classification of investment companies under the Investment Company Act of 1940. Open-end funds (mutual funds) and closed-end funds are subclassifications of management investment companies.

(Page 5)

5.   **A.**   A closed-end investment company does not redeem its own shares. The terms "mutual fund" and "investment company" are often used interchangeably.

(Page 6)

6.   **D.**   An open-end investment company can sell any quantity of new shares, redeem shares within seven days and provide for mutual ownership of portfolio assets by shareholders.

(Page 6)

7.   **B.**   A management company must be at least 75% invested, its investments must be diversified so that no more than 5% of its assets are in any one company and no single investment can represent more than 10% of the voting securities of another company.

(Page 7)

8.   **B.**   A diversified common stock fund will have stocks from many companies and many industries.   (Page 12)

9.   **D.**   Money-market instruments earn high interest rates but the rates are not guaranteed. Money-market funds are typically no-load funds with no redemption fee, but investors do pay a management fee. The interest earned on an investor's shares is computed every day and credited to the account at month end. An advantage of money-market funds is the ease with which shares can be purchased and sold.
                                                                              (Page 15)

10. **D.**   All of these items should be checked when assessing a fund.   (Page 16)

2 Mutual Fund Marketing, Valuation and Taxation

Key Terms

asset-based fee
back-end load
capital gains
capital losses
Class A shares
Class B shares
Class C shares
Class D shares
combination privilege
conduit theory
contractual accumulation plan
dividend reinvestment
dollar cost averaging
earned income
exchange privilege
forward pricing
front-end load

letter of intent (LOI)
lump-sum account
net asset value (NAV)
net investment income
no-load fund
passive income
portfolio income
public offering price (POP)
quantity discount
right of withdrawal
rights of accumulation
right to refund
spread load
voluntary accumulation plan
wash sale
withdrawal plan
withholding tax

Overview

This chapter will introduce some of the terminology used in explaining mutual funds. Understanding how mutual funds are marketed, priced and valued is important to brokers and investors alike. Of particular interest are the types of sales charges, discounts, and purchase and withdrawal plans offered by mutual funds.

Investors tailor decisions to take advantage of current tax structures, but must remain flexible enough to change as the laws change. Taxes levied by states and cities are less imposing than federal taxes, so investors spend more time and energy trying to minimize the impact of federal taxes.

Mutual Fund Marketing

Many words acquire new meanings when used in the securities industry. In order to understand the various rules and regulations covering sales charges, it is necessary to become familiar with the terms, interpretations and definitions used by the various regulatory organizations.

What follows is a brief glossary of the terms and phrases that will be encountered most frequently in any discussion of sales charges.

Definitions

Member. Any individual, partnership, corporation or other legal entity admitted to membership in the National Association of Securities Dealers, Inc. (NASD). Membership status with the NASD is independent of a broker-dealer's registration requirements with the Securities and Exchange Commission (SEC).

Nonmember. Any individual, partnership, corporation or other legal entity that has not been admitted to membership in the NASD, whether or not that person or company is registered as a broker-dealer with the SEC or other self-regulatory organizations (SROs). Among those falling into the category of nonmembers are:

- the public;
- broker-dealers who have been expelled from membership, who have had their membership suspended (they are nonmembers during the period of suspension but are automatically reinstated to membership after termination of the suspension period) or whose SEC registrations have been revoked;
- broker-dealers who have tendered their resignations from membership to the NASD; and
- members of a securities exchange, such as the New York Stock Exchange (NYSE), unless they also become NASD members.

The distinction between members and nonmembers is critical to understanding the way in which sales charges and discounts are to be applied, as well as to most other aspects of broker-dealer interaction.

Selling syndicate. An association of member broker-dealers formed to distribute an issue of securities to the public. The syndicate members are required to make a firm financial commitment as to the amount of securities each will purchase.

Selling group. An association formed in connection with a public offering to distribute an issue of securities to the public. No financial commitment to purchase a predetermined amount of the security offering is required. Each member of the group may elect to purchase as few or as many shares of an issue as that member desires to handle.

Sales load. The sales load (or sales charge) on an investment company transaction is the difference (or spread) between the public offering price (POP) of the security and its net asset value (NAV). Members of the selling syndicate or group are entitled to purchase investment company shares at a discount from the offering price. The shares are then resold to the public at the POP described in the prospectus. That part of the spread between the NAV and the POP that the broker-dealer keeps is known as the *concession*.

Customer. Any individual, person, partnership, corporation or other legal entity that is not a broker or dealer (i.e., the public).

Person. The word "person" is used frequently throughout securities law, and the principal must understand the exact meaning it has assumed in securities rules and regulations. In all cases, *person* includes any natural person, partnership, corporation, association or other legal entity. Included in the definition of "person" are:

- any individual;
- a joint account held by a combination of an individual, spouse and/or children; and
- a trustee or other fiduciary purchasing for a single trust, estate or fiduciary account.

The definition of "person" *does not* include:

- a group of individuals who combine funds in order to purchase investments (investment clubs);
- the trustee, agent, custodian or other representative of such a group;
- a company that has been in existence for less than six months with no purpose other than to purchase redeemable securities of a registered investment company at a discount; or
- any group of individuals whose sole common ground is that its participants are credit card holders, insurance policy holders or clients of an investment adviser.

Methods of Marketing Mutual Fund Shares

The 1940 act provides for price setting by a securities association such as the NASD. The NASD is charged with setting a minimum price at which members of the association can purchase investment company shares and a maximum price at which members may sell shares. This minimum and maximum price must bear a relationship to the current NAV of the investment company share.

An NASD member may purchase open-end investment company shares from an underwriter at a discount from the POP under certain conditions.

- The underwriter (sponsor) for the issuer (open-end fund) must be an NASD member.
- The broker-dealer buying the shares must be an NASD member.
- The securities must be used to fill a client's order or must be for the broker-dealer's own investment account (shares cannot be purchased for inventory).
- At the time of the sale, a written sales agreement must be in effect between the issuer and the broker-dealer.

If any one of these conditions is not satisfied, the transaction must be completed at the POP. The selling broker-dealer will not qualify for the member-to-member discount.

A fund can use any number of methods to market its shares to the public. A discussion of some of the marketing methods used by various firms follows.

Fund to Underwriter to Dealer to Investor

An investor gives an order for fund shares to a dealer. The dealer then places the order with the underwriter. To fill the order, the fund sells shares to the underwriter at the current NAV. The underwriter sells the shares to the dealer at the NAV plus the underwriter's concession (or at the public offering price less the dealer's allowance or discount). The dealer then sells the shares to the investor at the full POP.

Fund to Underwriter to Investor

An investor gives an order for fund shares to the underwriter (the underwriter acts as the dealer and uses its own sales force to sell shares to the public). To fill the order, the fund sells shares to the underwriter at the current NAV. The underwriter then adds the sales charge and sells the shares to the investor at the full POP. The sales charge is split among the various salespersons (underwriter as dealer, registered reps and so on).

Fund to Investor

Some funds sell directly to the public without the use of an underwriter or a sales force and without a sales charge. If an open-end investment company distributes shares to the public directly—that is, without the services of a distributor—and the fund offers its shares for sale at no load (without a sales charge) the fund is called a **no-load fund**. The fund pays all sales expenses.

Fund to Underwriter to Plan Company to Investor

Organizations that sell contractual plans for the periodic purchase of mutual fund shares are called *plan companies*. The mutual fund shares are purchased by the plan company and held in trust for the individual purchasing shares under the periodic payment plan. The maximum sales charge for contractual plans is 9% over the life of the plan.

Sales at the Public Offering Price

Any sale of fund shares to a *customer* (a member of the general public who is *not* a member of the NASD) must be made at the **public offering price** (**POP**). The route this sale takes (whether directly from the fund to the customer, from the fund through a dealer to the customer, etc.) is not important—the nonmember customer must be charged the POP. Only an NASD member acting as a dealer or an underwriter may purchase the fund shares at a discount from the issuer.

Determining the Value of Mutual Fund Shares

The act of 1940 requires mutual funds to calculate the value of the fund shares at least once per business day (because purchase and redemption prices are based on the NAV of the shares). Although funds may calculate the value more often, most wait until after the close of the NYSE (4:00 pm EST) before making their calculation.

Shares are purchased (or redeemed) at the NAV next determined after the request to purchase (or redeem) is received by the fund, a process known as **forward pricing**. Purchases are made at the NAV *plus* any sales charge and redemptions are made at the NAV *minus* any redemption fee. Funds vary in the amount of their purchase or redemption fees.

Net Asset Value per Share

A fund's NAV is the price on which sales of new shares to investors is based. The actual price is referred to as the POP, which is equal to the NAV plus a sales charge. When a customer sells, the liquidation price is always equal to the current NAV. To determine the NAV per share, the custodian bank totals the value of all assets and subtracts all liabilities, which results in the total NAV of the fund. The *NAV per share* is determined by dividing the total net assets by the number of shares outstanding.

$$\text{Assets (Cash + Current value of securities)} - \text{Liabilities} = \text{NAV of fund}$$

$$\frac{\text{NAV of fund}}{\text{Number of shares outstanding}} = \text{NAV per share}$$

To illustrate, assume that a mutual fund has $47.6 million in total assets and $7 million in total liabilities, with 2.5 million shares outstanding. The NAV per share would be $16.24:

$$\frac{\$47.6 \text{ million} - \$7 \text{ million}}{2.5 \text{ million shares}} = \$16.24$$

In working with NAV calculations, a fund's total assets include everything of value owned by the fund, not just the investment portfolio. This is why a mutual fund's NAV is analogous to a publicly owned corporation's book value.

Changes in NAV

The NAV can change daily because of changes in the market value of the fund's portfolio. If the number of shares remains constant while the portfolio value increases, the NAV will also increase. Likewise, if the value of the portfolio declines and the number of shares remains constant, the NAV will also decline.

The appreciation or depreciation of portfolio assets is also called *unrealized gain* or *loss*. For example, if the fund holds DWQ stock that it purchased for $100 per share and the market price of the stock increases to $110, the value of DWQ has appreciated. This appreciation is reflected in the fund's NAV. The gain is said to be unrealized because the fund did not sell the stock.

The events that may change a fund's NAV per share include but are not limited to:

- an *increase* in the NAV per share *if* portfolio securities increase in value or the portfolio receives income (interest on debt) from the securities held in the portfolio;
- a *decrease* in the NAV per share *if* portfolio securities decrease in value or portfolio income or gain is paid out to shareholders (dividends or gains distributions); and
- *no change* in the NAV per share *if* there is a sale (issuance) or redemption of fund shares or if there is a sale or purchase of portfolio securities (even if a previously unrealized gain or loss is realized). In these circumstances, the fund is exchanging securities for cash. The total net assets, therefore, remain unchanged.

An example may illustrate this last point more clearly. If the ArGood Mutual Fund has assets of $100 and ten shares outstanding, the NAV per share would be $10. If an investor wanted to purchase ten shares of ArGood Fund, excluding sales charges, the shares would cost $100. Now the fund has 20 shares outstanding, and because the fund receives the $100 for the shares purchased, it has assets of $200. The NAV per share remains at $10 ($200 ÷ 20 shares = $10 per share).

What has changed with this transaction is the proportionate ownership in the fund. Whereas prior to the sale of the new shares the ten shares outstanding represented a 100% ownership of the fund, ten shares now represent only a 50% ownership in the fund.

Sales Charges

As mentioned previously, the underwriter (or sponsor) is the key sales organization hired by the investment company. The underwriter is compensated for distributing the fund's shares by adding a sales charge to the NAV of the shares sold.

The NASD prohibits its members from assessing sales charges *in excess of 8.5%* of the POP on mutual funds purchases by customers. Broker-dealers are free to charge lower rates if they specify these rates in the prospectus, but they must never charge more than the 8.5% maximum.

Closed-end (publicly traded) funds do not carry a sales charge. The investor pays a brokerage commission to buy or to sell or a markup or markdown if a principal transaction is being executed.

All sales commissions and expenses are paid from the sales charges collected. Sales expenses include commissions for the managing underwriter, dealers, brokers and registered representatives, and all advertising and sales literature expenses. In most open-end investment companies, the underwriter is responsible for preparing sales literature because it is best equipped to prepare the literature in compliance with SEC rules and regulations.

Classes of Fund Shares

Mutual funds offer several classes of shares that allow the investor the opportunity to select the type of sales charge when investing in a mutual fund. The most common class types are referred to as *Class A, Class B, Class C* or *Class D* shares.

Class A shares have a *front-end load*—that is, the charge is paid at purchase; the charge is the difference between the purchase price and the net amount invested.

Class B shares have a *back-end load*—that is, the charge is paid at redemption; the charge is a contingent deferred sales load.

Class C shares have a *level load*—that is, the charge is an annually paid asset-based fee.

Class D shares have both an asset-based fee and a contingent deferred sales charge.

The class of share determines the type of sales charge only; all other rights associated with ownership of mutual fund shares remain the same across each class.

Front-end Loads

As defined by the NASD, front-end sales charges are the charges included in a fund's POP. The sales charges are added to the NAV of the shares at the time the investor purchases the shares. Front-end loads are the most common way of paying for the distribution services provided by a fund's underwriter. The bulk of this section will focus on calculation of this payment—the difference between the NAV and the POP.

Back-end Loads

Back-end sales loads (contingent-deferred loads) are those charged at the redemption of mutual fund shares or variable contracts. The sales load is a *declining percentage charge* that is reduced *annually* (for example, 8% the first year, 7% the second, 6% the third, etc.) and that is applied to the proceeds of any shares sold in that year. The back-end load is usually structured so that it has dropped to zero after an extended holding period (up to eight years), and the sales load schedule is specified in the fund's prospectus. For example, assume that ArGood Mutual Fund charges a back-end load and reduces it annually according to the following schedule:

Percentage	Year
8%	One
7%	Two
6%	Three
5%	Four
3%	Five
1%	Six
0%	Seven

Assuming that the POP for ArGood Mutual Fund shares is $10, an investment of $1,000 into the fund will purchase 100 shares. Should the investor decide to liquidate after six months (assuming there has been no change in NAV), the money returned will be $920 ($1,000 less the 8% back-end load of $80 equals $920). If the investor doesn't redeem the shares until the fifth year (again assuming there has been no change in NAV), he will receive $970 for the shares ($1,000 less the 3% back-end load of $30 equals $970).

12b-1 Asset-based Fees

An exception to the provision disallowing funds to act as distributors for their own fund shares is allowed under section 12b-1 of the Investment Company Act of 1940. Under this section, a company may collect a fee for promotion, sale or another activity in connection with the distribution of its shares. The fee is determined annually as a flat dollar amount or as a percentage of the company's average total NAV during the year. There are certain requirements:

- The percentage of net assets charged must be reasonable (typically 1/2% to 1% of the net assets). This annual fee cannot exceed 8.5% of the offering price on a per-share basis.
- The fee must reflect the anticipated level of distribution services.

The payments represent charges that would have been paid to a third party (underwriter) had sales charges been negotiated for sales promotion, services and related activities.

Approval. The 12b-1 plan must be approved initially and reapproved at least annually by a majority of the outstanding voting securities, the board of directors and those directors who are not interested persons of the company.

No-load Funds

If an open-end investment company distributes its shares to the public directly (i.e., without using a distributor), the fund must offer its shares for sale *with no load*—that is, without a sales charge. The shares are offered to the public at the fund's NAV).

Misuse of no-load terminology. A fund or contract that has a deferred sales charge or an asset-based 12b-1 fee of more than .25 of 1% of average net assets may not be described as a no-load fund. To do so violates the NASD's Rules of Fair Practice; the violation is not alleviated by disclosures in the fund's or contract's prospectus.

Mutual Fund Pricing

Closed-end investment companies (publicly traded funds) are bought and sold at market prices either on an exchange or in the OTC market—the same as corporate stock. Historically, closed-end funds trade below their book value, which is referred to as *NAV* when speaking of investment company securities.

In contrast, open-end investment company shares (mutual funds) are bought through broker-dealers that are authorized distributors of the fund and are sold as public offering securities at a fixed price (based on the NAV plus a sales charge). On the other side of the market, if a customer holding mutual fund shares wants to sell, normally the shares are tendered for redemption (at current NAV) rather than sold in the open market. Many mutual fund principal underwriters will buy shares from customers who want to sell in OTC transactions as an accommodation. But the price on such transactions is always based on the current NAV, not on an open market price.

Pricing Management Company Shares

The formula for determining the POP of mutual fund shares is:

$$\text{NAV} + \text{Sales charge (\$ amount)} = \text{Offering price}$$

The sales charge represents the money received by the underwriter for distributing fund shares. The charge collected includes the underwriter's concession and dealer discounts (if any) and pays for sales literature and advertising.

The basic formula for determining the sales charge on mutual fund shares is:

$$\text{Offering price} - \text{NAV} = \text{Sales charge (\$ amount)}$$

A mutual fund prospectus must contain a formula that explains how the fund computes the NAV and how the sales charge is added. The prospectus should also explain how often the fund makes these calculations.

Often, a representative will know only the NAV and sales load percentage of a mutual fund share. To determine the POP, divide the NAV by the complement of the sales load (100% − SL%). The formula is as follows:

$$\frac{\text{Net asset value}}{100\% - \text{Sales charge}\%} = \text{Public offering price}$$

It is important to use this formula because the sales charge is always based on the POP, not the NAV.

For example, if a fund's NAV is $10 per share and the sales charge is 7%, to calculate the POP divide the NAV by the complement of the sales load (100% − 7% = 93%, or .93); an NAV of $10 divided by 93% equals a POP of $10.75. In another example, if the NAV is $20 per share and the sales charge is the maximum 8.5%, the POP will be: $20 ÷ (100% − 8.5%) = $21.86.

Because of the possible high front-end sales charge, investment in mutual funds is recommended as a long-term investment. Short-term trading is considered an unsuitable practice.

Computing the Sales Charge Percentage

When the NAV and the POP are known, the sales charge percentage included in the POP can be determined this way:

$$\text{POP} - \text{NAV} = \text{Sales charge (\$ amount)}$$

$$\frac{\text{Sales charge (\$ amount)}}{\text{POP}} = \text{Sales charge \%}$$

For example, if the POP is $43.70 and the NAV is $40 per share, the sales charge percentage is calculated as follows:

$$\$43.70 - \$40.00 = \$3.70 \text{ Sales charge \$ amount}$$

$$\$3.70 \div \$43.70 = 8.5\% \ (8.46\%) \text{ Sales charge \%}$$

Reductions in the Permitted Maximum Sales Charge

The permitted maximum sales charge is reduced from 8 1/2% if certain provisions are not offered by the investment company. To qualify for the maximum 8 1/2% sales charge, the investment company must offer all of the following:

- automatic reinvestment of income distributions at net asset value (no sales charge);
- a scale of reduced sales charges for lump-sum investments; and
- rights of accumulation.

Dividend reinvestment. Dividend reinvestment must be made available to any person who requests such reinvestment. The company does have the right to limit the availability of dividend reinvestment to holders of securities with a minimum stated value (minimum not to exceed $1,200).

Quantity discounts. If quantity discounts are not made available to any person in terms at least as favorable as the schedules established for rights of accumulation, the maximum sales charge on any transaction will also be reduced.

Rights of accumulation. Rights of accumulation or discounts for cumulative purchases must be made available to any person for a period of not less than ten years from the date of first purchase according to a schedule established by the act of 1940. If rights of accumulation are not made available under terms at least as favorable as in the established discount schedules, the maximum sales charge on any transaction will be reduced accordingly.

Sales Charges and Quantity Discounts

Like most other businesses, open-end investment companies encourage large investments by offering discounts. The principle of *economy of scale* would dictate that the purchaser of one pair of shoes will pay more per pair than the purchaser of 1,000 pairs of shoes. The same is true for mutual fund share purchases. For example, there may be one sales charge percentage for investing $500 and a different sales charge percentage for investing $100,000, so that the sales charge would be considerably less per dollar of investment for the person investing $100,000.

Breakpoints

The schedule of discounts offered by a mutual fund is called the fund's **breakpoints**. Breakpoints are available to any person. The term "person," for this purpose, has a very loose definition. For example, most investment companies consider a family unit to be one person. However, a father and his 35-year-old son would not be considered a family unit qualifying for reduced sales charges because only minor children may be included in the family unit. Moreover, investment clubs or associations formed for the purpose of investing do not qualify for breakpoints. The following is an example of a breakpoint schedule:

Purchases		Sales Cost
$1 to $9,999	=	8 1/2%
$10,000 to $24,999	=	7 1/2%
$25,000 to $49,999	=	7%
$50,000 plus	=	6 1/2%

There are several ways an investor can qualify for breakpoints. As discussed, a large lump-sum investment would be one method. Mutual funds offer additional incentives for the investor to continue to invest and qualify for breakpoints, namely the statement of intention and rights of accumulation.

Statement of Intention (Letter of Intent)

Investors who do not have a large enough amount of money to invest at their initial purchase to qualify for a breakpoint may file a **letter of intent** (**LOI**). In the LOI, they indicate their intent to invest the additional funds necessary to reach the breakpoint at some time during the next 13 months.

The LOI is a unilateral contract that is binding on the fund only. The customer must complete the investment in order to qualify for the reduced sales cost, and the fund will hold the extra shares purchased from the reduced sales load in escrow. If the client deposits the money to complete the LOI, he receives the escrowed shares. Appreciation and reinvested dividends do not count towards the contract amount.

Assume a mutual fund offers breakpoints as follows:

Investment		Sales Charge
$1 to $9,999	=	8 1/2%
$10,000 to $24,999	=	7%
$25,000 to $49,999	=	6 1/2%

A client investing $9,000 is just short of the $10,000 breakpoint. In such a situation, a letter of intent may be an option. This statement of intention, promising to invest an amount qualifying for the breakpoint (in this case, an additional $1,000) within 13 months from the date of the letter, will allow the investor to qualify currently for the reduced sales charge. Each investment is charged the appropriate sales load at the time of purchase.

The letter is a unilateral contract, but the customer must complete the letter in order to receive the reduced load. The fund will hold in escrow some of the shares purchased because of the reduced load. If the client deposits the money to complete the letter, she receives the escrowed shares.

If at the end of the 13-month period the client has not completed the letter, she will be given the choice of sending a check for the difference in sales charges or cashing in enough of the escrowed shares to pay the difference.

Backdating the Letter

Because most investment companies are eager for people to become large investors, a fund often permits the client to sign a letter of intent as late as the 90th day after a purchase. The letter of intent is then backdated to the date of the original purchase. This means that if a client decides to sign the letter of intent after 60 days, she will have 11 months in which to complete the letter. The LOI may be backdated by up to 90 days to include prior purchases, but may not cover more than 13 months in total.

Rights of Accumulation

Rights of accumulation, like letters of intent, allow the investor to qualify for reduced sales charges. The client may qualify for reduced loads any time the aggregate value of shares previously purchased and shares currently being purchased in the account is over a breakpoint. For the purpose of qualifying for breakpoints, the investment company will base the quantity of securities owned on:

- the current value of the securities at either NAV or POP;
- total purchases of such securities at the actual offering price; or
- the higher of current NAV or the total of purchases made to date (typically how it is valued).

Assume an investment company offers breakpoints as follows:

Investment		Sales Charge
$1 to $9,999	=	8 1/2%
$10,000 to $24,999	=	7%
$25,000 to $49,999	=	6 1/2%

A client who originally invested $10,000, the value of which is currently $15,000, now wishes to invest an additional $10,000. Under rights of accumulation, the client will be charged 6 1/2% on the additional $10,000 investment. The original sales charge on the initial investment is not adjusted. Most funds set no limitations on the amount of time during which an investor can qualify for breakpoints under rights of accumulation.

Combination Privilege

Funds that have the same principal underwriter may grant an investor the privilege of combining separate investments in two or more funds under the same management towards a breakpoint. In this way, the investor would qualify for a reduced sales charge on his total investments.

For example, Randy Bear has invested $10,000 in the ACE Growth Fund for retirement and $10,000 in the ACE Income Fund for his children's education. The underwriter may offer Randy the privilege of combining the two separate investments into one investment totaling $20,000 for the purpose of calculating the sales charge. If the fund offers this privilege, it will be stated in the fund's prospectus.

Notifying Shareholders of Reductions in Sales Load

A mutual fund that grants any reduction in sales load to shareholders must notify all shareholders of this at least once a year.

Exchanges Within a Family of Funds

Sponsors frequently offer more than one fund and refer to these multiple offerings as their *family of funds*. One way that sponsors encourage customers to place additional money in their funds is by offering exchange (conversion) privileges within the family of funds.

Exchange privileges allow an investor to convert the value of shares held in one fund for an equal value of those of another in the same family. Some funds allow an investor to make this exchange with a phone call. The advantage to the investor of making an exchange within a family of mutual funds is that it is often accomplished without incurring an additional sales charge. (Keep in mind that any exchange of funds is considered a sale for tax purposes.)

As with any other aspect of securities sales, certain rules apply:

- Any purchases may not exceed the proceeds generated by the sale (or redemption) of the other fund.
- The redemption may not involve a refund of sales charges.
- The sale (or exchange) must take place within 30 days after the redemption.
- The sales personnel and dealers must receive no compensation of any kind from the reinvestment.

Redemption of Fund Shares

Forward Pricing

Under the 1940 act, an open-end investment company must redeem shares tendered to it *within seven days* of receipt of a *written request* for redemption (or, if the fund certificates are held by the customer, the date the certificates and instructions to liquidate arrive at the custodian). The customer's signature on the written request must be guaranteed. The price at which shares are redeemed is the NAV, which must be calculated at least once per business day. There are times when the redemption requirement may be suspended:

- the NYSE is closed other than for a customary weekend or holiday closing;
- trading on the NYSE has been restricted;
- an emergency exists that would make disposal of securities owned by the company not reasonably practical; or
- the SEC has ordered the suspension of redemptions for the protection of the securities holders of the company.

Otherwise, the fund must redeem shares upon request.

The redemption price is the NAV next calculated after the investment company receives the redemption request, known as **forward pricing**. For example, if a request to redeem shares were received by the fund today, that redemption request would be held until the fund next calculates the NAV per share. If the request were received after today's calculation had been made, the redemption would occur at the next calculation. (Forward pricing applies to the purchase of fund shares as well.) The fund may charge the investor a redemption fee, which is usually from 1/2 of 1% to 2% of the NAV.

With closed-end (publicly traded) funds, the NAV has no direct bearing on the market price because that price is determined by open market supply and demand. The NAV of a closed-end fund is one of many measuring tools for evaluating whether the current market price of the fund's shares are overvalued or undervalued.

Repurchase Agreement

Under a repurchase agreement, the principal underwriter will accept a wire order from the broker-dealer, and the transaction is completed at the next determined NAV. The dealer may charge a fee for repurchase above and beyond any redemption fee charged by the fund. Repurchase allows the investor to redeem shares immediately. Repurchase is offered by many companies but may be suspended or discontinued at any time.

Cancelation of Fund Shares

Once an open-end investment company share has been redeemed, it is destroyed. Unlike other corporate securities that may be transferred to other owners, mutual fund shares are not resold; they are *canceled*. An investor purchasing mutual fund shares receives new shares.

Mutual Fund Purchase and Withdrawal Plans

Open Account

When opening an account with an open-end investment company, the client will make an initial deposit of at least the minimum amount required by the fund. At this point, the account is open, and the client will determine if fund share distributions are to be received in cash or reinvested. If the client elects to receive distributions in cash rather than reinvesting them, his proportionate interest in the mutual fund will be reduced each time a distribution is made. The client can make additional investments to an open account at any time and without limit as to dollar amount—that is, no such limit is set by law, although each fund may set its own minimums.

For example, Tex Longhorn chooses to receive all distributions in cash, while June Polar elects to reinvest her distributions in shares. Both start with 100 shares. The next time a dividend distribution is made, June purchases more shares. Assuming an NAV of $10 and a dividend distribution equal to $1, June receives ten shares and Tex receives $100 in cash. Now June owns 110 shares, while Tex's account remains at 100 shares. Compared to June, Tex now has a lower proportionate ownership in the fund.

Accumulation Plans

Voluntary accumulation plan. Under a voluntary accumulation plan, the client opens an account and voluntarily commits to additional periodic investments. Many funds offer automatic withdrawal from customer checking accounts to simplify contributions. Most voluntary accumulation plans set up dividend and gains distributions on an automatic reinvestment basis. Because the plan is voluntary, should the client miss a payment, the fund can in no way penalize the investor. The plan may be discontinued at any time by the client. The plan is designed to help the investor form regular investment habits while still offering some flexibility.

Contractual accumulation plan. A contractual plan differs from a voluntary plan in that the investor signs an agreement to invest an agreed upon dollar amount over a specified period of time. Although called a contractual plan, the agreement is binding on the company only; the investor cannot be held to the contract.

Contractual plans may issue periodic plan certificates and use either of two methods of calculating sales charges. The choice is made by the investment company and is indicated in the prospectus. The Investment Company Act of 1940 allows a maximum of 9% in sales charges by contractual plans, although for large investments, the investor may qualify for lower sales charges by meeting breakpoint minimums.

Lump-sum accounts. Lump-sum accounts are also called regular accounts. The investor buys shares in the fund by depositing the entire amount he intends to invest all at once.

Periodic Payment Plans (Contractual Plans)

Periodic payment plans, also called *contractual plans*, enable the investor who would like to accumulate a sum of dollars over a fixed period of time to invest in a mutual fund on a periodic basis (usually monthly). A contractual plan allows an individual to invest an amount that is typically less than permitted under most minimum investment requirements of open-end funds. An investor may begin a contractual plan for as little as $20 per month, compared to typically higher minimum initial investments in an open-end fund. The investor will sign an agreement stating that she intends to invest a fixed number of dollars over a defined period of time. This agreement is not binding on the investor. The term "contractual plan" is really a misnomer because the agreement is unilateral; only the company is bound by the provisions. Finally, because sales charges are so heavy initially in these plans, some states do not allow their sale.

Characteristics of Contractual Plans

Separate products/separate prospectuses. When a contractual plan is sold, two interrelated sales are taking place. First, the customer is agreeing to make periodic payments to a contractual plan company (which is primarily a sales development company). Evidence of this agreement takes the form of a plan certificate issued by the contractual plan company. Second, as periodic payments are made by the customer, the plan company uses the money to buy shares in the mutual fund.

Contractual plan companies are organized as UITs. The customer's monthly payments to the plan buy dollar-denominated units that are credited to the customer's plan account. The dollars represented by these units, in turn, are invested in full and fractional shares issued by the mutual fund. The customer's units represent an undivided interest in the pool of underlying mutual fund shares.

Thus, there is a double sale—the sale of units in the plan account and the sale of shares in the fund. Therefore, two prospectuses exist.

Plan custodian. Plan companies also have their own plan custodian. The plan custodian has many of the same duties and functions as the investment company transfer agent. For instance, the plan company custodian is responsible for:

- safekeeping assets underlying the plan (held by the custodian, not by the investor);
- issuing a confirmation form to the customer designating the number of shares owned;
- taking care of any assignments or transfer of fund shares; and

- sending out the letter notifying the customer of the free-look period (45-day letter).

Front-end Load and Spread Load

Front-end load. Contractual plans may operate under one of two federal securities acts. The Investment Company Act of 1940 allows the company to charge up to 50% of the investor's deposits in the first year. These act of 1940 plans are known as **front-end load plans**. The seller is allowed to charge a maximum sales charge equal to 9% of the total payments stipulated in a contractual plan, as follows:

- 50% of the total payments made during the first twelve months (first year) may be deducted and applied against total sales charges due over the life of the plan. This 50% deduction must be applied evenly to twelve monthly payments.
- Over the remaining life of the plan, deductions for sales charges may be calculated in any reasonable manner (typically prorated over the payments remaining to the plan completion date).

If a person invests $100 a month under a front-end load plan ($1,200 the first year), the company could collect $600 in sales charges the first year.

Spread load. The Investment Company Act Amendments of 1970, which amends the 1940 act, allows the company to charge up to 20% of the investor's deposit in any one year as long as the average charge over the first four years does not exceed 16% annually. This arrangement is known as a **spread-load plan**.

- Over the *first four years* of the plan, *an average of 16%* of all payments made by the investor may be deducted and applied against the total sales charges called for over the life of the plan.
- In *each* of the *first four years*, the sales charge rate and dollar amount deducted for the year must be *uniformly applied* to each month's payment rather than bunched up and deducted from the first few months' payments.
- The rates at which sales charge deductions are made during each of the first four years are left to the seller's discretion, subject to the restriction that *the first year's deduction cannot exceed 20%* and the average over the four-year period cannot exceed 16%.

Figure 5 shows how a spread load might be scheduled.

Figure 5   Spread Loads

	Plan X	Plan Y	Plan Z
First year	20%	20%	20%
Second year	19%	18%	16%
Third year	18%	16%	15%
Fourth year	7%	10%	13%
Four-year average	16%	16%	16%

If a person invests $100 per month under a spread-load plan, the company might charge $240 the first year (20%), $228 the second year (19%) and $216 the third year (18%). The sales charge in the fourth year would be limited to 7%, or $84, because the average charge per year cannot exceed 16%. (Total sales charges of $768 equal 16% of the total amount contributed, $4,800.)

Whether the plan company operates under the act of 1940 or the act of 1970, the maximum sales charge allowable is 9% over the life of the plan. For example, if a client plans to invest $100 per month for ten years, her total investment over the life of the plan would equal $12,000. The maximum sales charge would be $1,080 (9% of $12,000). The main difference between the two acts is the method of reaching this maximum sales charge, either up front (50% front-end load) or spread out (20% spread load plan).

Figure 6 shows a comparison of contractual plans.

Investor Right to Terminate a Plan

Under the provisions of the Investment Company Act of 1940, a periodic payment plan (either front-end or spread load) must allow for the investor who reconsiders her purchase decision. The following opportunities must be made available to investors.

Right of withdrawal (45-day free look). The fund's custodian bank must furnish the investor with a written notice detailing the total sales charges that will apply over the life of the plan and must send that notice *within 60 calendar days* of the date a contractual plan certificate is issued to the customer.

Figure 6   Comparison of Contractual Plans

	Front-end Load	Spread Load
Max. sales charges (life)	9%	9%
Max. sales charges in any one year	50%	20%
Max. sales charges over four years	No limit set	16% average per year
45-day free-look letter	Refund of current NAV plus any sales charges	Refund of current NAV plus any sales charges
Termination within first 18 months	Refund of current NAV plus any sales charges in excess of 15% of total payments	Refund of current NAV only

The customer, if so inclined, may surrender the certificate and terminate the plan *within 45 days* from the mailing date of the custodian's written notice. If the customer does, in fact, surrender the certificate within that time, he is entitled to:

- a 100% refund of all sales charges paid to date, *plus*
- the current value of the investment.

The current value of the fund shares being liquidated at NAV may result in a profit or loss on the investment, depending on the NAV at the time of purchase and the current NAV.

Right to refund (18-month partial refund period). In a front-end load plan (but not in a spread-load plan), the right to refund provides that if a customer requests termination of a front-end load plan within the *first 18 months* from the issuance date of the periodic payment plan certificate, she is entitled to a refund of:

- all sales charges paid to date *in excess of 15% of the total (gross) payments* made to date, *plus*
- the current value of the investment, which is liquidated at current NAV (and may result in a profit or loss).

To illustrate how the sales charge refund works, assume that a customer bought a front-end load contractual plan that called for monthly payments of $100 for 15 years. After making twelve monthly payments, the customer decides to terminate the plan. From each of twelve $100 monthly payments, a 50% deduction for sales charges is made.

Total payments:	12 at $100	=	$1,200
Total deductions:	12 at $50	=	$600
Total investment:	12 at $50	=	$600

The customer refund consists of:

$ 600	Total sales charge deductions
− 180	15% of total payments ($1,200)
$ 420	Refund of sales charges
+ 600	Current market value of investment (assuming no gain or loss in NAV)
$1,020	Total refund due customer

As a second example, assume a client invests $100 a month for ten months in a contractual plan under the act of 1940. The client's current account value (NAV) is $750 when he terminates the plan. The refund provisions under the act of 1940 require the plan company to return the current value of the client's account ($750) plus all sales charges deducted in excess of 15% of the amount invested ($100/month × 10 months = $1,000). The client has invested $100 per month, of which $50 is a sales charge. Over ten months, the company has collected a total of $500 as a sales charge. The company may keep only $150 (15% of $1,000) and must return the balance of $350 ($500 − $150). Therefore, the client will receive a total refund of $1,100 ($750 NAV + $350 sales charge refund).

The right to refund policy also applies if the investor abandons the plan prior to the end of the 18-month refund period. Abandonment means that the customer simply stops making the monthly payments called for in the contract. In such instances, the custodian bank must take steps to notify the customer that payment is overdue and that the person's account may be closed.

Notice of right to refund. If a contractual plan has reached its *fifteenth-month anniversary* and the investor has missed *three or more* monthly payments, the custodian (or the plan company) must issue a **right to refund notice** to the investor. The custodian has 30 calendar days from the fifteenth-month anniversary date to mail the notice to the delinquent customer.

If the contractual plan is *past* its fifteenth-month anniversary date but has *not passed the eighteenth month*, and the customer now misses a payment (or has missed two payments in the past and now misses a third), the custodian must send a right to refund notice as promptly as possible.

Partial withdrawals. Plan companies may also allow for partial liquidation or withdrawal in the event of an emergency. The amount withdrawn may be reinvested at no additional cost or at a very reduced sales charge.

Plan Completion Insurance

With some funds, the client may purchase a decreasing term policy at group rates to ensure completion of the accumulation plan. The custodian is named as the insurance beneficiary. At the death of the participant, the fund custodian receives the insurance proceeds to complete the purchase of fund shares, which are distributed to the survivors.

Dollar Cost Averaging

One method of purchasing mutual fund shares (and a basic advantage of contractual plans) is called **dollar cost averaging**, an investment method that requires a person to contribute money to be invested in regular amounts over a period of time. This form of investing results in the investor purchasing more shares when prices are low and fewer shares when prices are high. In a fluctuating market, the average cost per share over a period of time will be lower for the investor than the average price of the shares for the same period. If prices are declining, however, this will not ensure the investor a profit. The following example illustrates how average price and average cost may vary with dollar cost averaging:

Month	Amount Invested	Price per Share	No. of Shares
January	$ 600	$ 20	30
February	600	24	25
March	600	30	20
April	600	40	15
Total	$2,400	$114	90

The average price per share equals $114 (the sum of the prices) divided by 4 (the number of purchases), which is $28.50 per share. The average cost per share equals

$2,400 (the total investment) divided by 90 (the total number of shares purchased), which is $26.67 per share.

Withdrawal Plans

In addition to lump-sum withdrawals (where a client requests that all of the shares he owns be sold and the proceeds distributed to him), mutual funds also offer **systematic withdrawal plans**. Not all mutual funds offer withdrawal plans, but those that do may offer plans based on a fixed-dollar, -percentage, -share or -time withdrawal.

Fixed dollar. A client may request the withdrawal of a fixed amount of money periodically. The fund will then liquidate enough shares to send that sum. The amount of money liquidated could be more or less than the earnings for the account during that period. If the amount requested is greater than the account's earnings, a portion of the principal will be liquidated.

Fixed percentage or fixed share. Under a fixed-percentage or fixed-share withdrawal plan, either a fixed number of shares or a fixed percentage of the account will be liquidated each period. The proceeds, whatever the dollar amount may be, are sent to the shareholder.

Fixed time. Under a fixed-time withdrawal plan, clients liquidate their holdings over a fixed period of time. For example, if a client wishes to receive the proceeds monthly for ten years, the fund will send an initial check equal to 1/120th of the client's current account value. Because the client has fixed the time, this type of withdrawal plan is considered self-exhausting; that is, for the above example, the client's account will be liquidated in ten years.

Regardless of the plan or plans offered by the fund, most open-end companies require a minimum amount of money to be invested before the plan may begin. Additionally, most funds discourage continued investment once withdrawals begin. (Withdrawals are at NAV; investments are at POP.)

Withdrawal plans are normally a free service offered by the open-end investment company.

Withdrawal Plan Sales Literature

Withdrawal plans are not guaranteed. With fixed-dollar plans, only the dollar amount to be received each period is fixed; all other factors (such as the number of shares liquidated or the time the plan will last) are variable. For a fixed-time plan, only the period of time is fixed; the amount of money the investor receives varies each period, and so on. Because withdrawal plans are not guaranteed, the SEC is very concerned that the benefits are not misrepresented.

- The registered rep can never promise the investor a guaranteed rate of return.
- The registered rep must stress to the investor that it is possible to exhaust the account by overwithdrawing.
- The registered rep must state that during a down market it is possible that the account will be exhausted if even a small amount is withdrawn.
- The registered rep must not use charts or tables unless the SEC specifically clears their use.

Mutual Fund Distributions

Mutual fund ownership has several economic advantages. Gains can be realized through the sale of the fund's portfolio securities themselves, and if the gains from the portfolio are reinvested or unrealized, the fund shares themselves will reflect the appreciation, and the shareholder can sell the fund shares for a gain. Appreciation of share values is not the only return possible from mutual fund investment; current income is often the stated objective. This income is paid in the form of dividends.

Net Investment Income

The investment company may pay dividends to each shareholder in much the same way corporations pay dividends to stockholders. According to the act of 1940, dividends are paid from the net investment income of the mutual fund. To calculate net investment income, the fund totals dividends received from common and preferred stock held in the portfolio and adds all interest income received from bonds and other debt instruments. The sum of dividends and interest equals the gross investment income of the fund. From gross investment income, the fund subtracts its expenses for operation (adviser's fee, custodial fee, utilities, salaries, accounting costs and so on). The result is net investment income.

Keep in mind that costs associated with selling shares to the public, such as advertising expenses and sales commissions, are collected as part of the sales load. They are not part of the fund expenses when calculating net investment income.

Calculating fund yields. Net investment income is dividends and interest received on portfolio securities, less operating expenses. The dividend paid from the net investment income is divided by the current offering price to calculate yield. All yield quotations must disclose the:

- general direction of the stock market for the period in question
- NAV of the fund at the beginning and the end of the period
- percentage change in the fund's price during the period

Advertising Returns

An investor's total return from a mutual fund investment will include income distributions, gains distributions and share appreciation, minus any sales charges and fees. However, average annual total return, as defined by the SEC, assumes reinvestment of all dividends and capital gains distributions, and does not deduct any sales charges or management fees. Advertisements that feature total return must also explain how the SEC calculates fund performance. If any performance figures are included in an advertisement, the minimum information provided must be one-, five- and ten-year (or life-of-fund) average annual total returns. Similarly, the SEC requires that current yield calculations be based only on income distributions for the past twelve months, divided by the current price of the share.

For example, if the ACE Mutual Fund has a current offering price of $10 and over the past twelve months has distributed dividends totaling $1 and capital gains totaling $.75, the current yield for this fund is only 10%, not 17.5%.

Should the board of directors declare a dividend, the dividend is paid from net investment income to shareholders according to their interest in the fund. Most mutual funds distribute dividends quarterly, although monthly and even daily dividends are not uncommon. The mutual fund must disclose the source of the dividend payment if it is from other than retained or current income (for example, if it is the result of a short-term gain).

The ex-dividend date for mutual funds (unlike that for other corporate securities) is set by the board of directors, and there is no two-day requirement. Normally, the ex-dividend date for mutual funds is the day after the record date.

Capital Gains Distributions

Capital gains distributions are derived from the activities of the investment adviser trading securities held in the fund's portfolio. It is hoped that the investment adviser will be purchasing stock that may appreciate in value. At the appropriate time, the adviser may sell the stock for a gain. If the fund has held the stock for a period of at least one year, the gain is a long-term capital gain. The investment company may retain the gain for further investment or may distribute the gain to shareholders in proportion to the number of shares owned. Capital gains distributions (long term) may not be made more frequently than once per year.

Any distribution of gains from an open-end investment company will be long term. Short-term gains are considered income distributions and will be identified and distributed as dividends.

Reinvestment of Dividend and Gains Distributions

Dividends and capital gains are distributed in cash. However, the shareholder may elect to reinvest the cash distributions to purchase additional shares of the mutual fund. This reinvestment of distributions is called *automatic reinvestment* and is similar to compounding interest at a bank; the reinvested distributions purchase additional shares, which then begin earning dividends or sharing in gains distributions.

Dividends may be systematically reinvested by customers at less than the POP, and can be used to purchase full and fractional shares as long as:

- shareholders who are not already participants in the reinvestment plan are given a separate opportunity to reinvest each dividend;
- the plan is described in the prospectus;
- the issuer of the securities bears no additional costs beyond those that would have been incurred in the normal payout of dividends; and
- all shareholders are notified of the availability of the dividend reinvestment plan at least once every year.

The mutual fund may apply a reasonable charge against each dividend reinvestment.

If the company wishes to establish a plan through which investors can reinvest their capital gains distributions (as opposed to their dividends) at a discount to the POP, the following rules apply:

- The plan must be described in the *prospectus*.
- All participants must be given a separate opportunity to reinvest capital gains at each distribution.
- All participants must be notified at least once a year of the availability of the distribution reinvestment plan.

Whether the distributions are taken in cash or reinvested to purchase additional shares, they are taxable to the shareholders. Distributions from net investment income are taxed as ordinary income. Long-term capital gains are taxed at the ordinary income tax rate.

Source of distributions. All dividends and capital gains distributions—whether retained for reinvestment purposes or disbursed to shareholders—must be clearly identified and accounted for separately at the time of the distributions.

A statement or transmittal letter must provide an accounting of each distribution, indicating whether the distribution represents:

- dividends (from accumulated undistributed net income or current income)
- undistributed profits (capital gains)
- paid-in surplus (return of principal)

In addition, while portfolio income may be distributed to shareholders' accounts as frequently as the fund sees fit, *capital gains must not be distributed more than once every twelve months*. Form 1099B is sent after the close of the year and details tax information related to distributions for the year.

Realized and Unrealized Appreciation

As stated earlier, the fund's investment adviser may sell stock that has appreciated in value, creating a gain. A gain on the sale of stock is realized appreciation and is passed through to the shareholders. If the fund held the stock for a year or less, the gain is a short-term gain and will appear as an income distribution on the shareholder's annual tax form. If the fund held the stock for more than a year, the gain is a long-term gain and will appear as a capital gain distribution on the shareholder's annual tax form.

The fund's investment adviser may decide to hold the appreciated stock, in which case the NAV of the fund shares increases to reflect the appreciated value. This increase in the value of the shares is unrealized appreciation and is not passed through to the shareholder. The shareholder incurs no tax liability if he does not sell his shares.

Income Taxes

Federal income taxes are imposed on three types of income: earned, passive and portfolio.

Earned income. Earned income includes salary, bonuses and income derived from active participation in a trade or business.

Passive income. Passive income and losses come from rental property, limited partnerships and enterprises (regardless of business structure) in which the individual is not actively involved. For the general partner, income from a limited partnership is earned income; for the limited partner, such income is passive. Passive income is netted against passive losses in order to determine net taxable income. Passive losses may be used to offset passive income only.

Portfolio income. Portfolio income includes dividends, interest and net capital gains derived from the sale of securities. No matter what the source of the income, it is taxed in the year in which it is received.

Individual Federal Income Taxes

The basic design of the tax return is:

	Earned income
plus	Passive income (netted against passive losses)
plus	Interest and dividends
plus / minus	Net capital gains / losses
	Adjusted gross income (AGI)
minus	Itemized or standard deductions
minus	Personal exemptions
	Taxable income
times	Tax rate
	Tax liability

Fund Share Liquidations to the Investor

Once an investor has decided to liquidate holdings (sell the shares) in an open-end investment company, he will have to establish his cost base in the shares in order to calculate tax liability.

A simple definition of cost base is: that amount of money invested that has already been taxed. Upon liquidation, cost base represents a return of capital and is not subject to a tax liability. The difference between cost base and the current value of the investor's shares represents his taxable gain (or loss if cost base is greater than the current value of the shares).

Valuing fund shares. The cost base of mutual fund shares includes the total cost of the shares, including sales charges, plus any reinvested investment income and capital gains. The cost base is compared to the amount of money received from the sale of the shares. If the amount received is greater than the cost base, the investor will report a taxable gain. If the amount received is less than the cost base, the investor has a reportable loss.

$$\text{Total value of fund shares} - \text{Cost base} = \text{Taxable gain}$$

The investor does not receive a tax form from the fund company for shares sold; the recordkeeping requirements are the responsibility of the investor.

Capital Losses

An investor can claim up to $3,000 in net losses to offset ordinary income in any one year. If the investor has more than $3,000 in losses, the amount exceeding the $3,000 limit can be carried forward to offset income in following years. The $3,000 limitation applies to net losses, long and short term. Short-term and long-term losses are deducted against ordinary income dollar for dollar.

For example, an investor with a $2,000 short-term loss and a $2,000 long-term loss could offset $3,000 of taxable income. The short-term loss is used first and, therefore, $1,000 of the long-term loss would be carried forward and applied in future years. There is no limit on the amount of loss that can be carried forward, nor on the number of years over which it is applied.

Wash sales. The IRS will disallow a loss if the investor repurchases a substantially identical security within 30 days before or after the sale of the security in which the loss was claimed. Substantially identical securities would include warrants, options, convertible securities or any security that might be exchanged for or represents the investor's original holding. Figure 7 illustrates the wash sale period.

Accounting Methods

Should the investor decide to liquidate on a per-share basis, the calculation of cost base can be accomplished by electing one of two accounting methods: first in, first

Figure 7   Wash Sale Period

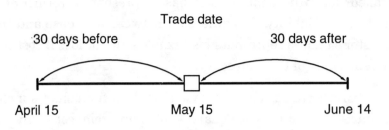

out (FIFO) or share identification. If the investor fails to choose, the IRS assumes the investor is liquidating shares on a FIFO basis.

Share Identification

Probably the more frequently used and advantageous method of determining cost on a per-share basis is share identification. The investor keeps track of the cost of each share purchased. Upon selling the shares, the investor decides which shares to liquidate. He then identifies the cost base of each share liquidated in whichever order provides the necessary tax benefit. Share identification is the most flexible of the two methods. For example, if the investor needs to report a loss, those shares with a higher cost base than the current NAV could be liquidated; if he can absorb a taxable gain, lower cost base shares could be liquidated.

Other Mutual Fund Taxation Considerations

Withholding tax. If an investor neglects or fails to include her tax ID number when purchasing mutual fund shares, the fund is required to withhold 31% of the distributions to the investor as a withholding tax.

Cost basis of shares transferred. The basis of property inherited is either stepped up or stepped down to its fair market value (FMV) at the date of the decedent's death. No adjustment of basis is necessary for the period prior to the decedent's death.

For example, June Polar inherited $10,000 worth of mutual fund shares from her father. At her father's death, the NAV of the shares was $11,500. June's basis in the shares is the FMV, or $11,500.

Dividend exclusions. TRA 1986 repealed the dividend exclusion for individual taxpayers and reduced the corporate dividend exclusion to 70%.

Taxation of investment returns. This can be summarized as follows:

Income distributions: taxed as ordinary income

Capital gains distributions: taxed as ordinary income

Profit or loss on sale: short- or long-term gain or loss; cost basis

Exchanges within a family of funds. Even though there is no sales charge on the exchange, for tax purposes, the IRS considers a sale to have taken place and the customer has some tax liability under IRS regulations. This tax liability can be significant, and shareholders should be aware of this potential cost of conversion.

Taxation of Mutual Funds

Investment Income: IRC Subchapter M

As a corporation or trust, the mutual fund is responsible for taxes on income earned from the securities held in the company's portfolio. Of concern to the investor, the taxation of income at the fund's level subjects the investment income to a tax liability on three levels: the corporate level of the individual company; the investment company; and the investor upon receiving the distribution.

Conduit (pipeline) theory. Triple taxation of investment income may be avoided if the open-end investment company qualifies under Subchapter M of the Internal Revenue Code (IRC). If a mutual fund acts as a conduit, or pipeline, for the distribution of net investment income, the fund may qualify as a regulated investment company and be subject to tax only on the amount of investment income retained by the company. The investment income distributed to shareholders escapes taxation at the investment company level. Subchapter M requires that the investment company distribute at least 90% of its net investment income to shareholders. If the company distributes 89%, the company is liable for tax on 100% of net investment income.

The definition of net investment income under IRC Subchapter M is interest and dividend income minus expenses. Gains are not included in the calculation of net investment income.

Since 1988, investment companies have been subject to an excise tax of 4%, if they do not distribute at least 98% (raised from 97%) of their income to their shareholders.

Capital Gains

If the investment company distributes capital gains to the mutual fund shareholder, the shareholder is responsible for taxes. If the investment company retains a capital gain and reinvests the gain in other securities, the shareholder is still liable for tax on the gain.

The investment company designates to the shareholder of record a proportionate share of the undistributed capital gain. This amount is included on the shareholder's 1040 as reportable income. The regulated investment company pays tax on amounts designated to shareholders, but the tax paid is treated as an advance payment by the shareholder. Because the tax rates on gains differ for corporate and individual taxpayers, the tax due from the shareholder is changed, as is the shareholder's cost basis in the fund portfolio.

Tracking Investment Company Securities

Investment company prices, like those for individual securities, are quoted daily in the financial press. However, because of the various methods used to calculate sales charges, as described below, the financial press uses footnotes to explain the type of sales charge used by the mutual fund issuer. The representative must understand the presentation and meaning of the footnotes associated with investment company quotes so that he can accurately describe the quotes to the investing public. An example of quotes and associated explanatory footnotes is shown in Figure 8.

Figure 8   Mutual Fund Quotations as They Might Appear in the Newspaper

Mutual Fund Quotations

Tuesday, September 13, 1998
Price ranges for investment companies, as quoted by the National Association of Securities Dealers. NAV stands for net asset value per share. The offering price includes net asset value plus maximum sales charge, if any.

	NAV	Offer Price	NAV Chg.		NAV	Offer Price	NAV Chg.
ArGood Mutual Funds				**FastTrak Funds**			
CapApp	4.80	5.04	+ .02	App	13.79	14.44	– .01
Grwth	6.87	7.21	+ .02	CapAp	22.13	23.17	+ .15
HiYld	10.28	10.79	+ .01	Grwth	18.33	19.24	– .10
TaxEx	11.62	12.20	– .04	**Z Best Invest**			
Best Mutual				Grth p	14.81	15.59	– .03
Balan	12.32	NL	– .06	HiYld p	9.25	9.74	+ .03
Canada	10.59	NL	– .04	Inco p	7.95	8.37	– .04
US Gov	10.49	NL	– .02	MuniB p	8.11	8.54	– .03

e- Ex-distribution. f- Previous day's quote. s- Stock split or div. x- Ex-dividend. NL- No load. p- Distribution costs apply, 12b-1plan. r- Redemption charge may apply.

Let's look at the family of funds called ArGood Mutual Funds. ArGood Growth Fund is a part of this group; its net asset value, offering price, and the change in its net asset value per share are listed. The offering price includes the NAV plus the *maximum* sales charge, if any. As stated previously, when there is a difference between the net asset value and the offering price, the fund is a load fund. A no-load fund is usually identified by the letters "NL" in the Offer Price column. Look at the Best Mutual funds; they are a family of no-load funds.

The final column shows the change in the net asset value of a share since the last trading date. A plus (+) indicates an upward move and a minus (–) indicates a downward turn.

From this information, you will be able to calculate the sale charge of any mutual fund. For example, find the FastTrak group of funds. The first entry is App. Remember the formula for calculating the sales charge.

$$\text{Sales charge} = \text{Public offering price} - \text{NAV}$$
$$= \$14.44 - \$13.79 = \$0.65$$

$$\text{Sales charge \%} = \text{Sales charge} \div \text{Public offering price}$$
$$= \$0.65 \div \$14.44 = 4.50\%$$

You will also be able to watch the movements of the fund's share value.

Stock guides such as Standard & Poor's include summaries of mutual funds for the year. Figure 9 shows a portion of a table taken from the *1991 Standard & Poor's Stock Guide;* you can use it to evaluate different mutual funds.

To the right of the third fund listed on the table, Alliance Fund, you will find the following information:

- **Principal objective of the fund**. "G" means Alliance is a growth fund. Other objectives might be income, return on capital, or stability; these are listed in the footnotes below the table.
- **Type of fund**. Alliance Fund is a "C," or common stock fund. As also listed in the footnotes, other types are:

B	– balanced	FL	– flexible
BD	– bond	H	– hedge
C	– common	L	– leverage
CN	– Canadian	P	– preferred
CT	– common, tax shelter	SP	– specialized
		TF	– tax free
CV	– convertible bond and preferred stock		

Figure 9   Mutual Funds Summary for 1991

Fund	Prin. Obj.	Type	Dec 31, 1991 Total Net Assets (MILS)	Cash & Equiv (MILS)	Net Assets per Share % Chg. from Prev. Dec. 31 At Dec. 31 1989	1990	1991	Min. Unit	Max. Sales Chg. %	$10,000 Invested 12-31-81 Now Worth	Price Record 1991 High	Low	NAV Per Sh as of 12-31-91 NAV per Shr.	Offer Price
Acorn	G	C	525.8	47.0	+ 3.9	+30.1	+15.4	$4,000	None	29,603	47.71	37.61	47.71	47.71
ALFA Securities	G	C	672.6	22.9	+33.5	+41.1	+21.6	$1,000	None	32,518	24.75	19.62	24.47	24.47
Alliance Fund	G	C	948.2	19.0	− 5.2	+29.5	+ 8.9	$250	5.5	24,661	9.67	6.96	9.45	10.00
Alliance Tech	G	C	200.8	10.0	−16.4	+26.1	+12.0	$250	5.5	....	36.47	23.44	34.24	36.23
Amer Balanced	IS	B	202.0	24.0	+ 7.7	+27.1	+15.8	$500	8.5	27,889	12.61	10.92	12.32	13.46
Amer Cap Corp Bond	IS	BD	136.0	16.0	+ 9.2	+24.6	+10.8	$500	8.5	23,457	7.51	7.12	7.12	7.48
Amer Cap Mun Bond	I	TF	187.0	7.0	+10.0	+22.0	+15.9	$500	4.75	22,897	21.74	18.53	19.14	20.09
Analytic Opt Equity	GI	C	85.7	11.7	+ 6.6	+15.5	+10.2	$5,000	None	20,662	15.59	13.88	15.45	15.45
Axe-Houghton Bond	SIR	B	204.5	4.0	+ 5.8	+31.6	+21.5	$1,000	None	27,766	12.16	10.26	11.93	11.93
Axe-Houghton Stock	G	C	93.4	2.0	−15.0	+31.1	+10.8	$1,000	None	28,394	11.46	8.25	11.13	11.13

Principal Objective: G-Growth; I-Income; R-Return on Capital; S-Stability; E-Objectives treated Equally; P-Preservation of Capital; Listed in order of importance. Type: B-Balanced; BD-Bond; C-Common; CV-Conv Bond and Prefd Stock; FL-Flexible; GB-Long-term Gov't; GL-Global; H-Hedge; L-Leverage; P-Preferred; PM-Precious Metals; O-Options; SP-Specialized; TF-Tax Free; ST-Short-term investments.

- **Total net assets**. This column lists total net assets at market value—that is, assets minus liabilities. Alliance Fund has total net assets of $948.2 million.
- **Cash and equivalents**. This column includes cash and receivables, short-term government securities and other money-market instruments less current liabilities. Cash and equivalents are part of the total net assets.
- **Percentage change in net assets per share**. These columns show the performance of a fund over a specific period—in this case, from the previous December 31st. For example, on December 31, 1990, Alliance Fund had a 29.5% increase in net asset value per share since December 31, 1989.
- **Minimum unit**. This is the minimum initial purchase of shares. For Alliance Fund, it is $250.
- **Maximum sales charge**. Alliance Fund charges 5.5%. If a fund is a no-load fund, there is no sales charge.
- **Current worth of $10,000 invested December 31, 1981**. This column provides a gauge of a fund's performance over several years. In this case, $10,000 invested in Alliance Fund on December 31, 1981, would have more than doubled, growing to $24,661.
- From the **price record** columns, you can learn the *percentage of appreciation of a share* from its low price of the year. To determine the percentage of appreciation, subtract the low price from the latest NAV per share and then divide the difference by the low price. For example, during 1991 Alliance Fund

sold at a low of 6.96. If on June 30, 1991 (the current date), its NAV per share was 9.67, the appreciation would be computed as follows:

$$
\begin{array}{lr}
\text{NAV} & 9.67 \\
\text{Low} & -\,6.96 \\
\hline
& 2.71
\end{array}
$$

$$2.71 \div 6.96 = 38.93\% \text{ Appreciation}$$

- **NAV per share.** In this column you will find the current NAV per share as well as the current POP.

After some practice at reading the tables of mutual funds, you will be able to distinguish the differences between the three management companies.

Q: Which of the following is most likely to be: (1) a closed-end fund, (2) an open-end fund and (3) a no-load fund?

	Fund	NAV	Offer Price
A.	IDS Fund	$ 5.84	$ 6.05
B.	Midwest Fund	$ 8.50	$ 8.20
C.	Apollo Fund	$10.10	$10.10

A: The IDS Fund is most likely an open-end fund because the offering price is higher than the NAV.

The Midwest Fund must be a closed-end fund because the offering price is less than the NAV. The fund is selling at a discount from its NAV.

The Apollo Fund is a no-load fund because the NAV and the offering price are the same, indicating that there is no sale charge. (There is a possibility that it is a closed-end fund that is trading for neither a discount nor a premium.)

Review Questions

1. The NAV of mutual fund shares is priced

    √A. daily
    B. monthly
    C. annually
    D. whenever the number of shares outstanding increases

2. A client decides to buy shares of an open-end investment company. When is the price of the shares determined?

    I. At the next calculation of net asset value on the day that the fund custodian receives the proper notification from the client
    II. At the next calculation of net asset value on the day that the broker-dealer wires the custodian on behalf of the client
    III. At the net asset value reported in the financial press at the time the client chooses to purchase the shares
    IV. At the net asset value reported to the broker's office on the daily price sheets

    A. I only
    B. I and II only
    C. II and III only
    D. I, II, III and IV

3. A sales load is defined as the

    A. difference between the public offering price and the net asset value
    B. commissions paid on the purchase or sale of securities
    C. fee paid to the investment adviser
    D. concessions allowed on the purchase or sale of securities

4. A 12b-1 plan must be approved at least annually by a majority of

    A. the outstanding voting shares of the company
    B. the board of directors
    C. the uninterested members of the board of directors
    D. all of the above

5. What services must a mutual fund sponsor offer in order to be permitted to charge the maximum allowable sales charge for the fund shares?

      I.   Rights of accumulation
      II. The privilege to reinvest dividend distributions at no sales charge
      III. Price breakpoints offering reduced commissions for larger purchases

      A. I and II only
      B. I and III only
      C. II and III only
      D. I, II and III

6. A letter of intent for a mutual fund does NOT contain which of the following provisions?

      A. The time limit is 13 months.
      B. The letter can be backdated 90 days to include a previous deposit.
      C. The fund can halt redemption during the period of time the letter of intent is in effect.
      D. The fund might keep some of the initially issued shares in an escrow account to ensure full payment of the full spread.

7. A customer canceling a contractual plan will have all of his sales charge refunded if he cancels the plan within

      A. 15 days of receiving the notice by the custodian bank
      B. 30 days of the mailing of the notice by the custodian bank
      C. 45 days of the mailing of the notice by the custodian bank
      D. 18 months of receiving the notice from the custodian bank

8. When calculating net investment income, an investment company would include

      A. only dividends
      B. only interest
      C. both dividends and interest
      D. both dividends and interest, minus operating expenses

9.   The conduit theory of taxation means that

    I.   the fund is not taxed on earnings it distributes
   II.   retained earnings are taxed as regular corporate income
  III.   the earnings distributed by a regulated mutual fund are taxed twice

    A.   I and II only
    B.   I and III only
    C.   II and III only
    D.   I, II and III

10.   The public offering price for a mutual fund as quoted in the financial press reflects

    A.   the maximum sales charge collected by the fund distributor
    B.   the average sales charge for the preceding twelve months collected by the fund distributor
    C.   the minimum sales charge collected by the fund distributor
    D.   no sales charge because the offering price depends upon the quantity purchased

Answers & Rationale

1. **A.** The NAV of a mutual fund is calculated according to a formula described in the prospectus, but under no circumstances may calculation occur less frequently than once per business day.   (Page 29)

2. **B.** The price for mutual fund shares is the next price calculated by the fund after receipt of the request (forward pricing). The price quoted in the financial press or on a broker's price list reflects the price calculated for orders received the previous business day.   (Page 29)

3. **A.** A sales load is the difference between the public offering price and the amount actually added to the investment company's portfolio (at the current NAV). Commissions, concessions and allowances are part of the sales load.   (Page 27)

4. **D.** A 12b-1 plan must be approved initially, and annually thereafter, by a majority vote of the shareholders, board of directors and uninterested members of the board of directors.   (Page 33)

5. **D.** NASD rules prohibit sales charges in excess of 8 1/2% on mutual fund purchases by public customers. Unless a mutual fund grants its shareholders certain privileges, the amount charged must be lower than 8 1/2%. To qualify for the maximum sales charge (8 1/2%), *all* of the following privileges must be extended to the fund's shareholders:

    - rights of accumulation
    - dividend reinvestment at net asset value
    - quantity discounts (breakpoints)

    (Page 36)

6. **C.** A letter of intent is not binding on the client in any way. Should the client decide to liquidate the account prior to completion of the letter, the company may reduce the redemption only by the amount of shares held in escrow.   (Page 37)

7. **C.** Under the Investment Company Act of 1940, contractual planholders must be allowed a full refund if they return their shares within 45 days of the mailing of the notice by the custodian bank.   (Page 46)

8.   **D.**   Net investment income is equal to gross investment income minus operating expenses. Gross investment income is interest and dividends received from securities in the investment company's portfolio. Capital gains are not included in investment income.   (Page 50)

9.   **D.**   Under the conduit (or pipeline) theory of taxation, which is applied to qualified regulated investment companies, the fund is liable for taxes only on the income retained. The investor benefits because the income is taxed only twice (at the corporate level and at the individual level) and not three times by adding taxation at the fund level.   (Page 57)

10.   **A.**   The public offering price for a quoted mutual fund includes the maximum sales charge that the fund distributor is permitted to charge.   (Page 59)

3

Investment Recommendations, Suitability and Ethics

Key Terms

balanced portfolio
breakpoint sales
call risk
capital risk
churning
credit risk
diversification
financial risk
holding period return
interest rate risk
internal rate of return (IRR)
legislative risk
liquidity

liquidity risk
marketability risk
market risk
nonsystematic risk
present value
purchasing power risk
reinvestment risk
Rules of Fair Practice
selection risk
selling dividends
speculation
suitability
systematic risk

Overview

Before appropriate recommendations can be made to customers, a sales rep must understand their financial objectives, financial status and investment needs and constraints. This chapter will explore the different factors that go into making an investment decision and recommendation that is appropriate for the investor. Helping a customer to understand investment risks and to analyze investment returns is very important to an ongoing financial relationship. Finally, this chapter covers the ethical standards that are expected and enforced by the securities and banking industry regulators.

Know Your Customer

Financial Profile

The more you know about your customer's income, current investment portfolio, retirement plans, net worth and other aspects of his current financial situation, the better will be your recommendations. The more your customer knows about the risks and rewards associated with each type of investment, the better will be his investment decisions.

Customer's Balance Sheet

Before you enter the first trade for a new customer, it is important to find out as much about that person's financial status as you can. Individuals, like businesses, have a financial balance sheet—a snapshot of their financial condition at a point in time. You can determine the status of your customer's personal balance sheet by asking questions similar to those in the following list:

- What kinds of assets do you own? Do you own your home? A car? Collectibles? A second home?
- What are your liabilities? Do you make mortgage payments on your home? Do you make car payments? Do you have any other outstanding loans or regular financial commitments, including credit cards?
- Do you own any marketable securities? What types of investments do you currently hold?
- Have you established any long-term investment accounts? Do you have an IRA, a Keogh or a corporate pension or profit-sharing plan? Are you contributing to any annuities? What is the cash value of your life insurance?

Customer's Income Statement

An important part of an individual's financial status is his personal income statement. For many people, this income statement takes the form of a monthly, quarterly or annual budget that measures the person's (or family's) income and outgo. In order to make appropriate investment recommendations, you need to determine what your customer's income statement looks like.

Gather information about your customer's financial responsibilities, projected inheritances, pending job changes and the like. You can do this by asking questions similar to those in the following list:

- What is your total gross income? What is your total family income? How stable is this income? Do you see major changes taking place over the next few years?
- How much do you pay in expenses each month? Is this a relatively stable figure? Do you anticipate any change in this amount over the next few years?
- What is your net spendable income after expenses? How much of this is available for investment?
- What is your net worth? How much of it is liquid?

Other Financial Elements

After you have gathered information on your customer's personal balance sheet and income statement, you will want to learn:

- whether the person owns his own home;
- how much and what type of insurance he has;
- his tax bracket and what changes may occur in it over the next few years; and
- whether he has experienced any credit problems.

Nonfinancial Investment Considerations

Once you have explored your customer's financial status and all of your questions have been answered, you can begin to gather information on his nonfinancial status. These nonfinancial considerations frequently carry more weight than the financial information. Some of the items you will want to ask your customer about include:

- age
- marital status
- number and ages of dependents
- employment
- employment of family members
- current and future family educational needs
- current and future family health care needs

Finally, no matter how much an analysis of a person's financial status tells you about his ability to invest, it is the customer's emotional acceptance of investing and his motivation to invest that will mold his portfolio. To understand better a customer's aptitude for investment, ask questions similar to the following:

- What kind of risks can you afford to take?
- How liquid must your investments be?
- How important are tax considerations?
- Are you seeking long-term or short-term investments?
- What is your investment experience?
- What types of investments do you currently hold?
- How would you react to a loss of 5% of your principal? 10%? 50%?
- What level of return do you consider good? Poor? Excellent?
- What combination of risks and returns would you feel comfortable with?
- What is your investment temperament?
- Do you get bored with stable investments?
- Can you tolerate market fluctuations?

Customer Investment Outlook

Contrary to what many investment professionals and most customers believe, people have many reasons for investing and many needs that must be met by their investments. By asking appropriate questions of your customers, you can uncover these reasons and needs—an important step because customers often do not know why they choose to invest the way they do. Most customers will claim that they invest so that their money will grow. By careful questioning, however, you may learn that because of tax status, income or other events, some growth investments are suitable, while others are not.

Some of the basic financial objectives customers may have are discussed in the following sections.

Preservation of capital. For many people, their single most important investment objective is to preserve the capital they have worked so hard to accumulate. A person with this as his most important objective would not be willing to invest in most equity securities, for example. In general, when clients speak of *safety*, they usually mean preservation of capital from losses due to credit, or financial, risk. Financial risk is the danger of losing all or part of the principal amount a person has invested.

Current income. Many investors, particularly retirees and others on fixed incomes, want to generate additional current income from their investments. Corporate bonds, municipal bonds, government and agency securities, income-oriented mutual funds, some stocks (including utilities and real estate investment trusts—REITs), money-market funds, annuities and some direct participation programs (DPPs) are among the investments that can contribute current income through dividend or interest payments.

Capital growth. Growth refers to an increase in the value of an investment over time. This growth can come from increases in the value of the security, the reinvestment of dividends and income, or both. Investors seek growth in order to meet a variety of needs (retirement planning, funding a child's education, travel or a vacation home, to name a few). The most common growth-oriented investments are common stock and stock mutual funds.

Tax advantages. Current tax rates—even though they were raised by the Revenue Reconciliation Act of 1993—are not as high as they once were. Nevertheless, as is always the case, investors seek ways to reduce their taxes. Some products and plans, like individual retirement accounts (IRAs) and annuities, allow interest to accumulate tax deferred (no taxes are paid until the investor withdraws money from the account). Other products, like many municipal bonds, offer tax-free interest income. (The tax advantages of municipal securities may vary depending on the state in which the investor resides.)

Portfolio diversification. An investor may have reasons based on other than personal or financial factors for choosing an investment. Investment professionals frequently encounter investors whose portfolios are concentrated in only one or a few securities or investments. Because such concentrations of investments expose these customers to much higher risks, portfolio diversification becomes an important objective. Typical of these customers are retirees with large profit-sharing distributions of one company's stock and investors with all of their money invested in CDs or U.S. government savings bonds.

Liquidity. Some people want immediate access to their money at all times. A product is liquid if the customer can sell it quickly at face amount (or very close to it) or at a fair market price without losing significant principal. Stock, for example, has varying degrees of liquidity (depending on many factors, including safety, number of shares outstanding and the market's perception of the issuer), while DPPs, annuities and bank CDs generally are considered illiquid. Real estate is the classic example of an illiquid product because of the time and money it takes to convert it into cash.

Speculation. Among the investment objectives a customer might have is the need to speculate—that is, gamble on higher than average returns in exchange for higher than average risks. Speculation is a legitimate investment objective, and most customers would be well advised to place some of their investable assets (typically 5% to 25%) in speculative, high-potential-return investments and securities.

Figure 10 illustrates the categories used in portfolio diversification.

Figure 10   Categories Used in Portfolio Diversification

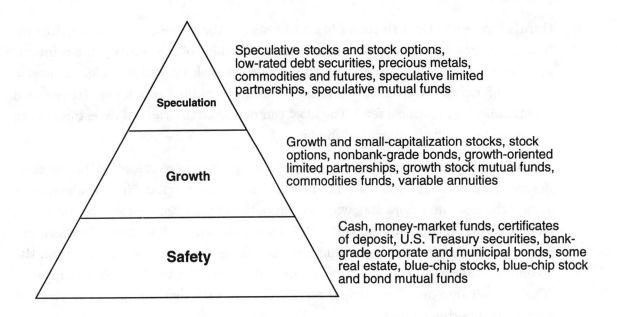

Suitability and Customer Recommendations

Suitability

Selecting suitable investments to meet investor needs is both an art and a science. The process is too complex to computerize; even the most sophisticated and expensive financial plans are only partially based on a computerized model. In the final analysis, recommending investments requires the finest computer in existence: the human brain. One of the key tasks of an investment adviser is to recommend suitable investments that best match the clients' unique characteristics, needs and objectives, including financial background and tax status. Customers should be guided to investments that make sense for them, not just for the broker.

Every investment should be fully explained, and the explanation should include a discussion of the investment's risks. At no time should customers own an investment which could put them at risk beyond their financial capacity.

Unsuitable Trades

Occasionally a customer will ask a registered rep to enter a trade for the customer's account that the rep feels is unsuitable. It is the rep's responsibility to discuss the trade with the customer, and explain why that particular trade might not be suitable. If the customer insists on entering the transaction, the registered rep should have the customer sign a statement acknowledging that the rep recommended against the trade, and the rep should mark the order ticket "unsolicited." In any event, the account belongs to the investor to do with as he pleases—while the rep may attempt to counsel the customer against unsuitable trades, the customer has the right to enter into any transaction he chooses and to be given good service on all transactions.

Customer Recommendations

Because of the inherently close relationship between recommending securities and receiving a commission from their sale, it is easy to see how unethical salespeople could manipulate the relationship to their advantage. It is the manager's responsibility to see that this does not happen.

Disclosure Requirements

Proposals and written presentations that include specific recommendations (sales literature) must have reasonable bases to support the recommendations, and the member firm must provide these in the proposal or other written document, or offer to furnish them upon request. In any event, the rep should have reasonable grounds for believing that a security is a suitable investment for a customer before recommending its purchase.

A recommendation typically takes the form of a simple summary of what the customer said his investment needs were and what he wants to accomplish, coupled with an explanation of the recommendation being made and how it relates to the customer's needs and wants.

A recommendation of a corporate stock must include the stock's current price. If, in recommending a security, a firm uses material referring to the performance of past recommendations, it must reveal certain information. In particular, it must disclose:

- the price (or price range) of the recommended security at the date and time that the recommendation is made;
- the general direction of the market;
- the availability of information supporting the recommendation;

- any recommendations made of similar securities within the past twelve months (including the nature of the recommendations—buy, sell or hold);
- whether the firm intends to buy or sell any of the recommended security for its own account;
- whether the firm is a market maker in the recommended security;
- whether the firm or its officers or partners own options, rights or warrants to buy the recommended security;
- whether the firm managed or co-managed a public offering of the recommended security or any other of the same issuer's securities during the past three years; and
- all recommendations (gainers and losers) made by the firm over the period of time in question.

The time span covered in the list of recommendations must run through consecutive periods, without skipping periods in an attempt to hide particular recommendations or negative price performance data.

The above is the type of information a knowledgeable investor can use to determine whether a recommendation is appropriate for his situation. In addition to meeting these requirements, the company making the recommendation must not:

- imply that there are any guarantees accompanying the recommendation;
- compare the recommended security to dissimilar products;
- make fraudulent or misleading statements about the recommended security; or
- make any predictions about the future performance or potential of the recommended security.

Special Bank Considerations

Banks have a special responsibility to explain investment risks because they offer both insured and noninsured products. Bank customers are ingrained with the idea that bank products are insured.

The sale of mutual funds in banks is regulated by the Federal Reserve Board (FRB), the Office of the Comptroller of the Currency (OCC), the Office of Thrift Supervision (OTS) and the Federal Deposit Insurance Corporation (FDIC). These organizations have strict guidelines that banks must follow when selling mutual funds.

The two greatest concerns of the regulatory organizations are customer confusion between insured deposit and noninsured nondeposit products (mutual funds) and mismanagement of the sales process. Sound compliance policies and procedures will protect a bank from exposure to the risk of customer recourse offered by federal securities laws.

Separation at all levels of insured deposits and noninsured nondeposit products will substantially limit a bank's exposure to the risks associated with customer confusion about the *safety* of nondeposit investments. Employees who accept deposits should be prohibited from selling nondeposit investments or giving any kind of investment advice. Other bank personnel with customer contact should be trained in the differences between products so that customers may be directed to the appropriate area of the bank.

An area of special concern is the separation of the physical areas where employees accept deposits and where nondeposit investments are sold. The best solution is for the areas to have different entrances, be separated by walls and doors and be easily distinguished by signs to avoid customer confusion.

Investment suitability and disclosure issues will certainly impact the overall success of the bank retail investment program. Risk disclosure protects the customer and the bank. Customers must be made to understand and accept that mutual funds:

- are not bank deposits or bank obligations
- are not insured by the FDIC
- are not guaranteed
- are subject to investment risks, including loss of principal

Banks are prohibited from engaging in any practice that could mislead customers about the risk of investing in uninsured products. Customers must be advised of the risk of loss of some or all principal due to market fluctuations. The bank should require a signed acknowledgement from each customer that such disclosure has been made and understood at the time the account is opened. A copy should be filed with the account documentation.

Recommending Investment Company Products

Whenever an investment company or a broker-dealer develops advertisements or sales literature for a mutual fund, it must comply with all of the rules designed to protect the public. It is the manager's duty to see that all public communications containing recommendations are developed in accordance with these rules and that the registered reps using them to sell investment products use them properly.

When recommending mutual funds to clients as investments and when using advertisements or sales literature developed for those investments the broker-dealer should:

- use charts or graphs showing the fund's performance covering a period of time long enough to reflect variations in value under different market conditions, generally a period of at least ten years;
- reveal the source of the graphic;
- separate dividends from capital gains when making statements about the fund's cash returns;
- not state that a mutual fund is similar to or safer than any other type of security (including government bonds, insurance policies or annuities, or corporate bonds);
- reveal the fund's highest sales charge, even if the client appears to qualify for a breakpoint; and
- not make any fraudulent or misleading statements or omissions of facts.

Periodic Investment Plans

Mutual fund plans that fall into the periodic payment category (frequently sold in this manner to receive the benefits of *dollar cost averaging)* cannot be described in advertisements or sales literature without the disclosure that:

- a profit is not assured;
- they do not provide protection from losses in a declining market;
- the plan involves continuous investments regardless of market fluctuations; and
- the investor should consider his financial ability to continue purchases during periods of declining prices.

Analyzing Financial Risks and Rewards

Because all investments involve trade-offs, the task of the registered representative or the investment adviser is to select securities that will provide the right balance between investor characteristics on the one hand and investment capabilities on the other.

Investment Risks

In general terms, the greater the risk assumed by the investor, the greater the potential for reward. There are several risks to consider in determining the suitability of various types of investments when building a financial portfolio.

Call Risk

Call risk is the risk that a bond might be called before maturity and investors will be unable to reinvest their principal at the same (or a higher) rate of return. When interest rates are falling, bonds with higher coupon rates are most likely to be called. Thus, investors will lose their steady stream of income. Investors concerned about call risk should look for call protection—a period of time during which a bond cannot be called. Most corporate and municipal issuers generally provide some years of call protection.

Capital Risk

Capital risk is the potential for an investor to lose all of her money or capital under circumstances unrelated to the financial strength of the issuer. For example, when options expire out-of-the-money, buyers lose all of their capital (the cost of the premium) even though the underlying security may be solvent.

Credit Risk

Credit risk (also called *financial risk* or *default risk)* involves the danger of losing all or part of one's invested principal through failure of the issuer. Credit risk varies with the investment product. Bonds backed by the federal government or municipalities tend to be very secure and have low credit risk. Long-term bonds involve more credit risk than short-term bonds because of the increased uncertainty that results from holding bonds for many years. Preferred stocks generally are safer than common stocks. Mutual funds offer increased safety through diversification. On the other hand, penny stocks, nonbank-grade bonds and some options positions can be quite risky, yet right for some customers.

Bond investors concerned about credit risks should pay attention to the ratings. Two of the best known rating services that analyze the financial strength of thousands of corporate and municipal issuers are Moody's Investors Service and Standard & Poor's Corporation. To a great extent, the value of a bond depends on how much credit risk investors are taking. The higher the rating, the less likely the bond is to default and, therefore, the lower the coupon rate. Clients seeking the highest possible yield from bonds might want to buy bonds with lower ratings. The higher yields are a reward for taking more credit risks.

Inflation Risk

Also known as *purchasing power risk,* **inflation risk** measures the effects of continually rising prices on investments. If an investment's yield is lower than the rate of inflation, the client's money will have less purchasing power as time goes on. A client who buys a bond or a fixed annuity may be able to purchase far less with the invested funds when the investment matures.

Interest Rate Risk

Interest rate risk refers to the sensitivity of the price or value of an investment to fluctuations in the current level of interest rates; also, the risk that involves the competitive cost of money. This term is generally associated with bond prices, but it applies to all investments. In bonds, the price carries an interest risk because if bond prices rise, outstanding bonds will not remain competitive unless their yields and prices are adjusted to reflect the current market.

Legislative Risk

Congress has the power to change existing laws affecting securities. The risk that such a change in law might affect an investment adversely is known as **legislative risk** or **political risk**. For example, by changing the tax consequences of passive income from DPPs, Congress affected the viability of many deep tax shelter programs. Similarly, a client who goes short against the box to postpone capital gains might be disappointed if Congress changes the taxation of such gains. When recommending suitable investments, you should warn clients of any pending changes in the law that may affect those investments.

Liquidity Risk

The risk that a client might not be able to liquidate her investment at a time when she needs cash is known as **liquidity risk** (or *marketability risk).* The marketability of the securities you recommend must be related directly to the client's liquidity needs. Government bonds, for instance, are marketed easily; on the other hand, DPPs are illiquid and extremely difficult to market. Municipal securities have a regional rather than a national market; therefore, they may be less marketable than more widely held securities.

Market Risk

Both stocks and bonds involve some degree of **market risk**—that is, the risk that investors may lose some of their principal due to price volatility in the market (also known as **systematic risk**). Stocks tend to be more volatile than bonds; stock prices can rise or fall dramatically due to changing investor demand.

Prices of existing bonds can fluctuate with changing interest rates. There is an inverse relationship between bond prices and bond yields: as bond yields go up, bond prices go down (and vice versa). In order to maintain a competitive yield, the market price of existing bonds drops as new bonds are issued with higher coupon rates.

All things being equal, deep discount bonds are more responsive to changes in market yields than bonds selling at par or at a premium. Compared to other bonds, deep discount bonds tend to appreciate faster as interest rates fall and drop faster as interest rates rise. The most deeply discounted bonds (zero-coupon bonds) are the most susceptible to market risk. Of course, clients will receive face value for their bonds at maturity. If they should sell their bonds before maturity, however, they risk losing some of their principal. This particularly affects clients who invest in bonds with long maturities. They have stable income, but risk losing some principal if they sell the bonds before maturity. Furthermore, if interest rates rise considerably after a bond is issued, the holder may be stuck with a low interest rate until the bond matures, which may be in 20 years.

For bonds with short maturities, the opposite is true. Their price remains fairly stable because investors generally will not sell them at deep discounts or buy them at high premiums. A client's income from short maturities, however, will vary with prevailing interest rates.

Reinvestment Risk

Because bond investors typically seek a steady flow of income, they risk not being able to reinvest their interest income or principal at the same rate. This is known as **reinvestment risk** and is of particular concern during periods of falling interest rates. If interest rates decline, it is extremely difficult for bond investors to maintain the same level of current income without increasing their credit or market risks. Zero-coupon bonds are not susceptible to reinvestment risk because periodic interest payments have been eliminated.

Selection Risk

When all other factors have been accounted for and an investor chooses (or has recommended to her) an investment, there is always the possibility that the choice will be a poor one. Even when an industry is expected to outperform the market and an investment in a company within that industry seems to be a sure thing, the company chosen might be the one company that files for protection under bankruptcy laws. This is known as **selection risk**.

Timing Risk

As in most encounters with today's world, timing is everything. Even an investment in the soundest company with the most profit potential might do poorly simply because the investment was timed wrong. The risk to an investor of buying or selling at the wrong time and incurring losses or lower gains is known as **timing risk**.

Analyzing Investment Returns

Regardless of whether an investor is pursuing aggressive investment strategies (those that entail high levels of risk in return for potential high rewards) or defensive investment strategies (those that emphasize preservation of capital and guaranteed returns), the key question remains: What returns have been made on the investment in securities?

Holding period return. The easiest (and most misleading) method of identifying investment returns is to compute the holding period rate of return. This involves calculating the total return from capital gains and dividend income without taking into consideration how long the investment was held. For example, assume an investor bought 100 shares of stock at $10 per share, sold them for $15 and received $100 in dividends. This is a 60% total return ($500 capital gains + $100 dividend income ÷ $1,000 initial investment = 60%).

A 60% return is fine if the holding period is a year or less. But if this investment were held for ten years or more, a 60% return would not be that impressive. (The investor might do better in a bank savings account, at 5 1/4% interest, offering guaranteed safety of principal and full liquidity.) Thus, the holding period return can be misleading because it fails to take into account the time value of money.

Present value. The concept of present value is based on the time value of money. Receiving a dollar today is preferable to receiving a dollar at some future date. Present value calculates today's value of a future payment or stream of payments, discounted at a given compound interest rate. For example, assume that a customer is offered a zero-coupon bond maturing in one year at $1,000. What price should the customer pay for the bond? Certainly not $1,000. Assume that the interest rate for this type of security is 5%. The price the customer would pay would be $1,000 divided by 1.05, or $952.38. This is the bond's present value.

Internal rate of return. A related concept is the internal rate of return (IRR). This theoretical investment value is most commonly used to calculate the potential return from an investment. The IRR is the discount rate at which the present value of future cash flows of an investment equals the cost of that investment. It is found by trial and error. When the present value of cash outflows (costs) equals cash inflows (returns), the investment is valued at the IRR and there will be no profits. When the IRR is greater than the investor's required rate of return, the investment is acceptable.

Portfolio Analysis

A **portfolio** is the combined holdings of stocks, bonds, cash equivalents, packaged investment products and other investment securities of an individual or a business. Most portfolios are built over time, and their compositions change as purchases and sales of the underlying securities are made. By its very nature, a portfolio of securities offers the investor **diversification**.

Many things can influence the makeup of a portfolio, including both personal and market factors. An investor's portfolio changes as he grows older and his investment needs change. A portfolio of securities appropriate for a 25-year-old unmarried man may not be appropriate for a 45-year-old married man with two children in college or a 65-year-old woman facing retirement. Similarly, a portfolio built during a recessionary period with safety- and income-oriented bonds may be inappropriate at a later date when the economy is experiencing inflation and stocks are showing healthy growth.

Aggressive Investment Strategies

Investors willing to take risks with their capital in order to maximize the returns on their investment portfolios adopt what are known as *aggressive* investment strategies. Aggressive investors place a high percentage of their investable assets in equity securities in the belief that the stock markets will provide the best growth opportunities. These investors keep a much lower percentage in safer debt securities and cash equivalents that provide lower returns. Aggressive investors pursue aggressive policies to buy and sell securities, including:

- selecting stocks with high betas (volatility)
- buying securities on margin
- using put and call option strategies
- employing arbitrage techniques

Defensive Investment Strategies

Not all investors are financially and temperamentally able to withstand the risks that accompany aggressive strategies. These investors are more likely to adopt *defensive* investment strategies in making their investment decisions. Defensive investors are willing to accept potentially lower total returns in order to minimize investment risk and preserve their capital. Investors who apply defensive strategies to their portfolios place a high percentage of their investable capital in bonds, cash equivalents and stocks that are likely to fare well in recessionary times, including stocks in energy, food, pharmaceuticals and other defensive industries.

Balanced Investment Strategies

Most investors adopt a combination of aggressive and defensive strategies when making decisions about the securities in their portfolios. A **balanced portfolio** (also known as a *mixed portfolio)* contains securities of many types, including bonds, stocks, packaged products and cash equivalents. The investor who creates a balanced portfolio will have securities that provide a hedge against the market—no matter what its course.

Modern Portfolio Theory

Modern portfolio theory is a fairly sophisticated approach to choosing investments that allows investors to quantify and control the amount of risk they accept and return they achieve in their portfolios. It differs from traditional securities analysis in that it shifts the emphasis away from analyzing the specific securities to determining the relationship between risk and reward in the total portfolio.

Systematic and Nonsystematic Risk

When investing in equity and debt securities, clients risk losing some of their principal due to fluctuations in market value. Analysts distinguish between **systematic risk** (risk common to all stocks or bonds) and **nonsystematic risk** (risk specific to a particular stock or bond).

Systematic risk. The tendency for security prices to move together is known as systematic risk (also known as **market risk**). Investors cannot avoid this risk—not even through diversification. In bull markets, the prices of individual securities tend to rise with the market. In bear markets, the prices of individual securities tend to decline, regardless of the financial condition of the company that issued the security.

Nonsystematic risk. Nonsystematic risk is associated with the underlying investment itself. Strikes, natural disasters, operating losses and many other factors may cause an individual security's price to decline when the market as a whole is rising. And the introduction of a new product line or an attempted takeover may cause an individual security to rise even when the market is declining. The larger and more diversified an investor's portfolio, the less subject it is to nonsystematic risk.

Risk Management Techniques

Diversification. While investors can do little to avoid systematic risk or inflation, they can temper nonsystematic risk. One important investment strategy is diversification. A portfolio can be diversified in many ways, including:

- type of instrument (equity, debt, packaged and so on)
- industry
- companies within an industry
- length of maturity
- investment rating
- geography

By mixing industries and types of assets, investors spread their risk. A particular event (deregulation of the airline industry, for example) will have less impact if an investor's portfolio consists of a wide assortment of securities than if the investor buys only airline stock.

Dollar cost averaging. A common defensive technique investors use to manage the risk in their portfolios is dollar cost averaging. To apply a dollar cost averaging strategy, an investor makes periodic purchases of a fixed dollar amount in one or more common stocks or mutual funds. In a fluctuating market, the average *cost* of the stock purchased in this manner is always less than the average market *price*. Dollar cost averaging is not a guarantee that the investor will not suffer a loss (and it would be fraudulent for a registered rep to imply so), but it does help control the cost of investing.

Constant ratio plan. The strategy behind a constant ratio plan is that securities should be bought and sold in such a manner as to keep the portfolio balanced between equity and debt securities. The investor initially sets an equity-to-debt ratio (as an example, 60% equity to 40% debt). Purchases and sales are then made as necessary to maintain the ratio between debt and equity securities.

Constant dollar plan. An often used defensive strategy is the constant dollar plan. This strategy's primary goal is to buy and sell securities so that a set dollar amount remains invested at all times. As an example of a constant dollar plan strategy, assume that a customer wants to keep her portfolio at a constant level of $100,000. Under a constant dollar plan, if the value of her portfolio reaches $110,000, the investor will liquidate $10,000 worth of securities. Conversely, if her portfolio slips to $95,000, she will buy $5,000 worth of securities. This forces the investor to sell when the market is high and buy when it is low.

By employing this technique, the client is selling as prices rise and buying as prices fall. A problem with this strategy is that in an extended bull market, the investor keeps liquidating more and more equities to stay at the constant dollar level. By doing so, she may not be taking advantage of the bull stock market.

Ethics in the Securities Industry

The securities industry is a highly competitive business; at times, the participants' desire to succeed seems to outweigh all other considerations. Despite this enormous personal pressure to succeed, the industry is governed by a very strong code of ethics. There is agreement on what constitutes acceptable behavior, and those who engage in unacceptable behavior risk sanctions ranging from fines and reprimands all the way to expulsion from the industry. There are clear standards against which business behavior and practices are measured for fairness and equity.

Ethics in Securities Transactions

A problem in evaluating ethical behavior in securities transactions is the speed at which the industry operates. Decisions are made in split seconds, transactions occur almost instantaneously and millions of pieces of paper are generated and handled daily. If there are questions about the propriety of any transaction or agreement, it is nearly impossible to address them before the fact. This has caused some concern in the investing population—that in the shortness of time available to conduct business, there is also a shortness of time for considering the ethical consequences of actions.

Securities and banking industry regulators are very active in detecting and preventing unethical behavior. Regulators systematically examine activity at all levels—from large firms to banks to investment advisers to registered reps to individual investors. Even the most junior of employees of brokerage firms or commercial banks is expected to employ high standards of business ethics and commercial honor in dealing with the public, customers, the firm or bank and the industry.

Corporate Ethics and Responsibility

The rules that guide relationships between members of the securities industry and all of the other participants are set by the states, the North American Securities Administrators Association (NASAA), the NASD, the SEC, the FRB, the OCC and other regulatory bodies and exchanges throughout the country. The federal securities acts, the state laws, NASAA's *Statement of Policy on Unethical Business Practices of*

Investment Advisers, the *NASD Manual*, the *NYSE Constitution and Rules*, the *Interagency Statement on Retail Sales of Nondeposit Products* issued by the FRB, OCC, OTS and FDIC, together with various other legislative acts governing securities, contain guidelines for what is and what is not acceptable behavior. It is the responsibility of broker-dealers, investment advisers, registered reps and others in the securities industry to be familiar with and follow these guidelines.

There is more to corporate responsibility than complying with rules, however. The first responsibility of any company, including a broker-dealer or bank, is to its stockholders. Broker-dealers and banks must be profitable so as to provide the long-term stability and security needed for a strong, viable securities market.

One part of corporate responsibility for ethical behavior involves a commitment to self-regulation. Every broker-dealer and bank has the responsibility of supervising all associated persons. Each firm must have a written procedures manual and must designate a supervisor (principal) or bank officer who is responsible for enforcing the rules in the manual. The individual charged with oversight responsibility must review and approve all correspondence and keep a record of all securities transactions and correspondence. The management must regularly review the activities of all branch offices. Individuals within the firm who engage in unethical behavior must be detected and their behavior corrected, or they risk being removed from their jobs. Compliance departments generally are the center of member firms' and banks' continuing effort to self-police. Employees need to know that compliance with regulations is important, and that noncompliance is dealt with swiftly.

Through self-regulation, broker-dealers and banks protect customers. Protecting customers includes ensuring they are fully informed about their investments, have access to the information they need to make good investment decisions, and receive value for the commissions and fees they pay. Customers deserve fair and equitable treatment; without it, the industry would lose credibility with the public.

Employee Ethics and Responsibility

The various federal and state securities regulations, the NASD Rules of Fair Practice, the Interagency Statement on Retail Sales of Nondeposit Products and other laws cover employees as well as broker-dealers and banks. Those who work for a broker-dealer, bank or investment adviser represent their employer in all that they do. Employees, both producers and nonproducers, are responsible for ensuring that their activities fall within the guidelines set by regulators and by their companies.

Many firms and banks view the regulations as minimum standards, and set stricter policies for internal behavior. Employees are responsible for knowing their firm's particular policies as these relate to the job they do. Even a well-intentioned employee of a broker-dealer, bank or investment adviser can sometimes run afoul of the regulations. For example, a customer might suggest that an employee deliver a security in person, saving the time and expense of registration and registered-mail delivery. But in most firms and banks, delivering securities in this fashion is strictly against policy, and any person doing so could be subject to dismissal. Shortcuts are rarely a good idea—policies and regulations protect the employee, the firm and the customer.

Employees also have a responsibility to the industry. Serving on industry committees, assisting with public education, and self-education are all part of service to the industry; other examples include representing the firm or bank and the industry in community activities and attending industry conferences and seminars.

Customer Ethics and Responsibility

Practices that would tend to give select investors an unfair advantage over the general public are prohibited by regulations; a prime example of such practices is insider trading. It is the responsibility of the individual investor to abide by these regulations.

The customer also should make full and honest disclosure to the registered representative. This information is all the representative or investment adviser has on which to base recommendations. Such information also may be important in gaining permission to engage in specific kinds or sizes of trades. A customer who fails to disclose relevant information could jeopardize the career of the representative or investment adviser. Failure on the part of a customer to provide information is often the first signal to compliance departments of potential trouble.

Prohibited Practices

The following is a list of trading practices that broker-dealers are prohibited by the NASD (as well as by NASAA and other SROs) from engaging in at all times. The prohibitions apply to all dealings with customers.

Manipulative and Fraudulent Devices

Without exception, NASD member firms are strictly prohibited from using manipulative, deceptive or other fraudulent tactics or methods to effect a transaction or in an attempt to induce the sale or purchase of a security. In recent years, the SEC has stepped up both enforcement and penalties for violations of this rule. A customer may bring suit for damages under the act of 1934 within three years of the alleged manipulation and within one year of discovering it. There is no dollar limit placed on damages in lawsuits based on allegations of manipulation.

Fair Dealing

The NASD's Rules of Fair Practice and the laws of most states require broker-dealers, registered reps and investment advisers to inquire into a customer's financial situation before making any recommendation to purchase, sell or exchange securities. The representative must determine such things as the client's other security holdings, income, expenses and financial goals and objectives. The following activities are considered violations of the rules regarding fair dealing:

- recommending speculative securities without finding out the customer's financial situation and being assured that the customer can bear the risk;
- short-term trading of mutual funds;
- setting up fictitious accounts to transact business that otherwise would be prohibited;
- making unauthorized transactions or use of funds;
- recommending purchases that are inconsistent with the customer's ability to pay;
- committing fraudulent acts (such as forgery and the omission or misstatement of material facts); and
- trading mutual fund positions with the same or similar objectives for the purpose of generating commissions (switching).

Excessive Trading: Churning

The practice of engaging aggressively or excessively in trading a customer's account primarily to generate commissions, rather than to help achieve the customer's stated investment objectives, is an abuse of fiduciary responsibility known as *churning*. Churning can take the form of both excessive frequency (trading in and out of corporate bonds in a retirement account on a weekly basis could be a form of churning) and excessive size (recommending securities purchases to a customer that are so large that they require the liquidation of established positions in order to complete). As one method of preventing such abuses, self-regulatory organizations require that all accounts in which a registered rep or investment adviser has discretionary authority be reviewed frequently by a principal of the member firm.

Selling Dividends

If an investor purchases fund shares just before the dividend distribution date (the ex-dividend date), she is at a double disadvantage. Not only does the market value of the fund shares decrease by the amount of the distribution, but the investor also incurs a tax liability on the distribution. A registered representative is forbidden to encourage investors to purchase fund shares prior to a distribution because of this tax liability, and doing so is known as **selling dividends**.

Breakpoint Sales

Breakpoint sales are those in which a customer unknowingly buys investment company shares in an amount just under a dollar bracket amount that would qualify the investment for a reduction in sales charges. As a result, the customer pays a higher dollar amount in sales charges, which reduces the number of shares purchased and increases the cost basis per share. Encouraging a customer to make purchases in such a manner, or remaining silent when a customer unknowingly requests such a transaction *in order to make the higher commission*, is unethical and a violation of the NASD's Rules of Fair Practice.

The NASD considers this practice contrary to just and equitable principles of trade; it is the responsibility of all parties concerned, particularly the principal, to see that such practices are eliminated.

Misrepresentations

Registered reps and investment advisers are prohibited from misrepresenting themselves or their services to clients or potential clients. Included in this prohibition are misrepresentations covering:

- qualifications, experience and education
- nature of services offered
- fees to be charged

It would also be considered a misrepresentation to either inaccurately state or fail to state a material fact regarding any of the above. Without a full and accurate view of the facts and circumstances surrounding a professional relationship, a client would have difficulty comparing the services of professionals in the business.

Guarantees and Sharing in Customer Accounts

Broker-dealers, investment advisers and registered reps must not guarantee any customer against a loss or guarantee that a gain will be achieved in his account. Except in limited circumstances, members, advisers and representatives are also prohibited from sharing in any profits or losses in a customer's account. An exception will be made if a joint account has received *prior* written approval, and the registered representative shares in the profits and losses only to the extent of his *proportionate contribution* to the account.

If the member firm authorizes such a **shared account**, any or all such sharing must be directly proportionate to the financial contributions made by each party. However, in the case of an account being shared by a member or associated person and a member of that person's immediate family, directly proportionate sharing of profits and losses is not mandatory.

Immediate family members include parents, mother- or father-in-law, husband or wife, children, or any relative to whom the officer or employee in question contributes financial support.

Information Obtained as a Fiduciary

Confidentiality of customer information. Customers expect and deserve a high level of confidentiality. Employees of broker-dealers and investment advisers may not divulge personal information about customers without the express permission of the customer. This includes such information as security positions, personal and financial details and trading intentions. The securities industry depends on the trust of its customers; the employee is responsible for meeting and keeping that trust.

Legal Recourse of Customers

The Securities Exchange Act of 1934, and the acts of 1933 and 1940, all contain sections prohibiting the use of any fraudulent or manipulative device in the selling of securities to the public.

The rules make it unlawful for any person to use the mails or any facilities of interstate commerce to "… employ, in connection with the purchase or sale of any security … any manipulative or deceptive device … in contravention of such rules and regulations as the Commission may prescribe as necessary." In essence, this passage states simply that an act is unlawful if the SEC says it is, and the enforcement of the intent of the act is not to be limited by the letter of the law.

Any client may sue for damages if he believes that the broker-dealer or bank employed any form of manipulative or deceptive practices in the sale of securities. The client must bring the lawsuit within three years of when the manipulative act occurs and within one year of his discovery of the manipulation or deception.

Criminal Penalties

The criminal penalties for violations of securities laws were increased through an amendment to the act of 1934. If a person is convicted of willfully violating federal securities regulations, or of *knowingly* making false or misleading statements in a registration document, that person can be fined up to $1,000,000, sentenced to prison for not more than ten years, or both; the maximum fine is $2,500,000 for other than a natural person.

Review Questions

1. To open a new account, the registered representative must obtain information about the client's

    I.   financial needs
    II. investment objectives
    III. financial condition

    A. I and II only
    B. I and III only
    C. II and III only
    D. I, II and III

2. As a rep, if a customer wishes to place an order that you feel is unsuitable for her, you should advise the customer of your opinion and

    A. refuse to execute the order
    B. execute the order only after approval of a principal
    C. execute the order only after MSRB approval
    D. execute the order as directed by the customer

3. Any recommendations made to customers by a broker-dealer must be suitable for the customer based on an investigation of the customer's

    I.   investment objectives
    II. financial background
    III. tax status

    A. I only
    B. I and II only
    C. II and III only
    D. I, II and III

4. In recommending securities to customers, a member firm must

    A. not make guarantees as to future performance
    B. have a suitable basis for the recommendations
    C. disclose or offer to disclose supporting documentation
    D. comply with all of the above

5. When a member firm refers to its previous recommendations, it must also

    I.   indicate that the market was generally rising if such is the case
    II. show all of its recommendations of the same type of securities made within the previous twelve months
    III. indicate the date and price of the security at the time of recommendation
    IV. give the amount of profit or loss that would have been realized had an individual acted on all of the recommendations

    A. I, II and III only
    B. II and III only
    C. I, II, III and IV
    D. None of the above

6. Which of the following best describes "market risk"?

    A. The risk of losing some or all principal due to failure of the issuer
    B. The risk of not being able to convert the investment into cash when needed
    C. The risk of losing some or all principal due to price volatility in the market
    D. The risk of incurring losses or lower gains by buying or selling at the wrong time

7. The NASD Rules of Fair Practice govern the actions of its members. All of the following are considered violations of the rules EXCEPT

    A. churning accounts
    B. the blanket recommending of low-price speculative stocks
    C. using discretionary authority
    D. guaranteeing a customer against loss

8. The term "churning" refers to

    A. excessive trading in a customer's discretionary account for the express purpose of generating commissions
    B. the practice of freeriding in more than one customer's account at a time
    C. manipulation of market prices by a firm
    D. making false or misleading statements to a customer for the purpose of inducing the customer to purchase or sell a security

9. To what does the term "selling dividends" refer?

   A. Encouraging mutual fund customers to sell their holdings just before the fund declares a dividend payment
   B. Enticing customers to buy mutual fund shares just before a dividend payment date
   C. Withdrawing dividends rather than reinvesting these amounts in additional shares
   D. Encouraging investors to postpone purchases of mutual fund shares until after the ex-date for a dividend distribution

10. Encouraging a customer to purchase mutual fund shares in an amount just under the next dollar volume bracket, which entitles the customer to a reduction in sales charges, or remaining silent on the matter, is called

    A. breakpoint sales
    B. boiler room selling
    C. double-dip selling
    D. low-ball sales

Answers & Rationale

1. **D.** Under Rule 405 (the NYSE "Know Your Customer" Rule), all of this information is considered essential before opening an account.   (Page 67)

2. **D.** The customer controls the account ultimately, but in circumstances such as this it would be wise to have the customer put the order in writing, noting the fact that you advised against it.   (Page 73)

3. **D.** The MSRB requires that financial status, tax bracket and objective be taken into consideration when recommending a security.   (Page 72)

4. **D.** Answers A through C are applicable to customer recommendations.   (Page 73)

5. **A.** When referring to past recommendations, a member must show the whole universe of recommendations in the past year, not only the winners. A member must indicate whether the overall market was generally rising and the date and price of the security at the time of recommendation.   (Page 73)

6. **C.** Answer C describes market risk. Answer A describes credit risk; answer B describes liquidity risk; and answer D describes timing risk.   (Page 79)

7. **C.** Use of discretionary authority is not a violation of the Rules of Fair Practice, but abuse of that authority by excessive trading and the misuse of a customer's funds or securities is. Answers A, B and D are clear violations. Recommendations should be based on the customer's financial status and objectives. Low-priced stocks may result in a higher percentage of commission. Brokers that make a practice of selling low-priced stocks are often called *penny brokers*.   (Page 88)

8. **A.** "Churning" describes trading that is excessive in light of a particular customer's circumstances or trading more excessive than what would normally be considered suitable. This is equally true for both discretionary and nondiscretionary accounts.   (Page 88)

9.   **B.**   "Selling dividends" is an unethical sales practice in which a seller intentionally or unintentionally misleads customers into believing they will be getting the equivalent of a rebate on their investments because the fund will soon be paying a distribution. The customers suffer out-of-pocket losses because the cash immediately coming back is dividend income, subject to tax.   (Page 89)

10. **A.**   "Breakpoint sales" are those in which a customer unknowingly buys investment company shares in an amount just under a dollar bracket amount that would qualify the customer's investment for a reduction in sales charges. As a result the customer pays a higher dollar amount in sales charges, which reduces the number of shares purchased and results in a higher cost basis per share.   (Page 89)

4 Investment Company Regulation, Registration and Management

Key Terms

advertising materials
affiliated person
cooling-off period
custodian
Glass-Steagall Act of 1933
hot issue
indication of interest
interested person
interlocking directorate
investment adviser
Maloney Act

preliminary prospectus
red herring
registration statement
sales literature
Securities Act of 1933
Securities Exchange Act of 1934
selling group
sponsor
tombstone
underwriter

Overview

This chapter introduces you to the regulation of investment companies, beginning with a review of the stock market crash of 1929—the calamity that precipitated the legislation now governing securities trading. From there, the chapter discusses rules for communicating with the public, investment company registration and, finally, investment company management structure.

The Regulation of New Issues

The Crash of 1929

During the early 1900s, America enjoyed a long-term bull market that promised to last forever. Attracted by the dream of easy money, Americans turned en masse to Wall Street, poring over stock price tables and learning the language of trading operations. For the first time, the general public became a significant factor in the market; but often they purchased securities knowing little or nothing about the issuing company or its plans for spending their money.

Investors borrowed heavily (that is, they bought securities *on margin*). Doing so was an act of faith in the perpetual bull market and an outcome of generous credit policies that allowed investors to borrow most of the purchase price of stock. By the summer of 1929, over a million Americans held stock on margin.

The rest is familiar history. Stock prices reached new heights in early September 1929. Then things fell apart. By the third week of September, tumbling prices brought the Dow Jones averages down 19 points. A month later, averages were 50 points below the September high mark. The downward spiral of prices gained momentum, breaking through crumbling layers of anticipated buying support.

Rapidly declining prices meant investors' stocks were no longer adequate security for the loans they had taken out to buy them. Securities purchased on very low margins, therefore, were sold to raise money, and this caused even deeper drops in market prices. Stock dumping destroyed grassroots investors and wealthy traders alike, including those supposedly safe investment trusts, which unloaded their holdings for whatever they could bring.

The Legislative Reaction

After the crash, the market continued to decline for several years. During that time, Congress examined the causes of the debacle and passed several laws meant to prevent its recurrence. This legislation included, among other acts, the Securities Act of 1933, the Glass-Steagall Act of 1933, and the Securities Exchange Act of 1934.

The Securities Act of 1933. The Securities Act of 1933 requires issuers of securities to provide sufficient information for investors to make fully informed buying decisions. This information must be registered with the federal government and published in a prospectus. The act outlaws fraud committed in connection with the underwriting and issuing of all securities (including exempt securities).

The Glass-Steagall Act (Banking Act) of 1933. Securities firms were not the only financial companies to go belly-up in the early 1930s. Banks, too, went broke in vast numbers. Congress concluded that one factor in the general financial collapse was the fact that commercial bankers engaged in investment banking. In their role as commercial bankers, they took deposits and financed commercial enterprises. As investment bankers, they underwrote stocks, using deposits to finance their securities ventures. Losses on the investment side of the bank, therefore, affected the health of the commercial operations.

With the Glass-Steagall Act (Banking Act) of 1933, Congress attempted to erect a wall between commercial banking and investment banking. The act forbids commercial banks to underwrite securities (except municipal general obligation bonds) and denies investment bankers the right to open deposit accounts or make commercial loans.

The Securities Exchange Act of 1934. The Securities Exchange Act of 1934 addresses secondary trading of securities, personnel involved in secondary trading and fraudulent trading practices. It also created the Securities and Exchange Commission (a government agency) to oversee the industry.

In 1938, the act was broadened when it was amended by the **Maloney Act**, which provides for the establishment of a self-regulatory body to help police the industry. Under the provisions of the Maloney Act, the NASD regulates OTC trading in much the same way as the exchanges regulate their members.

The Trust Indenture Act of 1939. The Trust Indenture Act of 1939 was created, in part, to provide the same sort of protection to the purchasers of debt securities as is afforded to investors in equities. The term "debt securities" includes all notes, bonds, debentures and other similar evidences of indebtedness. The term "trust indenture" covers any mortgage, trust or other indenture, or any similar instrument or agreement.

As its major focus and means of protecting the public interest, the act prohibits the sale of any corporate debt security unless it has been issued under a **trust indenture**. In addition to full disclosure about the nature of the debt issue and the issuer, the trust indenture identifies the rights and powers of the trustee, as well as the trustee's responsibilities.

The trust indenture is the contract that gives the appointed trustee the powers necessary to enforce the issuer's obligations and the debt holders' rights. Among the trustee's responsibilities is the representation of the future investors in the preparation of the indenture.

The Investment Company Act of 1940. The Investment Company Act of 1940 was created to regulate investment companies, protect investors from unfair dealings and provide investors with current information.

The Legislation

The Securities Act of 1933 regulates new issues of corporate securities sold to the public. The act is also referred to as the *Full Disclosure Act*, the *New Issues Act*, the *Truth in Securities Act* and the *Prospectus Act*. The main purpose of the act is to ensure that the investing public is fully informed about a security and its issuing company when the security is first sold (in the **primary market**). The act requires the registration of new issues (both debt and equity) of nonexempt securities with the SEC if the mails or any other means of interstate commerce are used to offer or sell the security to the public. It also requires that a prospectus (which contains information derived from the registration statement) be given to buyers.

The 1933 act protects the investor who is considering purchase of new issues by:

- requiring registration of new issues that are to be distributed interstate;
- requiring the issuer to provide full and fair disclosure about itself and the offering;
- requiring the issuer to make available all material information necessary for the investor to judge the merit of the issue;
- regulating the underwriting and distribution of primary and secondary issues; and
- providing criminal penalties for fraud in the issuance of new securities.

When a corporation wants to issue its securities to the public, the SEC requires it to use *due diligence* to:

- supply detailed information about itself and its securities to the SEC; and
- supply the relevant portion of that information to the general investing public.

A **registration statement** disclosing material information must be filed with the SEC by the issuer. Part of the registration statement is a prospectus, which must be provided to all purchasers of the new issue. A prospectus contains much of the same information included in the registration statement, but without the supporting documentation. The registration statement must contain:

- a description of the issuer's business;
- the names and addresses of key people in the company, officers and directors, their salaries and a five-year business history of each;
- the amount of corporate securities owned by these key people and by owners of 10% or more of the company;
- the company's capitalization, including its equity and the amount of funded debt;
- a description of how the proceeds will be used; and
- whether the company is involved in any legal proceedings.

Communications with the Public

The Prospectus

The preliminary prospectus. After an issuer files a registration statement with the SEC, a **cooling-off** period begins. During the cooling-off period (a 20-day period during which the SEC reviews a security's registration statement), a registered rep may discuss the new issue with clients and provide them with a **preliminary prospectus** (also known as a **red herring**). A registered rep *may not* send any other material to potential customers with the preliminary prospectus, including research reports, *Value Line* sheets, marketing letters and so on.

A red herring need not include the final price of the securities, commissions, dealer discounts or net proceeds to the company (although pricing formulas and other information are often included). The document must carry a legend to the effect that a registration statement has been filed with the SEC, but is not yet effective. By law, this disclaimer message must be printed in red ink.

SEC rules prohibit the sale of public offering securities other than by prospectus, which means that no sales are allowed unless and until the buyer is furnished with a final prospectus (that is, securities may be *sold by prospectus only)*.

However, the SEC does allow the use of preliminary prospectuses (essentially all the same information found in a final prospectus, but with only an offering price range or no price at all) as prospecting tools. The underwriters and selling group members thus have a document to use as they test for investor receptivity and gather **indications of interest**.

An indication of interest is just that—a broker-dealer's or investor's declaration that it might be interested in purchasing some of the security from the underwriter after the security comes out of registration. An indication of interest on the part of the broker-dealer or investor is *not* a commitment to buy because sales are prohibited until after the registration becomes effective (the *effective date)*.

The final prospectus. When the registration statement does become effective, the issuer amends the preliminary prospectus and adds information, including the effective date, final offering price and underwriting spread. This revised report becomes the final prospectus. Registered representatives may then take orders from those customers who indicated an interest in buying during the cooling-off period.

A copy of the final prospectus must precede or accompany all sales confirmations. The prospectus should include all of the following information:

- description of the offering
- price of the offering
- selling discounts
- date of the offering
- use of the proceeds
- description of the underwriting, but not the actual contract
- statement of the possibility that the issue's price may be stabilized
- history of the business
- risks to the purchasers
- description of management
- material financial information
- legal opinion concerning the formation of the corporation
- SEC disclaimer

SEC review. The SEC reviews the prospectus to ensure that it contains whatever material facts the SEC deems necessary, but it does not guarantee the accuracy of the disclosures. Further, the SEC does not approve the issue, but simply clears it for distribution. Implying that the SEC has approved the issue is a violation of federal law. Finally, the SEC does not pass judgment on the investment merit of the issue. The front of every prospectus must contain a clearly printed SEC disclaimer clause specifying the limits of the SEC's review procedures. A typical SEC disclaimer clause reads as follows:

> These securities have not been approved or disapproved by the Securities and Exchange Commission nor has the Commission passed upon the accuracy or adequacy of this prospectus. Any representation to the contrary is a criminal offense.

The information supplied to the SEC becomes public (accessible to anyone) once a registration statement is filed. (This is one of the reasons why issuers seek ways to sell securities to the public without having to file registration statements.)

The critical path from the registration of securities to their effective date is shown in Figure 11.

NASD Rules Concerning Public Communications

Many rules and regulations regarding securities transactions were conceived and written into law in order to offer the general public some form of protection from unscrupulous investment professionals. In recognition of the power of the various media to persuade people, the NASD and the SEC strictly enforce all of the rules and regulations designed to protect the public.

The two main problems addressed by the NASD's code of professionalism in advertising and sales literature are omissions and distortions of material facts. In general, all communications from a member to the public must be based on principles of fair dealing and good faith. The communication should provide a sound basis for evaluating the facts in regard to the product, service or industry promoted. Exaggerated, unwarranted or misleading statements or claims are strictly prohibited.

Figure 11   Critical Path from Securities Registration to the Effective Date

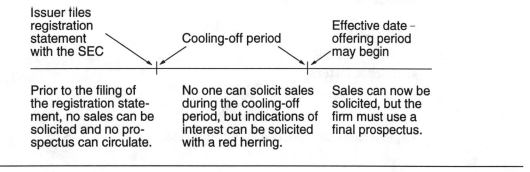

In an attempt to guide members in creating and producing advertising and sales literature that meet the Association's professional standards, specific requirements apply.

Identification of source. In general, sales literature (including market letters and research reports) must identify: the name of the member firm; the person or firm that prepared the material if copy was prepared outside; and the date the material was first used.

If the literature cites price or market performance data that are not current (or any other noncurrent information), that fact should be stated in the material. Copy created for paid advertising need carry only the name of the member firm.

Advertising and Sales Literature

Advertising materials. "Advertising" includes copy and support graphics and/or other support materials intended for:

- publication in newspapers, magazines or other periodicals;
- radio or television broadcast;
- prerecorded telephone marketing messages and tape recordings;
- videotape displays;
- signs or billboards;
- motion pictures and filmstrips;
- telephone directories; or
- *any other use of the public or electronic media.*

Sales literature. "Sales literature" is *any written communication distributed to customers* (or to the public in general) or available to people upon request, and that does not meet the definition of "advertising." Standardized sales pitches, telephone scripts and seminar tapes are all classed as sales literature, and are therefore subject to the same rules and regulations that apply to printed literature. Sales literature includes materials such as:

- circulars;
- research reports;
- market letters;
- form letters;
- options worksheets;
- performance reports and summaries;

- text prepared and used for educational seminars;
- telemarketing scripts;
- prepared scripts for public interest radio and television interview programs; and
- reprints and excerpts from any advertisement, sales literature or published news item or article.

Sales literature can be distributed in either written, oral or electronic form. It must always be preceded or accompanied by a prospectus.

Generic advertising (Rule 135a). Generic (or institutional) advertising is a special type of advertising that is used to promote securities as an investment medium but that does not make reference to any particular security. The rules that regulate generic advertising are similar to those that govern tombstones, except that they specifically mention investment company advertising. Institutional advertising uses general terms and phrases and often includes information about:

- the securities offered by investment companies
- the nature of investment companies
- services offered in connection with the described securities
- explanations of the various types of investment companies
- descriptions of exchange and reinvestment privileges
- where the public can write or call for further information

All generic advertisements must contain the name and address of the registered sponsor of the advertisement and can be placed only by a firm that actually offers the type of security or service described. For example, a discount brokerage firm would not be permitted to advertise no-load mutual funds if it does not sell them.

Tombstones. Tombstones are advertisements that adhere to the content restrictions of Rule 134 (**Rule 134 advertisements**); this differentiates them from prospectuses. Rule 145 makes it unlawful to solicit stockholders unless a prospectus accompanies the solicitation. An underwriter is limited in what he can publicly state about a security in registration when advertising or otherwise gathering indications of interest for an upcoming public offering. Under Rule 134, advertising copy and other sales materials will not be deemed a prospectus (which means they need not be filed with the SEC as part of the registration statement) if the body copy is limited to the following:

- the name and address of the issuer of the securities being offered (or the name and address of the person or company whose assets are to be sold in exchange for the securities being offered);
- a brief description of the business of the person making the offer;

- the date, time and place of the meeting at which stockholders are to vote on or consent to the proposed transaction (exchange of securities or sale of assets);
- a brief description of the planned transaction (material facts and financial information); or
- any legend or disclaimer statement required by state or federal law.

Any advertising copy in a tombstone must also contain the following disclaimers:

- that the registration statement has been filed by the issuer but is not yet effective;
- that the communication does *not* represent an offer to sell the securities described—securities are **sold by prospectus only**;
- the name and address of the person (or firm) to contact for a prospectus; and
- that a response to this advertisement does not obligate the prospect to a buying commitment of any kind (i.e., that it represents only an **indication of interest**).

Advertisements and other promotional materials created in support of open-end investment company securities being sold on a continuous new-issue offering basis are also covered by this rule.

Approval and Filing Requirements

Approval

Each advertisement and piece of sales literature must be approved *prior to use* and *prior to filing with the NASD* by the signature or initial of a registered principal of the member. For advertisements or sales literature specific to options, the advertisement or sales literature must be approved by a registered options principal (ROP) or compliance ROP (CROP). Research reports must be approved by a *supervisory analyst* acceptable to the NYSE.

Advertisements and sales literature relating to investment company securities (mutual funds, variable contracts and unit investment trusts) must be filed with the NASD's advertising department within ten days of first use or publication by the member, and each filing must include an actual or anticipated date of first use. Advertisements and sales literature used and filed previously and without change do not have to be refiled. If the advertisement or sales literature refers to investment company products solely as part of a listing of services or products offered, the filing requirement will not apply.

Figure 12 shows an example of an advertisement for a mutual fund.

Figure 12   Example of a Mutual Fund Tombstone

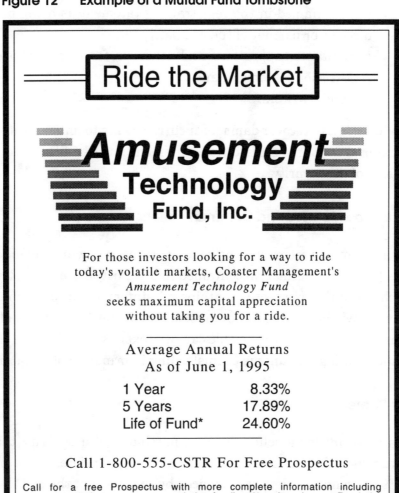

Civil Liabilities under the Act of 1933

Untruths in Registration Statements

If a registration statement contains untrue statements of material fact or omits material facts, any person acquiring the security may sue any or all of the following:

- those who signed the registration statement;
- directors and partners of the issuer;
- anyone named in the registration statement as being or about to become a director or partner of the company;
- accountants, appraisers and other professionals who contributed to the registration statement; and
- the underwriters.

A civil lawsuit to recover damages incurred owing to untrue statements or omissions of material facts in a registration statement must be filed within three years after the sale of the security.

Untruths in Prospectuses and Communications

The seller of any security being sold by prospectus (which includes oral communications based on information contained in a security's prospectus) will be liable to the purchaser if the prospectus contains misstatements or omissions of material facts. To avoid civil liability, the seller must prove that he did not know of the misstatements or omissions and that reasonable care was exercised at the time of the sale to prevent communicating any untrue or misleading information of a material nature.

Unlawful Representations

It is unlawful for a seller to tell a purchaser of a security that the information contained in the registration statement (and, therefore, in the prospectus) must be 100% true and complete as evidenced by the fact that the SEC has not issued a stop order.

Investment Company Registration

A company must register as an investment company with the SEC if:

- the company is in the business of investing, reinvesting, owning, holding or trading in securities; or
- 40% or more of the company's assets are invested in securities. (Government securities and securities of majority-owned subsidiaries are not used in calculating the 40% limitation.)

Registration of Investment Companies

Before a company may register as an investment company with the SEC, certain minimum requirements must be met. A management company (or any other type of investment company, for that matter) is not allowed to issue securities to the public unless it has:

- private capitalization (seed money) of at least $100,000
- 100 investors
- clearly defined investment objectives

If the investment company does not have 100 shareholders and $100,000 in assets, it can still register a public offering with the SEC provided that it can meet these requirements within 90 days of registration.

The company must clearly define an investment objective under which it plans to operate. Once defined, the objective, whether growth, income or whatever, may only be changed with a majority vote of the company's outstanding shares.

Open-end companies. In addition, the act of 1940 requires open-end companies to have the following:

- no more than one class of security
- a minimum asset-to-debt ratio of 300%

Because open-end investment companies may issue only one class of security (common stock), they are permitted to borrow from banks. They cannot issue preferred stock or bonds, but may borrow money as long as the company's asset-to-debt ratio is not less than 3-to-1 (that is, debt coverage by assets of at least 300%).

SEC Registration and Public Offering Requirements

Investment companies must file registration statements with the SEC, provide full disclosure and generally follow the same public offering procedures that other corporations and noninvestment companies follow when issuing securities. In filing for registration as an investment company with the SEC, a corporation must provide the following information in its registration form:

- the type of investment company it intends to be (i.e., open-end or closed-end);
- any plans the company has to raise money by borrowing;
- the company's intention (if any) to concentrate its investments in a single industry;
- any plans for investing in real estate or commodities;
- conditions under which investment policies may be changed by a vote of the shareholders;
- the full names and addresses of each affiliated person; and
- a description of the business experience of each officer and director during the preceding five years.

The investment company is considered registered upon the receipt of its notification of registration by the SEC. Once a corporation has met the above tests for registration as an investment company, the SEC allows it certain rights and places certain prohibitions on its activities. While operating as an investment company, corporations are strictly prohibited from:

- seeking to gain control of other companies
- acting in the capacity of a broker by trading securities for a commission
- acting as a bank, insurance company or savings and loan
- operating with fewer than 100 shareholders or less than $100,000 in assets

There are exceptions to these guidelines. Under the act, the following corporations are exempt from registration as investment companies with the SEC, even if more than 40% of their assets are invested in securities:

- underwriters and brokers
- banks, insurance companies and bank investment advisory accounts
- mortgage bankers
- security holders protective committees
- real estate investment trusts (REITs)

Continuous Public Offering Securities

The sale of open-end management company shares is treated by the SEC as a continuous public offering of shares, which means that the shares must be sold by prospectus only. All sales must be accompanied by a prospectus. With publicly traded (closed-end) funds, only the initial public offering stock is sold with prospectus.

Purchasing mutual fund shares on margin. Because a mutual fund is continually issuing new shares, and it is considered a continuous primary offering, mutual fund shares may not be purchased on margin; that is, an investor may not borrow from the broker-dealer to buy the securities. Mutual fund shares may be used as collateral in a margin account, however, if they have been held fully paid for 30 days.

Registration of Investment Company Securities

In addition to filing as an investment company under the act of 1940, the investment company, like any other corporation, must register with the SEC any securities that it intends to issue. The registration of shares takes place under the Securities Act of 1933.

Registration Statement—Prospectus

The registration statement a corporation must file consists of two parts: part 1 is the prospectus, a copy of which must be furnished to every person to whom the securities are offered; and part 2 is the document containing information that need not be furnished to every purchaser, but that must be made available for public inspection. In general, the prospectus must contain any information that the SEC decides should be revealed in the best interest of the public. The fact that all publicly issued securities must be registered with the SEC does not mean that the SEC in any way *approves* the securities. For that reason, every prospectus must contain a disclaimer on its front cover.

Securities Issued by Investment Companies

Common stock (equity securities). Investment companies, both open-end and closed-end, allow investors to participate in their portfolios by selling shares of the fund. The shares of common stock represent an undivided interest in the company's portfolio. The investor's interest in the portfolio is proportionate to the number of shares owned.

Open-end companies are not allowed to issue senior securities, such as bonds and preferred stock, but are permitted to borrow from banks. A 300% asset-to-debt coverage ratio applies to open-end companies borrowing from banks.

Bonds (debt securities). Only closed-end investment companies are permitted to issue debt securities (senior securities are issued under the Trust Indenture Act of 1939). A closed-end company may issue either bonds or debentures, provided that, after they have been issued, the company maintains an asset-to-debt coverage ratio of at least 300%.

As an example, if a closed-end investment company has $200 million in common stock outstanding, it can issue up to $100 million in bonds. After the bonds are issued, it will have $200 million in assets represented by the stock and $100 million in cash from the bond sale, for a total ratio of $300 million in assets to $100 million in debt (or 300% coverage). From another perspective, the company is allowed to issue bonds worth up to 50% of the value of its outstanding common stock.

Preferred stock (equity securities). A closed-end investment company can also issue preferred stock with the approval of its common shareholders. Restrictions similar to those covering the issuance of bonds exist, and the principal must become familiar with those restrictions.

In order to conduct an offering of preferred stock, the company must be able to maintain a 200% asset-to-preferred-stock coverage ratio. That is, the company can issue preferred stock in an amount equal to 100% of the value of its outstanding common stock. Any preferred stock that the investment company issues must be a cumulative preferred; the preferred stock must have the right to receive all scheduled dividends (including defaulted dividends) before any dividends are distributed to the common shareholders. After any distributions are made, the company must still maintain at least a 200% asset coverage.

Restrictions on Operations

Functions and Activities of Investment Companies

The act of 1940 sets out rules, restrictions and regulations under which investment companies must operate. These rules and regulations were written to protect the investor and have been amended and updated frequently. The SEC has identified certain activities of mutual funds as having high risk potential. Examples of such activities include:

- making securities purchases on margin
- selling securities short
- participation in joint investment or trading accounts
- acting as distributor of its own securities, except through an underwriter

These high-risk activities are restricted, but not prohibited, by regulations issued under the 1940 act. It is clear that the fund must specifically disclose these activities and the extent to which it plans to engage in these activities in its prospectus.

Changes in the Registration Statement

Shareholders' Right to Vote

Whatever is stated in the prospectus as the management company's purpose for existence, its investment objectives, capital formation methods, organizational structure, shareholder services, and so on, can be changed only by a *majority of shares outstanding* being voted in favor of the changes.

Before any change can be made to the published bylaws or objectives of the fund, the approval of the shareholders is mandatory. In voting matters, it is the *majority of shares voted* for or against a proposition that counts, *not the majority of people voting*. Thus one shareholder holding 51% of all the shares outstanding can determine the outcome of a vote.

Among the changes that would require a majority vote of the shares outstanding are the following:

- changes in *borrowing* by open-end companies (open-end management companies are permitted to borrow cash from banks; closed-end companies are prohibited from borrowing money);
- *issuing or underwriting* other securities (closed-end companies are allowed to raise capital through the issuance of senior securities, either debt or preferred stock; open-end companies are prohibited from issuing senior securities);
- purchasing or underwriting *real estate;*
- making *loans;*

- a change of *subclassification* (for example, from open-end to closed-end, or from diversified to nondiversified);
- a change in *sales load policy* (for example, from a no-load fund to a load fund);
- a change in the *nature of the business* (for example, ceasing business as an investment company); and
- a change in *investment policy* (for example, from income to growth, or from bonds to small capitalization stocks).

In addition to the right to vote on these items, stockholders retain all rights normally accorded to the holders of any corporate stock.

Investment Company Management

Like publicly owned corporations in general, a management company has a CEO, a team of officers and a board of directors, all in place to serve the interests of the investors.

Board of Directors

The officers and directors concern themselves with investment objectives, long-term strategy, portfolio funding and cash flow matters, accounting and business administration duties. But they themselves do not manage the investment portfolio. As with any other type of corporation, the shareholders of an investment company elect the board of directors to make decisions and oversee operations. The shareholders of a management investment company must approve the election of the fund's board members, as well as any additions or replacements to the board.

The only exception to this rule is that any vacancies that occur after the initial election may be filled in any legal manner as long as at least two thirds of the directors have been elected by the shareholders. The board may be divided into classes, provided that no one class of directors is elected for a period shorter than one year or longer than five years.

The act of 1940 places restrictions on who is eligible to sit on the board of directors of an investment company. A section of the act, called **interlocking directorate**, requires that at least 40% of the directors must be independent (noninterested persons). This means that no more than 60% of the board members may be interested persons, including attorneys on retainer, accountants and any persons employed in similar capacities with the company (see "Affiliated and Interested Persons" later). For example, if a fund has ten directors, at least four of the directors can hold no other position within the fund.

The second restriction is that no one may serve on a board of directors who has been convicted of either a felony (of any type) or of a misdemeanor involving the securities industry.

The third restriction to be aware of is that no person who has been either temporarily or permanently enjoined from acting as an underwriter, broker, dealer or investment company by any court can be elected to a term on a board.

Investment Adviser

Once an investment company is registered as such and has elected its board of directors, the board then contracts with an outside **investment adviser** (portfolio manager). The fund's investment adviser may be an individual or an investment advisory company. Once hired, the adviser is responsible for investing the cash and securities held in the fund's portfolio, implementing investment strategy, clearly identifying the tax status of any distribution made to shareholders as a result of activity in the fund's portfolio, and managing the day-to-day trading of the portfolio. Naturally, the adviser must adhere to the objective as stated in the fund's prospectus (only a majority vote of the shares can alter a fund's objective). The adviser cannot transfer the responsibility of portfolio management to anyone else. The simple fact that an investment adviser is elected does not relieve the directors of their responsibility of adhering to the fund's objective.

Investment advisers earn management fees for their services, typically a set annual percentage (such as .5% of the portfolio asset value being managed) which is paid from the net assets of the fund. In addition, if an investment adviser consistently outperforms a specified market performance benchmark, he will typically earn an incentive bonus. (But the sword is double-edged; if the adviser underperforms, his management contract may not be renewed.)

In choosing an investment adviser, the company must select the best, most qualified adviser it can find without regard to former, current or future ties or business the adviser might have with the company. To protect the shareholders of the investment company, the act of 1940 requires:

- a written contract, which must be approved initially by a vote of the shareholders; and
- that the advisory contract has a *maximum life of two years,* after which time it may be extended on a year-to-year basis by the annual approval of the directors and/or a majority vote of the shares.

The **contract** must also include:

- a precise description of all compensation to be paid the investment adviser;
- a provision that the contract may be terminated by the board of directors or by a majority vote of the shares with 60 days notice;
- the stipulation that the contract will be terminated if the investment adviser assigns its contract to another person (note: *assignment* means any transfer of a controlling interest in the management group, of which the investment adviser is a part);
- the requirement that any such assignment be approved by the shareholders of the investment company; and
- the requirement that any amendment or renewal of the advisory contract be approved by a majority of the noninterested (independent) directors.

Similarly, the terms under which the principal underwriter handling the continuously issued and publicly offered shares will be compensated must also be in writing and approved by a majority of voting shares outstanding.

An investment company is prohibited from contracting with an investment adviser who has been convicted of a securities-related felony unless it has received an exemption from the SEC. In addition, an investment company is prohibited from lending money to its investment adviser.

Affiliated and Interested Persons

The act of 1940 and subsequent amendments identify certain categories of individuals and entities that have control over or may influence the operation of an investment company. The identification of these persons is critical, as the act regulates and places restrictions on their activities. The act broadly defines two classes of persons: affiliated and interested.

An *affiliated person* is in a *control* position within the company; in general, an affiliated person controls the investment company's operations. An *interested person* is in a position to *influence* the operations of an investment company.

Affiliated Persons

Anyone who could have any type of control over an investment company's operations is called an **affiliated person**. The act has set forth a series of regulations that effectively prohibit affiliated persons from using the control they have for their personal benefit. Those persons considered affiliated include:

- anyone with 5% or more of the outstanding voting securities of the investment company;
- any corporation in which the investment company holds 5% or more of its outstanding securities;
- any person (an individual or a corporate entity) controlled in whole or in part by the investment company;
- all officers, directors, partners and employees of the investment company;
- the investment adviser; and
- in the absence of a board of directors, the individual who deposits the assets into the account at the custodial bank (also known as the *depositor)*.

Interested Persons

Introduced by the 1970 amendments to the act, the designation **interested person** broadens the category of people whose actions are restricted or regulated by the SEC. The list of restricted persons now includes broker-dealers, legal counsels and immediate family of affiliated persons, as well as anybody else whom the SEC wishes to designate as such. All of the following are considered interested persons:

- person associated with the investment company, its investment adviser or its principal underwriter, including the immediate families of any affiliated person;
- person employed by the investment company, the investment adviser or the principal underwriter;
- person who, within the last two years, has acted as legal counsel to any affiliated person;
- broker-dealer registered under the Securities Exchange Act of 1934; and

- any other person deemed to be interested by the SEC because of business dealings with the company, its investment adviser or its principal underwriter.

The directors of an investment company are specifically excluded from the definition of an interested person. The directors are, however, affiliated persons (see the restrictions of director membership under "Board of Directors" previously).

Restrictions

In addition to any other restrictions, an affiliated or interested person is prohibited from:

- borrowing money from the investment company; or
- selling any security or other property to the investment company or to any company controlled by the investment company.

Custodian

As a means of safeguarding investors' assets, the act of 1940 requires each investment company to place its securities in the custody of a bank (with assets of at least $500,000) or a stock exchange member broker-dealer. The bank or broker-dealer performs an important safekeeping role as custodian of the company's securities and cash and receives a fee for its services (which, like the adviser's fee, is paid from the net assets of the fund). Often, the custodian will handle most of the clerical functions the investment company might need. The custodian may, with the consent of the investment company, deposit the securities it is entrusted to hold in one of the systems for the central handling of securities established by the NASD or the NYSE. These systems make it easier to transfer or pledge securities. Once securities are placed in the system, most such transfers can be accomplished with a simple bookkeeping entry rather than actual physical delivery of the securities.

Once a custodian has been designated by an investment company (and assets are transferred into its safekeeping), it is required to follow certain rules and regulations as specified by the act. The custodian must:

- keep the investment company's assets physically segregated at all times;
- allow withdrawal only under the rules of the SEC; and

- restrict access to the account to certain officers and employees of the investment company.

The board of directors designates, by majority vote, which employees it wishes to have access to the account. As a further safeguard, the act specifies that at least two of these designated employees must be present each time the account is opened. The only other people the custodian is permitted to allow access to the account are the independent public accountants verifying the securities and any authorized employees of the SEC.

The securities in the account must be verified by an independent public accountant at least three times a year. One accounting is performed for the annual report; the other two are held at the accountant's request without advance notice to the company.

Transfer Agent (Customer Services Agent)

The functions of the transfer agent are manifold; they include, among other duties, issuing and redeeming fund shares, sending out customer confirmations and sending out fund distributions.

The transfer agent can be the fund custodian or a separate service company. The fund pays the transfer agent a fee for these services.

Underwriter

The underwriter (often called the *sponsor* or *distributor*) markets fund shares, prepares sales literature and, in return, receives a percentage of the sales charge paid by the client. The underwriter's compensation is part of the sales load paid by the customer when shares are purchased. Sales fees are not part of the fund's expenses.

In general, open-end investment companies (issuers) may not also act as the distributor (underwriter). For example, the distributor for the ArGood Mutual Fund must be a separate and distinct entity from the ArGood Mutual Fund (even though it may be called ArGood Distributors). The underwriter (distributor) of funds receives a fee for selling and promoting the fund shares to the public. This fee is in the form of a sales charge. Except for offerings defined as *contractual plans*, sales charges cannot exceed

8.5%. The underwriter is hired as the head salesperson for the investment company. Obviously, this is an ongoing and important position. The board of directors will appoint an underwriter (sponsor, or distributor) to sell fund shares to the public. The open-end investment company will sell its shares to the underwriter at the current NAV but only as the underwriter needs the shares to fill customer orders. The underwriter is prohibited from maintaining an inventory in open-end company shares. The underwriter is compensated by adding a sales charge to the share's NAV when sales are made to the public.

Under the 1940 act, the contract between the investment company and the underwriter must be in writing and must have a maximum term of two years, after which time it may be extended on a year-by-year basis by the annual approval of the board of directors and/or a majority vote of the outstanding shares.

Figure 13 illustrates how a typical fund is organized.

Figure 13   Organization of a Mutual Fund

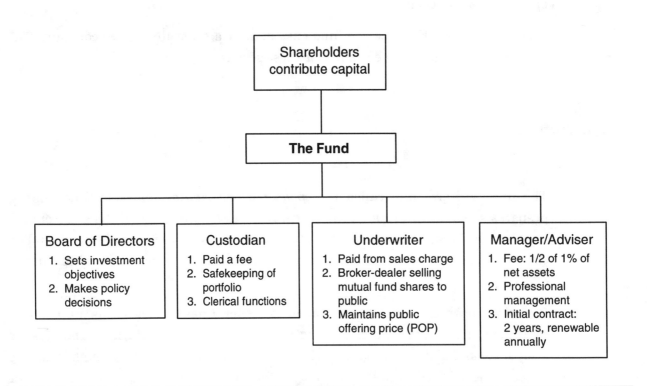

Bonding of Directors and Employees

The investment company, as well as each officer or employee of an investment company who has access to the cash or securities of the company, must be bonded. The company may purchase separate bonds for each individual to be covered, or it may purchase a single bond that lists by name each employee to be covered within the company.

The amount of the bond must be determined by a majority of the noninterested directors at least once every twelve months. The SEC has set forth a schedule of minimum bonding requirements, determined by the investment company's gross assets at the end of the most recent fiscal quarter. A copy of the bond must be filed with the SEC. If a claim is made under the bond, the investment company must notify the SEC in writing of the nature and amount of the claim. The SEC must also be notified within five business days of the terms of a settlement of any such claim.

Officers and directors may be covered by the bond only for negligence. No bond protects an officer or director from acts of willful malfeasance, bad faith or gross negligence or reckless disregard of his duties in the conduct of his office.

Information Distributed to Investors

Prospectus

In an effort to simplify and enhance its readability, the prospectus distributed to investors may come in two parts: the prospectus (called an *N1-A prospectus* or a *summary prospectus)* and a statement of additional information. The prospectus must be distributed to an investor prior to or during any solicitation for sale. The statement of additional information may be obtained by the investor upon request from the fund.

The prospectus contains information on the fund's objective, investment policies, sales charges and management expenses, services offered and a ten-year history of per share capital changes (performance). The statement of additional information typically contains the funds consolidated financial statements including the balance sheet, statement of operations, income statement and portfolio list at the time the statement was compiled.

Financial Reports

The act of 1940 requires that shareholders receive financial reports at least semiannually (every six months). These reports must contain:

- the investment company's balance sheet;
- a valuation of all securities in the investment company's portfolio on the date of the balance sheet (a portfolio list);
- the investment company's income statement;
- a complete statement of all compensation paid to the board of directors and to the advisory board; and
- a statement of the total dollar amount of securities purchased and sold during the period.

It is the principal's responsibility to see that each of these reports is current and accurately reflects the state of the company at the end of the reporting period. In addition, the company must send a copy of its balance sheet to any shareholder who makes a written request for one at any time between semiannual reports.

The investment company must be audited at least annually and distribute an audited annual report to every investor once a year.

Additional Disclosure Requirements

The SEC, in a continuing effort to give investors more information on which to evaluate the performance of mutual funds, requires the fund to include in its prospectus or annual reports:

- a discussion of those factors and strategies that materially affected its performance during its most recently completed fiscal year;
- a line graph comparing its performance to that of an appropriate broad-based securities market index; and
- the name(s) and title(s) of the person(s) who are primarily responsible for the day-to-day management of the fund's portfolio.

Fund Performance

Fund management is required to discuss what happened to the fund during the previous fiscal year and why it happened. In its review, management is not obligated to evaluate the effectiveness of its strategies or investment techniques employed to achieve its performance.

Financial Highlights

A simplified "per share" table of condensed financial information must be provided in the prospectus. The table will enable an investor to track the operating performance of the fund on a per share basis from its beginning net asset value to its ending net asset value. A line graph comparison of the per share performance of the fund to an appropriate broad-based securities market index must be provided. For example, a broadly diversified common stock fund touting an 18% rise in share value may lose some of its appeal when compared to the S&P 500 which has risen 26% during the same time frame.

Disclosure of Advisers

Many investment advisers who have achieved stellar returns have attained celebrity status. Funds marketing their portfolios will advertise the fund as managed by the adviser "star," when in fact the fund is managed by a committee that may or may not include the personality advertised. To clarify and eliminate the potential for abuse, the prospectus must disclose the person(s) responsible for the day-to-day management of the fund's portfolio. Money-market and index funds are excluded from this requirement.

Review Questions

1. The Securities Act of 1933 covers all of the following EXCEPT

   A. due diligence
   B. prospectus requirements
   C. full and fair disclosure
   D. blue-sky laws

2. A prospectus must include

   I. the effective date of the registration
   II. whether the underwriter intends to stabilize the issue if necessary
   III. a statement indicating the SEC has not approved the issue
   IV. disclosure of material information concerning the issuer's financial condition

   A. I, II and IV only
   B. I and IV only
   C. II and III only
   D. I, II, III and IV

3. If the SEC has cleared an issue, which of the following statements is true?

   A. The SEC has guaranteed the issue.
   B. The underwriter has filed a standard registration statement.
   C. The SEC has endorsed the issue.
   D. The SEC has guaranteed the accuracy of the information in the prospectus.

4. Which of the following are included under the terms "advertising" and "sales literature" with respect to mutual funds?

    I.   Commercial messages broadcast on radio and television
    II. "Sales ideas" and marketing literature sent by issuers to broker-dealers to be used as internal sales development materials
    III. Sales aids and product literature distributed to broker-dealers by a fund's principal underwriter, such materials to be sent to prospective buyers or displayed for their viewing
    IV. Written communications such as direct mail pieces sent to the general public

    A. I and III only
    B. I, III and IV only
    C. IV only
    D. I, II, III and IV

5. Which of the following is classified as sales literature?

    I.   Prospecting letter stating opinions on securities that is mailed to a mass audience
    II. Listing in the telephone directory that reveals that a firm is a member of the NYSE and the CBOE
    III. Market letter that contains buy and sell recommendations on securities
    IV. Market letter that makes specific recommendations on trading strategies

    A. I, II and III
    B. I, II and IV
    C. I, III and IV
    D. III and IV

6. A tombstone advertisement may include all of the following EXCEPT

    A. the issuer's name and address
    B. the investment's financial information
    C. the investment's past performance
    D. any disclaimer required by law

7. Under NYSE rules, prior approval of sales literature and research reports must be given by a(n)

    I. chartered financial analyst
    II. supervisory analyst
    III. CROP
    IV. ROP

    A. I
    B. I, III and IV
    C. II and III
    D. II, III or IV

8. Sales literature pertaining to open-end investment company funds must be filed with the

    A. SEC five days before first use
    B. SEC within ten days after first use
    C. NASD within five days after first use
    D. NASD within ten days of first use

9. An open-end investment company may do all of the following EXCEPT

    A. continuously offer shares
    B. borrow money
    C. lend money
    D. issue bonds

10. Under the Investment Company Act of 1940, shareholders must receive financial reports

    A. monthly
    B. quarterly
    C. semiannually
    D. annually

Answers & Rationale

1. **D.** Blue-sky laws are state laws and are not covered under the federal securities act. (Page 100)

2. **D.** Choices I and IV should be obvious. If underwriters intend to engage in activities that are designed to stabilize the price of the security, disclosure in the prospectus is required. The SEC disclaimer is required to appear on every prospectus and states that the SEC has neither approved nor disapproved the issue. (Page 102)

3. **B.** The SEC does not approve, endorse or guarantee the accuracy of a registration statement. (Page 102)

4. **B.** The terms "advertising" and "sales literature" refer only to materials prepared for publication or broadcast to a mass audience or investors in general. Materials intended for internal use within a broker-dealer's organization are not considered advertising or sales literature—assuming, of course, that the firm keeps them away from customers. (Page 104)

5. **D.** Advertising is defined as any sales material that reaches a mass audience through public media or through written sales communications. Market letters are defined as sales literature. A listing in a telephone directory that includes a firm's exchange memberships is not considered sales literature. (Page 104)

6. **C.** Companies are not permitted to describe past performance or make predictions about future performance in a tombstone advertisement. (Page 105)

7. **D.** The NYSE rules require that all sales literature and research reports be approved prior to use by an NASD member, such as a registered options principal (ROP) or a compliance registered options principal (CROP), or a supervisory analyst. A chartered financial analyst is not qualified to approve reports. (Page 106)

8. **D.** Sales literature by a mutual fund issuer or underwriter must be filed with the NASD within ten days of its first use. (Page 106)

9.   **D.**   A mutual fund is prohibited from issuing any senior securities, although it may purchase just about any type of security as an investment. All shares of a mutual fund must be of the same class.   (Page 112)

10.   **C.**   Investment company shareholders must receive financial reports at least semiannually (that is, every six months).   (Page 122)

5　Issuing and Trading Mutual Funds

Key Terms

agent	INSTINET
American Stock Exchange (AMEX)	investment banker
auction market	market maker
broker	market order
Consolidated Tape	New York Stock Exchange (NYSE)
dealer	over-the-counter (OTC) market
Exchange Act	parity
exchange market	position trading
fourth market	specialist
inside market	third market

Overview

In general, securities come to market in one of two ways: as new issues (primary distributions) from a corporation, a municipality or the federal government, or in secondary trades between investors. This chapter explains the process of issuing investment company securities and the sales agreement between the issuer and the broker-dealers participating in the distribution.

Wall Street is a marketplace where merchants, agents and customers of the financial industry meet to buy and sell stocks, bonds and other securities, including mutual funds. This chapter introduces the terminology, language and regulation of trading securities.

Much buying and selling of stocks and bonds takes place on exchanges, where they are traded in a two-way auction process; a number of closed-end mutual funds are exchange traded. Open-end mutual funds (and some closed-end funds) trade in the nationwide network of broker-dealers known as the *over-the-counter market*.

The Underwriting Process

The first successful securities underwriting in the United States is attributed to Jay Cooke. During the Civil War, he and his force of bond salesmen placed over $2 billion in U.S. government bonds with private investors throughout the North. By fostering these financial ties between government and investors, Cooke's sales force reinforced the loyalty and patriotism of many investors.

After the war ended, securities underwriting continued to be critical to the economic development of the United States. Today, publicly owned and financed corporations dominate U.S. business. Each year, the underwriting activities of investment bankers provide billions of dollars in new equity and debt financing.

Investment Banking

A business or branch of municipal government that plans to issue securities usually works with an **investment banker**, a securities broker-dealer that may also specialize in underwriting new issues by helping to bring securities to market and sell them to investors.

An investment banker's functions may include:

- advising corporations on the best ways to raise long-term capital
- raising capital for issuers by distributing new securities
- buying securities from an issuer and reselling them to the public
- distributing large blocks of stock to the public and to institutions

Participants in a Corporate New Issue

Securities and Exchange Commission. When a corporation issues new securities, the SEC is responsible for the following:

- reviewing the registration statement filed for the offering (accomplished during the cooling-off period between the filing date and the effective date);
- sending a deficiency letter to the issuer if the review uncovers problems, thus halting the review until deficiencies are corrected, at which point the cooling-off period continues; and

- declaring the registration statement effective—that is, releasing the securities for sale.

The issuer. The issuer is the party selling the securities to raise money. The issuer's duties include:

- filing the registration statement with the SEC;
- filing a registration statement with the states in which it intends to sell securities (also known as *blue-skying the issue);* and
- negotiating the price of the securities and the amount of the spread with the underwriter.

National Association of Securities Dealers. The NASD Committee on Corporate Financing reviews the underwriting spread to determine fairness and reasonableness of underwriting compensation.

Figure 14 illustrates the payments made in a mutual fund underwriting.

Figure 14   Who Gets What in a Mutual Fund Underwriting

$10,000,000 gross from
the sale of the issue
to the public.

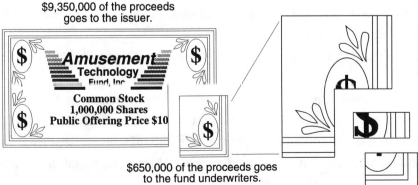

$9,350,000 of the proceeds
goes to the issuer.

$400,000 selling concession
paid to syndicate members and
selling group members based on
the number of shares of the fund
sold by each firm.

$120,000 management fee paid to the
fund's managing underwriter.

$650,000 of the proceeds goes
to the fund underwriters.

$130,000 underwriting fee
paid to all syndicate members
based on their pro rata
underwriting participation.

The individual states. State security laws, also called **blue-sky laws**, require state registration of new issues. The issuer or investment banker may blue-sky an issue by one of the following three methods:

- **Qualification**. The issue is registered with the state independent of federal registration, meeting all state requirements.
- **Coordination**. The issuer registers simultaneously with the state and the SEC. Both registrations become effective on the same date.
- **Filing**. Certain states allow some new issues to blue-sky by having the issuers notify the state of registration with the SEC. In this case, no registration statement is required by the state, although certain other information must be filed.

The underwriter. The underwriter not only assists with registration, but also may advise the corporate issuer on the best way to raise capital.

Issuing Investment Company Securities

The Sales Agreement

The written sales agreement between the issuer and those broker-dealers participating in the distribution of the new securities (either as part of the selling syndicate or as part of the selling group) must contain certain provisions.

- It must set forth selling concessions to be received by the broker-dealer (that is, it must contain a complete description and schedule of available discounts, as well as qualification requirements).
- It must provide that all parties involved in the transaction will abide by the act of 1940.
- It must contain a provision that, if any security is repurchased by the issuer, or by the underwriter for the account of the issuer, or is tendered for redemption within seven business days after the date of transaction, then the dealer or broker shall refund to the underwriter the full concession allowed to the dealer or broker on the original sale.

- The dealer or broker must be notified by the underwriter of any repurchase or redemption within ten days of the date on which the certificate or written request for redemption is received by the underwriter or issuer (the underwriter shall pay to the issuer the underwriter's share of the sales charge on the original sale by the underwriter, and also any refund received from the dealer or broker when received).
- If the original sale was made directly to the investor by the principal underwriter, the entire sales charge must be paid to the issuer by the principal underwriter.

These last three provisions are intended to prevent any one party from profiting from reneged trades. Additional restrictions concerning the sales agreement include the following:

- No member that is party to a sales agreement may purchase an open-end investment security from a record holder at a price lower than the bid price next quoted by or for the issuer.
- No member that is a principal underwriter for an open-end investment company security may repurchase the security from a dealer that is not a party to the sales agreement with the underwriter.
- The underwriter may not repurchase the security from an investor unless the dealer or investor is the owner of record.
- No member that is a principal underwriter may participate in an offering if the issuer voluntarily redeems or repurchases its securities from a dealer acting as principal that is not party to the sales agreement or from an investor that is not the record owner of the security.

Transactions in Investment Company Securities

Participation in Underwriting

A member is strictly prohibited from entering into a joint account, underwriting syndicate or selling group with any nonmember broker or dealer, or with any member of a national securities exchange who is not also a member of the NASD, for the purpose of acquiring and distributing an issue of securities.

The rule further states that members are prohibited from joining with nonmembers in a group "contemplating the distribution to the public of any issue of securities." This emphasis in the rule specifically prohibits a broker or dealer whose membership has been suspended (a nonmember by definition) from participating in an underwriting of securities, even if the suspension period will terminate prior to the actual distribution date of the securities.

Suspension After Group Formation

If a dealer is suspended or expelled after having joined an underwriting group (syndicate), the effective date of the order of suspension or expulsion determines how transactions are to be completed with the suspended or expelled dealer.

Prior to the effective date of the suspension or expulsion, the dealer can accept delivery from the issuer of the securities that the dealer had underwritten and pay to the issuer its commitment without violation of the rules by any of the members.

However, after the effective date of the order, and during the period of suspension (or expulsion), members may only buy and sell securities from or to the dealer at the POP, regardless of whether the NASD members were also members of the underwriting group. Suspended members are treated as nonmembers.

If a dealer is suspended or expelled after having joined a selling group, NASD members, including underwriters and other selling-group members, are prohibited from selling securities to or buying securities from the dealer at any price other than the POP.

Sales to Banks or Trusts

A member participating in the distribution of an issue of securities as an underwriter or in a selling group may not allow any selling concession, discount or other allowance in connection with the sale of the securities to any bank or trust company. A bank or trust is excluded from the definition of a broker or dealer.

Member-to-member Pricing

A member may only grant selling concessions, allowances or discounts to other members who are party to a written sales agreement. An NASD member must deal with nonmember broker-dealers at the same prices and for the same fees and commissions as the member deals with the general public. All other transactions must be conducted at the POP.

Commissions in Transactions with Nonmembers

An NASD member may not pay a nonmember to execute trades in the over-the-counter market, but a nonmember may pay a member to execute such a trade.

Commissions and Fees Paid to Suspended Members

If a member renders advisory services for a fee and thereafter is suspended or expelled from the NASD, another member may continue to pay the suspended or expelled dealer an investment advisory fee as long as the transactions in securities made with the adviser are at the same price and terms accorded the public.

The fee cannot be used to disguise compensation for transactions in securities. A member may also pay commissions to a suspended member if:

- the commissions resulted from transactions that occurred prior to the member's suspension; or
- the suspension period expires prior to the close of the selling period, and the commissions are earned after the expiration of the suspension.

Transferability of Shares

A registered open-end company may restrict the transferability or negotiability of a security of which it is the issuer only if the restriction is contained in the registration statement and is not in contravention of SEC rules and regulations.

Reciprocal Brokerage Rule

The choice by the investment company of a broker-dealer to handle portfolio transactions and investments must be made strictly on the basis of the broker-dealer's professional capabilities. Any transactions must be justified on the basis of the value and quality of the brokerage services rendered, and not on the basis of the dollar amount of sales of the investment company shares.

Members may compensate their sales personnel based on their total sales of investment company shares using overrides, accounting credits or other reasonable compensation methods. A member's retail sales of shares of the investment company should be based on suitability—which funds best fit the objectives of the specific client involved. These funds should not be selected on the basis of additional brokerage commissions generated by fund portfolio transactions.

To enforce the above principle, the Board of Governors of the NASD has issued the following interpretations. With respect to member retail sales of investment company shares, the member *may not:*

- provide a salesperson or other sales personnel any incentive or additional compensation based on the amount of brokerage commissions received from any investment company (bonuses, preferred compensation lists, sales incentive campaigns or contests based on brokerage commissions are included in this prohibition);
- recommend specific investment companies to sales personnel or establish recommended, selected or preferred lists if such companies are selected on the basis of brokerage commissions received or expected;
- grant to any salesperson a participation in the brokerage commission if such commissions are identified with the sale of shares of the investment company; or
- use the sales of shares of any investment company in negotiating the amount of brokerage commissions to be paid on any portfolio transaction.

Withholding Orders

NASD regulations prohibit members from offering mutual funds at a price other than that described in the current prospectus, and from withholding orders for any mutual funds in order to profit by such withholding.

The NASD has also ruled that members may only purchase investment company shares for investment purposes or to cover customer orders. In addition, if the member is accepting a conditional order from a customer, it may do so only at a specified price.

Changes in Sales Charges

Each principal underwriter of a mutual fund, single-payment UIT or variable contract must file the details of changes or proposed changes in the schedule of sales charges with the investment company department of the NASD prior to any implementation. This document must be clearly identified as "Amendment to Investment Company (Unit Investment Trust) (Variable Contract) Sales Charges."

The Regulation of Trading

After the Securities Act of 1933 was enacted regulating primary issues of securities, attention turned to the need for regulating secondary trading. The intent of the Securities Exchange Act of 1934 is to maintain a fair and orderly market for the investing public. It seeks to attain this goal by regulating the securities exchanges and the over-the-counter markets. Commonly called the **Exchange Act**, it formed the Securities Exchange Commission and gave the Commission authority to oversee the securities markets and to register and regulate the exchanges.

According to the Securities Exchange Act of 1934, several other entities must also register with the SEC, including exchange members and broker-dealers that trade securities OTC and on exchanges and individuals who effect securities trades with the public.

The Securities Exchange Act of 1934, which has much greater breadth than the act of 1933, addresses the:

- creation of the SEC
- regulation of exchanges
- regulation of credit by the Federal Reserve Board
- registration of broker-dealers
- regulation of insider transactions, short sales and proxies
- regulation of trading activities
- regulation of client accounts
- customer protection rule
- regulation of the OTC market
- net capital rule

The Securities and Exchange Commission

The SEC, created by the act of 1934, was given responsibility and authority to regulate the securities markets. The SEC is made up of five commissioners appointed by the president of the United States and approved by the Senate. One of the primary responsibilities of this group is to enforce the act of 1934.

The SEC has established rules regarding net capital requirements for broker-dealers, the hypothecation of customer securities, the commingling of broker-dealer securities with those of customers, the use of manipulative and deceptive devices and broker-dealer recordkeeping. The SEC enforces the Securities Exchange Act of 1934 (and others) by providing rules and prescribing penalties for violations.

The SEC may make any additional rules and regulations applicable to investment companies, principal underwriters and broker-dealers (whether or not these are members of a registered securities association).

Registration of Exchanges and Firms

Under the 1934 act, the national securities exchanges must file a registration statement. When they register, the exchanges agree to comply with and help enforce the rules of this act. Each exchange gives the SEC copies of its bylaws, constitution and articles of incorporation. Any amendment to rules must be disclosed as soon as it is adopted. The exchange must also institute and enforce disciplinary procedures for members who do not use just and equitable practices.

In addition to the registration of exchanges, the act of 1934 requires companies that list securities on those exchanges to register with the SEC. Each listed company must file quarterly and annual statements (Form 10Q and 10K, respectively) informing the SEC of its financial status (as well as other information).

Many firms with securities that are traded OTC must also register. Those firms with 500 or more stockholders and assets of $5 million or more are required to do so. Exchange members who do business with the public must register as well as broker-dealers that do business OTC or that use the mail (or telephone, television, radio, etc.) to conduct OTC business.

The Maloney Act, an amendment to the Securities Exchange Act of 1934, permitted the establishment of a national securities association of broker-dealers transacting business in the OTC market. According to the act, SROs such as the NASD could be established and registered with the SEC.

There are also some exemptions from registration, including small local exchanges and any broker-dealer that deals only on an *intra*state basis. An *intra*state firm, however, cannot use the mail or other instruments of *inter*state commerce and still qualify for the exemption from registration.

Net Capital Rule

To ensure broker-dealer solvency, the act of 1934 states that broker-dealers must maintain a certain level of net capital. A firm must not let its debts exceed 15 times its net capital.

Financial Statements Sent to Customers

Every broker-dealer must furnish financial statements to customers. A customer is any person for whom the broker-dealer holds funds or securities or anyone who has made a securities transaction at any time up to one month before the date of the financial statement. Excluded from the definition of "customer" are other broker-dealers, partners or officers of the broker-dealer, and subordinated lenders. NASD rules require a broker-dealer to provide a copy of its current balance sheet to any active customer who makes a written request for one.

Regulation of Credit

The act of 1934 empowered the FRB to regulate margin accounts (that is, to regulate credit extended in the purchase of securities). Within FRB jurisdiction are:

- **Regulation T**—regulates the extension of credit by broker-dealers
- **Regulation U**—deals with the extension of credit by banks
- **Regulation G**—deals with the extension of credit by anyone else

Securities Markets and Broker-Dealers

Securities Markets

A market is the exchange (or system) in which trades of securities occur. The market in which securities are bought and sold is also known as the **secondary** market (as opposed to the **primary** market where new issues are sold). All of the securities transactions in which people, corporations, governments and institutions engage take place in one of four trading markets.

Exchange Market

The NYSE and other exchanges on which *listed* securities are traded compose the **exchange market**. The term "listed security" refers to any security listed (quoted) for trading on an exchange. Some closed-end mutual funds are exchange traded.

Over-the-counter Market

The dealer market in which *unlisted* securities (securities not listed on any exchange, also known as *nonexchange securities*) are traded is called the *over-the-counter market*.

The OTC market is a computer- and telephone-connected interdealer market representing hundreds of securities dealers across the country. The number of different securities that are traded OTC far exceeds the number registered for listed trading on the various exchanges. OTC-traded securities include all municipal securities, U.S. government securities and open-end mutual funds, as well as many closed-end funds.

Third Market (OTC-listed)

The **third market** is a trading market for institutional investors in which *exchange-listed* securities are bought and sold (usually in large blocks) in the OTC market. These transactions are arranged and negotiated through the services of a broker-dealer registered as an OTC market maker in listed securities.

All securities listed on the NYSE and American Stock Exchange (AMEX) plus most exclusively traded securities listed on the regional exchanges are eligible for OTC trading, provided that trading information (volume and execution price) is reported for public display on the **Consolidated Tape** within 90 seconds after the execution of any transaction.

Fourth Market (INSTINET)

INSTINET is a market for institutional investors in which large blocks of stock (both listed and unlisted) change hands in privately negotiated transactions between banks, mutual funds, pension managers and other types of institutions, unassisted by a broker-dealer.

Registered with the SEC as a broker-dealer, INSTINET includes among its subscribers a large number of mutual funds and other institutional investors. All INSTINET members are linked by computer terminals. Subscribers can display bid and ask quotes, and their sizes, to others in the system.

Trading Hours

Exchange business hours. Both the NYSE and AMEX begin trading at 9:30 am EST each business day and close trading at 4:00 pm EST.

OTC business hours. Normal hours for retail OTC trading are the same as those of the NYSE: 9:30 am to 4:00 pm EST, Monday through Friday.

To accommodate institutional investors in the third market, NASD members functioning as registered market makers in listed securities may remain open for business beyond the normal 4:00 pm market close until 6:30 pm EST. However, if a registered market-maker broker-dealer stays open beyond 4:00 pm, but *not* until the 6:30 pm final close, the NASD requires orderly closing times on the hour or half hour, from 4:00 pm to 6:30 pm.

Comparison of Listed and OTC Markets

Listed Markets

Location. Listed markets (such as the NYSE or AMEX) have a central marketplace and trading floor facilities.

Pricing system. Listed markets operate as **double-auction markets**. Floor brokers compete among themselves to execute trades at prices most favorable to the public.

Price dynamics. When a floor broker representing a buyer executes a trade by taking stock at a current offer price higher than the last sale, a plus tick occurs (market up); when a selling broker accepts a current bid price below the last sale price, a minus tick occurs (market down).

Major force in the market. The **specialist** is charged with maintaining an orderly market and providing price continuity. The specialist fills limit and market orders for the public and trades for his own account to either stabilize or facilitate trading when serious supply and demand imbalances occur.

Transactions away from the main market. As a rule, dealers do not maintain inventories in listed stocks and do no principal business in them, except in connection with third market transactions. Customer orders are routed to an exchange trading floor for execution, and the originating firm charges a commission for services rendered.

OTC Markets

Location. There is no central marketplace for OTC trading. Trading takes place over the phone, over computer networks and in trading rooms across the country.

Pricing system. The OTC market works through an **interdealer network**. Registered market makers compete among themselves to post the best bid and ask prices.

Price dynamics. When a market maker raises its bid price to attract sellers and outpace other market makers, the price of the stock rises; when a market maker lowers its ask price to attract buyers and outpace other market makers, the price of the stock declines.

Major force in the market. The **market makers** post current bid and ask prices. The best price at which the public can buy (best ask) and the best price at which the public can sell (best bid) are called the **inside market**.

Subject to certain minimum capital requirements, any NASD member can apply for registration as a market maker in any number of OTC securities.

Transactions away from the main market. Unlike the situation in listed stocks, many dealers maintain inventories in OTC stocks (or stand ready to buy or sell for their own accounts) without registering as market makers. Such firms have the choice of filling customer orders either as principal trades (from inventory) or as agency trades (executed with a registered market), similar to the way listed stocks are handled.

Role of the Broker-Dealer

Those engaged in buying and selling securities must register as broker-dealers. Most firms act both as brokers and dealers, but not in the same transaction.

Brokers. Brokers are agents that arrange trades for clients and charge them a commission. The broker does not buy shares, but simply arranges a trade between a buyer and seller.

Dealers. When firms act as dealers (or principals), they buy and sell securities for their own accounts (inventory). A broker-dealer that is buying and selling for its own account is sometimes said to be **position trading**. A position in a security also can be referred to as being *in control* of that amount of the security. Members may not trade excessively for their own accounts because that would obstruct the maintenance of a fair and orderly market. Any trading practice that manipulates the market or deceives the investing public is a violation of SEC regulations.

When selling from their inventory, dealers charge their clients a markup rather than a commission. A markup is the difference between the current interdealer offering price and the actual price charged the client. When a price to a client includes a dealer's markup, it is called the *net price*. The dealer does not just arrange a trade, but actually sells the client shares from its inventory.

Filling an order. A broker-dealer may fill a customer's order to buy securities in any of the following ways:

- The broker may act as the client's agent by finding a seller of the securities and arranging a trade.
- The dealer may buy the securities from the market maker, mark up the price and resell them to the client on a dealer basis.
- If the dealer has the securities in its own inventory, it may sell the shares to the client from that inventory.

Broker-dealer role in transactions. A firm is prohibited from acting as both a broker and a dealer in the same transaction. For example, your firm cannot make a market in a stock, mark up that stock and add an agency commission. If the firm acts as a broker, it may charge a commission. If it acts as a dealer, it may charge a markup (or markdown). A violation of this practice is called making a *hidden profit*.

The following chart compares brokers and dealers:

Broker	Dealer
Acts as an agent, transacting orders on behalf of the client.	Acts as a principal, dealing in securities for its own account and at its own risk.
Charges a commission.	Charges a markup or markdown.
Is not a market maker.	Makes markets and takes positions (long or short) in securities.
Must disclose to the client its role and the amount of its commission.	Must disclose to the client its role, but not necessarily the amount or source of the markup or markdown.

An easy way to remember these relationships is to memorize the letters "BAC/DPP." The letters stand for "**B**rokers act as **A**gents for **C**ommissions/**D**ealers act as **P**rincipals for **P**rofits."

Review Questions

1. A broker-dealer selling open-end investment company shares will be required to return its entire selling concession if the principal underwriter has to repurchase those shares from a customer within how many business days of the sale?

    A. 7
    B. 15
    C. 30
    D. 60

2. During a period of suspension, a member must

    A. have no securities dealings of any kind
    B. restrict activities with members solely to investment banking
    C. restrict activities with customers solely to investment companies
    D. be treated as a nonmember by other members

3. Which of the following is(are) regulated or mandated by the Securities Exchange Act of 1934?

    I.   Full and fair disclosure on new offerings
    II.   Creation of the SEC
    III. Manipulation of the market
    IV. Margin requirements on securities

    A. I
    B. I, II and III
    C. II
    D. II, III and IV

4. The Securities Exchange Act of 1934 covers which of the following?

    I.   Trading of government securities
    II. Trading of corporate securities
    III. Issuance of financial reports by corporations
    IV. Issuance of government securities

    A. I, II and III
    B. I, II and IV
    C. I and III
    D. II and IV

5. When selecting a broker-dealer to execute trades for its portfolio, a mutual fund should

    A. consider only a broker-dealer with sound and reputable qualifications
    B. base its selection on the volume of fund shares a broker-dealer has sold
    C. base its selection on the length of time a broker-dealer has sold fund shares
    D. consider only a broker-dealer with which it does not have an underwriting agreement

6. Which of the following statements about transactions in the different securities markets is(are) true?

    I.   Transactions in listed securities occur primarily in the exchange markets.
    II. Transactions in unlisted securities occur primarily in the OTC market.
    III. Transactions in listed securities that occur in the OTC market are said to take place in the third market.
    IV. Transactions in listed securities that occur directly between customers or institutions without using broker-dealers as intermediaries are said to take place in the fourth market.

    A. I only
    B. I and II only
    C. II and III only
    D. I, II, III and IV

7.   An open-ended investment company bought preferred utility stock from a bank through INSTINET. This trade took place in the

    A.   primary market
    B.   secondary market
    C.   third market
    D.   fourth market

8.   The *broker* part of the term "broker-dealer" indicates which of the following?

    A.   Acting for others in both purchase and sale
    B.   Acting for others in both purchase and sale, and selling from inventory
    C.   Acting for the firm and for others in both purchase and sale
    D.   None of the above

9.   Your firm, Serendipity Discount Securities, has received an order from one of your customers to buy 300 shares of DWQ at the market. Serendipity goes into the market and buys 300 shares of DWQ from another broker-dealer for its own inventory. It then takes those shares out of inventory and sells them to the account of the customer. Serendipity's role in this transaction is that of a

    A.   broker acting as an agent for a commission
    B.   dealer acting as a principal for a profit
    C.   broker acting as an agent for a profit
    D.   dealer acting as a principal for a commission

10. ALFA Securities, a broker-dealer that is a member of the NYSE, is a position trader. This means that ALFA Securities

    A.   is trading for its own account
    B.   is in violation of NYSE regulations
    C.   is underwriting securities in the primary market
    D.   acts as a broker for customers

Answers & Rationale

1.   **A.**   Customers have the right to redeem their shares, with full sales charges rebated, within seven days of purchase. Because the principal underwriter must return the full sales charge, any selling concession or discount earned by a member of the selling group would also have to be returned.   (Page 132)

2.   **D.**   A suspended member is not a member. Any firm that is not a member (for whatever reason) must not be granted any of the rights or privileges of NASD membership.   (Page 134)

3.   **D.**   The Securities Exchange Act of 1934 set up the SEC and regulates the market. The Securities Act of l933 requires full and fair disclosure.   (Page 137)

4.   **A.**   The Securities Exchange Act of 1934 regulates secondary trading or trading markets, while the Securities Act of 1933 regulates the primary, or new issue, market. Trading of corporates and governments would therefore fall under the 1934 act, as does corporate financial reporting. The 1933 act covers the issuance of new securities. Governments are exempt securities under the 1933 act.   (Page 137)

5.   **A.**   A broker-dealer's reputation and qualifications are the only criteria a mutual fund may use when selecting an executing broker-dealer.   (Page 135)

6.   **D.**   Listed securities traded on exchanges compose the exchange market. Unlisted securities traded over the counter are the OTC market. Listed securities traded OTC compose the third market. Securities bought and sold without the aid of a broker-dealer compose the fourth market. INSTINET is a reporting service used by many institutions to locate other parties for fourth-market equity transactions.   (Page 140)

7.   **D.**   The fourth market consists of direct trades between institutions, pension funds, broker-dealers and others. Many of these trades use INSTINET. (Page 140)

8.   **A.**   When the term "broker" is used, it means that the firm is acting as an agent and is bringing a buyer and a seller together. Answers B and C describe a dealer.   (Page 143)

9.   **B.**   Your firm was acting as principal in first acquiring the 300 shares of DWQ for its inventory before selling them to the customer. The way to remember the difference between brokers and dealers is through the letters BAC/DPP. This acronym stands for "Brokers act as Agents for Commissions/Dealers act as Principals for a Profit." *Profit* is another way of saying *markup*.   (Page 143)

10. **A.**   "Position trading" is simply trading as principal, or dealer, for the firm's own account. The opposite role is that of a broker (or agent) trading securities in the secondary market for customers.   (Page 142)

6 Customer Accounts

Key Terms

administrator
cash account
corporate account
credit agreement
custodial account
custodian
discretionary account
donor
executor
fiduciary account
full power of attorney
guardian
hypothecation agreement
joint account
joint tenants in common (JTIC)

joint tenants with right of
  survivorship (JTWROS)
limited power of attorney
loan consent agreement
margin account
new account form
Regulation T (Reg T)
retirement account
single account
special cash account
third party account
trading authorization
trustee
Uniform Gifts to Minors Act
  (UGMA)

Overview

The customer account (and any statements generated by it) serves as a record of the customer's investment activity. The account also functions as a file in which the company can record all of the information it requires about the customer. There are several types of accounts that a representative can open for a customer. Among the variables to be considered are the type of investing the customer intends to do, the number of people who will have access to the account, and whether the customer intends to borrow money in the course of investing.

Each transaction in each type of account has its own recordkeeping requirements. Some account and order forms provide companies with the information they need in order to keep track of the daily business of their customers; others are required by the SEC, the NASD, or the other SROs and government agencies, such as the OCC, as a means of monitoring industry practices.

New Accounts

For every type of account (and for every variation of every type), there are specific forms and paperwork that must be filled out, filed, sent to the appropriate regulatory body and/or kept on file by the broker. Some forms, such as the new account form (or card), need to be filled out for every account opened. Other forms have their own specific applications, including:

- customer agreements
- loan consent agreements
- IRA contracts
- Keogh forms
- partnership agreements
- corporate charters
- simplified employee pension plan (SEP) applications
- annuity contracts
- trust documents
- mutual fund applications
- full or limited powers of attorney

Classification of Accounts

Account ownership. Procedures and relevant regulations vary according to the type of person, group or business that owns the account. The principal types of ownership are:

- individual
- joint (for example, a husband and wife or two business associates)
- corporate
- partnership

Trading authorization. The primary types of trading authorization are:

- **Discretionary**. After receiving written authority from the customer, the registered representative enters trades without having to consult the customer before each trade.

- **Fiduciary**. The individual given fiduciary responsibility enters the trades for the account.
- **Custodial**. The custodian for the beneficial owner enters all trades.

Payment method. Customers may pay for securities in one of two ways: cash or margin. In cash accounts, customers must pay the full purchase price of securities. In margin accounts, customers may borrow part of the purchase price of a security from the broker-dealer.

Securities traded. Customers must have special approval to make certain types of trades in their accounts, and additional special requirements exist for options accounts.

Opening New Accounts

Before opening any new account, the broker-dealer and registered representative should evaluate the prospective customer as to character and credit references, financial reliability and specific financial goals and objectives.

Required information. According to NYSE Rule 405 ("Know Your Customer"), exchange members must exercise due diligence to learn essential facts about every customer and account. General guidelines suggest the registered rep interview the customer in order to obtain an inventory of the customer's present holdings and discover the customer's financial situation, needs and objectives.

Generally, any competent person may open an account. Any person declared legally incompetent may not open an account. Fiduciary or custodial accounts may be opened for minors or legally incompetent individuals.

Approval and Acceptance of an Account

Without exception, every new account must be approved by a partner, officer or principal of the firm, in writing on the account form, prior to or promptly after completion of the first transaction in that account. The principal may initial the form to indicate that the account is approved and that the firm has accepted the account.

Documenting New Accounts

New account form. The registered rep must fill out a new account form for every new account she opens. An example of a new account form is shown in Figure 15. On the form the rep should enter certain details regarding customer identification and information concerning suitability. The firm must have a record of the following information about each customer who will have access to the account:

- full name;
- address and telephone number (business and residence numbers);
- Social Security or tax identification number;
- occupation, employer and type of business;
- citizenship;
- whether the customer is of legal age;
- financial information (estimated income and net worth);
- investment objectives;
- bank and brokerage references;
- whether the customer is an employee of a member broker-dealer;
- how the account was acquired;
- name and occupation of the person(s) with authority to make transactions in the account; and
- signatures of the representative opening the account and a principal of the firm (the customer's signature is not required on a new account form).

If the customer refuses to disclose or provide all of the financial information requested by the firm, the firm may still open the account if it determines by other means that the customer has the financial resources to carry the account and that whatever trades the customer seeks to enter are suitable.

Customer information should be updated periodically as situations change. Transactions placed by the customer and judged unsuitable by the registered rep may still be entered by the customer. For unsuitable trades (as well as for any trade requested by a customer without the rep's recommendation), the rep should note on the ticket that the transaction was unsolicited. If the ticket is not marked, the trade will be assumed to be solicited.

Figure 15   Example of a New Account Form

Worthmore, Moola, Inc.

Staking Your Financial Future
12654 Futurity Blvd.
Belmont, CA 99462

NEW ACCOUNT FORM

TAXPAYER ID NUMBER	☐ SSN ☐ TAX ID	AGE	BRANCH# RR#	ACCOUNT#	DATE

LEGAL NAME(S) AND MAILING ADDRESS   ☐ HOME   ☐ BUS

ACCOUNT TYPE   ☐ CASH   ☐ OPTION
☐ MARGIN   ☐ COMMODITY

MARITAL STATUS   ☐ MARRIED   ☐ SINGLE
☐ DIVORCED   ☐ WIDOWED

ACCOUNT REGIS.   ☐ SINGLE   ☐ JTWROS
☐ JTIC   ☐ INV CLUB
☐ CORP   ☐ PARTNER
☐ RETIRE   ☐ OTHER

TELEPHONE NO. ☐ HOME ☐ BUS	TELEPHONE NO. ☐ HOME ☐ BUS	DIVIDENDS ☐ HOLD ☐ MAIL	U.S. CITIZEN? ☐ YES ☐ NO ___

IS THE CUSTOMER OR SPOUSE EMPLOYED BY, OR RELATED   ☐ YES   DUPLICATE ☐ YES   **ATTACH SPECIAL INSTRUCTIONS**
TO AN EMPLOYEE OF, ANY FINANCIAL INSTITUTION?   ☐ NO   CONFIRMS? ☐ NO

EMPLOYMENT

EMPLOYER'S NAME   YEARS EMPLOYED

ADDRESS

TYPE OF BUSINESS   CLIENT'S OCCUPATION

DOCUMENTATION			OTHER (DESCRIBE)
MARGIN AGR	☐ PEND	☐ RCVD	___
JOINT ACCT	☐ PEND	☐ RCVD	___
TRADING AUTH	☐ PEND	☐ RCVD	___
CORP/PART AGR	☐ PEND	☐ RCVD	___
RETIRE ACCT	☐ PEND	☐ RCVD	___
SIG CARD	☐ PEND	☐ RCVD	___

REFERENCE

BANK NAME AND ADDRESS   ☐ CHECKING   ☐ VERIFIED
☐ SAVINGS   ☐ NOT VERIFIED

DOES CLIENT HAVE AN ACCOUNT   ☐ YES   IF YES, WITH WHAT FIRM?
WITH ANOTHER BROKERAGE FIRM?   ☐ NO

SPOUSE

NAME   OCCUPATION   AGE

EMPLOYER   ADDRESS   ANNUAL INCOME

INVESTMENT EXPERIENCE

INVESTMENT OBJECTIVES
☐ GROWTH ☐ SPECULATION
☐ INCOME ☐ RETIREMENT
☐ GRO/INC ☐ TAX

HOME ☐ OWN ☐ RENT
NO. OF DEPENDENTS ___
ANNUAL INC ___
NET WORTH ___

DOES CLIENT OR SPOUSE HAVE
ANOTHER ACCOUNT WITH US?
☐ YES   ☐ NO
IF YES, LIST:
___
___

IS CLIENT NOW OR HAS CLIENT
EVER BEEN A CORPORATE
OFFICER OR OWNER OF 10%
OF ANY CORPORATION'S
SECURITIES?
☐ YES   ☐ NO
IF YES, NAME:
___

HOW WAS ACCOUNT ACQUIRED?
☐ WALK IN ☐ REFERRAL
☐ PHONE IN ☐ PROSPECT
☐ OTHER ☐ ACQUAINTANCE
INITIAL TRANSACTION
☐ BUY   DESCRIBE:
☐ SELL
☐ OTHER
INITIAL DEPOSIT

DISCRETIONARY AUTHORIZATION
☐ FULL ☐ LIMITED ☐ NONE

OPTION TRADES ANTICIPATED
☐ BUY ONLY ☐ STRADDLES
☐ COV CALLS ☐ SPREADS
☐ COV PUTS ☐ COMBINS
☐ UNC OPTS ☐ OTHER
IS CLIENT FAMILIAR WITH
OPTIONS?
☐ YES   ☐ NO
HAS CLIENT RECEIVED OCC
PROSPECTUS?
☐ YES DATE ___
HAS CLIENT PREVIOUSLY
TRADED OPTIONS?
☐ YES   ☐ NO
ARE OPTIONS SUITABLE?
☐ YES   ☐ NO

RR SIGNATURE	AGENT'S NAME AND ADDRESS
BRANCH MGR APPROVAL DATE	ROP SIGNATURE (OPTIONS APPROVAL)

Signature Cards

Many firms ask their customers to fill out a signature card. Although the customer is not legally required to fill one out for a cash account, the card provides both protection and convenience; it enables a customer to send written orders to the registered rep or sponsor, who can then verify the accuracy of the order by comparing the signature on the letter to the one that the firm has on file.

Mailing Instructions

When a new account form is filled out, the customer gives specific mailing instructions. Statements and confirms may be sent to someone other than the customer (his agent or attorney, for example) if the customer requests it in writing or if duplicate confirms are also sent to the customer. A member firm may hold the customer's mail for up to two months if the customer is traveling in the United States, and for up to three months if the customer is abroad.

Cash Accounts and Margin Accounts

When a customer has opened an investment account with a brokerage firm, the account will be designated as either a cash account or a margin account. Each type of account carries certain rights and responsibilities, depending on how the customer chooses to pay for any securities purchased.

Cash Accounts

The cash account (also known as the **special cash account**) is the securities industry's basic investment account. Anyone who is eligible to open an investment account can open it as a cash account. In a cash account, a customer is expected to pay in full for any securities purchased.

Certain accounts may be opened *only* as cash accounts; among these are personal retirement accounts (such as IRAs and Keoghs), corporate retirement accounts and custodial accounts (UGMAs).

Margin Accounts

The margin account came into being as a way for customers to borrow money for the purpose of investing. The term "margin" refers to the minimum amount of cash or marginable securities that a customer is required to deposit on the purchase of securities.

The Federal Reserve Board's Regulation T

Because leveraging is a two-way street, several rules apply to margin accounts. The Securities Exchange Act of 1934 grants the Federal Reserve Board (FRB) authority to regulate credit extended in the purchase of securities. The FRB established Regulation T, which sets forth the equity or margin required in a purchase of securities in a margin account. Regulation T prevents the overextension of credit in securities transactions. It also stipulates which securities may be purchased on margin. The board establishes the rules and regulations governing margin accounts, and then delegates the enforcement of them to the SEC.

Opening a Margin Account

If a customer wishes to open a margin account, the firm holding the account first satisfies itself that the customer can meet certain minimum financial requirements (the securities industry's equivalent of a credit check). After that, the customer is allowed to place orders for investments and is asked to deposit only a percentage of their cost (and to pay interest on the unpaid balance). The securities purchased are held for the customer in the account in street name. The rate of interest on margin accounts is based on the broker call rate, a rate typically more favorable than the rates offered by banks and savings institutions for similar loans.

Documenting a margin account. When opening a margin account, the customer signs a margin agreement disclosing the terms under which credit will be extended. The margin agreement contains a credit agreement, a hypothecation agreement and an optional loan consent.

- The **credit agreement** discloses the terms under which credit is extended. The SEC requires that the firm disclose the annual rate and method of computing interest and the conditions under which interest rates and charges will be changed. The firm is also required to send the customer an assurance that statements accounting for interest charges will be sent at least quarterly. If the firm fails to make these disclosures, changes in interest rates are permitted only with 30 days' notice to the customer.

- The **hypothecation agreement** gives the firm permission to pledge (or hypothecate) securities held on margin. The hypothecation agreement is a mandatory part of the margin agreement.
- The **loan consent agreement** gives the firm permission to lend the customer's securities held in a margin account to other brokers (usually for delivery on short sales). A customer signature to a loan consent is not mandatory under NASD rules. A typical loan consent would read as follows:

> Until you receive written notice of revocation from the undersigned, you are hereby authorized to lend to yourselves as brokers, or to others, any securities held by you on margin for the account of, or under the control of, the undersigned.

Retirement Accounts

Each separate type of personal and corporate retirement account has its own forms and applications. The most important ones are those that establish the firm's custodial relationship with the owner of the retirement account, necessary for IRS approval.

Business Accounts

When a registered rep opens a business account of any type, it is necessary to establish three items:

1. the business's legal right to open an investment account;
2. any limitations that the owners, stockholders, a court or any other entity has placed on the investments in which the business will be allowed to invest; and
3. who will be allowed to represent the business in transactions involving the account.

A copy of the legal documents that established the business will usually contain this information and must be kept on file together with all other account forms.

Trading Authorization/Power of Attorney

Any time a power of attorney or a discretionary power to the broker has been established for an investment account, a signed copy of that document must be kept on file.

Opening Accounts for Employees of Other Brokers

The NASD, NYSE and MSRB all have rules that require broker-dealers to give special attention to accounts opened by certain individuals. This special attention typically involves permission from or written notification to some other broker-dealer regarding the establishment of the account. Accounts opened by the following individuals fall within these rules:

- employee of a broker-dealer
- spouse or minor child of an employee of a broker-dealer

NASD requirements. NASD rules do not require the employee of one NASD member firm to get the employer's permission to open an account with another NASD member. The rules do require the firm opening the account to notify the customer's employer. The employee is responsible for disclosing that she is an NASD member when opening the account. Duplicate confirmations and statements must be sent to the employer broker-dealer only if the employer requests them.

Types of Accounts

When an account is opened, it is registered in the name(s) of one or more people. They are the owners of the account and are the only individuals who will be allowed access to and/or control of the investments in the account. When a representative opens an account, he asks the customer to specify the names in which the account is to be registered.

Single Accounts

In general, if the customer will be the only person who has access to the account, his name is the only one that appears on it, and it is known as a **single account**. In a single account, there is only one beneficial owner. The account holder is the only person who can:

- control the investments within the account
- request distributions of cash or securities from the account

"Single account" refers only to the number of owners and does not limit in any way the owner's ability to trade or margin the securities in the account.

Joint Accounts

If the names of two or more people appear on the account and each will be allowed some form of control over the account (that is, two or more individuals are co-tenants or co-owners of the account), it is called a **joint account**.

In addition to the appropriate new account form, a joint account agreement must be signed, and the account must be designated as either joint tenants in common (JTIC), or joint tenants with right of survivorship (JTWROS).

The account forms must be signed by all owners. Both types of joint account agreements provide that any or all tenants may transact business in the account. Checks must be made payable to the name(s) in which the account is registered (and must be endorsed for deposit by all tenants), although mail need only be sent to a single address. To be in good delivery form, securities sold from a joint account must be signed by all tenants.

Joint tenants in common. JTIC ownership provides that a deceased tenant's fractional interest in the account is retained by that tenant's estate and is not passed to the surviving tenant(s), if any. As an example, if a JTIC agreement provides for 60% ownership interest by one owner and 40% ownership interest by the other, that is the fraction of the account that would pass into the deceased owner's estate if he died. The JTIC agreement may be used by more than two individuals.

Joint tenants with right of survivorship. JTWROS ownership stipulates that a deceased tenant's interest in the account passes to the surviving tenant(s).

Power of Attorney

An individual will occasionally want another person to have trading authority in (access to or control of) her investment account. If that person is not named on the account as an owner, custodian, trustee or some other form of legal account manager, then the customer must file written authorization with the broker-dealer giving that person access to the account. This trading authorization usually takes the form of a power of attorney. There are two basic types of trading authorization: full and limited powers of attorney.

Full Power of Attorney

The beneficial owner of an account can direct the broker-dealer to allow another person access to her account. The account owner does this by supplying the broker-dealer with what is known as a *full power of attorney*. A full power of attorney allows someone who is not the beneficial owner of an account to:

- deposit or withdraw cash and/or securities; and
- make investment decisions for the owner of the account (i.e., buy, sell, trade or in any other manner affect the account's holdings).

Custodians, trustees, guardians and other people filling similar legal duties typically have been given full power of attorney.

Limited Power of Attorney

If the beneficial owner of an account would like another individual to have some (but not total) control over the account, he will file a *limited power of attorney* with the broker-dealer that clearly states the rights and responsibilities he is giving this person. Limited powers of attorney must include signed authorizations by customers who want to give their brokers discretionary power over their accounts.

Discretionary Accounts

Customers occasionally want to give a registered rep the authority to make transactions on their behalf without having to ask for specific approval each time. An account set up with this type of preapproved authority is known as a *discretionary account*. "Discretion" is defined as the *authority to decide*:

- the security
- the number of shares (or units)
- whether to buy or sell

Discretion *does not* apply to decisions regarding only the *timing* of the investment or the *price* at which it is acquired. An order from a customer worded: "Buy 100 shares of Datawaq for my account whenever you think the price is right" is not a discretionary order.

Discretionary authority. There are a number of rules and regulations regarding discretionary accounts of which the principal must be aware. A customer can give a registered rep discretionary power over his account(s) only by filing a trading authorization or a limited power of attorney with the registered rep's broker-dealer. No transactions of a discretionary nature can take place without this document on file. Once trading authorization has been given, the customer is legally bound to accept the registered rep's decisions.

The customer may only give authority to make decisions for the account to specific individuals, and cannot give blanket authorization to the firm. If the registered rep (or other person named in the power of attorney) leaves the firm or in any other way stops working with the account, the discretionary authority does not pass on to the next account representative. It ends immediately and will not restart unless the account owner files a new power with the company.

The power of attorney remains in force for no more than three years (and must be kept on file for at least three years), at which point it can be renewed at the discretion of the customer.

In addition to other information required, on every discretionary account the registered rep needs to record whether the customer is of legal age and the occupation of the customer, as well as the signature of each person authorized to exercise discretion in the account. The account file must also include the signature of the registered rep who introduced the account and the signature of the member, partner or other company officer who accepted the account for the firm.

Uniform Gifts to Minors Act Accounts

Until the Tax Reform Act of 1986 changed the favorable tax status of the **Uniform Gifts to Minors Act** (**UGMA**) and its successor, the Uniform Transfers to Minors Act (UTMA) adopted by the National Conference of Commissioners of Uniform State Laws in 1983, many people used these accounts as a means of transferring highly taxable income and capital gains to a child in a lower tax bracket through gifts of money or securities (children are normally in a low tax bracket and subject to lower taxes on most types of income).

The regulations surrounding these gifts are very specific in their application. They were developed over time as a means of protecting the interests of the recipient (the minor), the gift giver (the donor) and the custodian of the account.

UGMA and UTMA accounts require an adult (or bank trust department) to act as custodian for a minor (the beneficial owner). Any kind of security—cash, life insurance, annuity contracts and other forms of property—may be given, and there is no limitation on the dollar amount of the gift.

Donating Securities

When a person makes a gift of securities to a minor under the UGMA laws, that person is referred to as the **donor** of the securities. A gift under UGMA is a complete, irrevocable donation of the donor's interest to another person. Once the gift is donated, the donor gives up all rights to the property.

A gift to a minor through an UGMA gives the minor what is known as **indefeasible title**; that is, title that cannot be made null or void. The minor is considered the beneficial owner of the account and its contents. The gift is *irrevocable*: the donor may not take back the gift, nor may the minor return the gift until she has reached the age of majority or the age that the laws of her state have set as the age when the custodianship will terminate. When the minor reaches the specified age, the property in the accounts is transferred into her name.

Bearer securities are generally not permitted but, if they are, gifts of bearer securities must be accompanied by a *deed of gift*.

Custodian

Any securities given to a minor through an UGMA account are managed by a custodian until the minor attains the age of majority. The custodian may be either the donor or a person appointed by the donor, but not necessarily a family member. The custodian has full control over the minor's account and can:

- buy or sell securities
- exercise rights or warrants
- liquidate, trade or hold securities

The custodian may also use the property in the account in any way that person deems proper for the support, education, maintenance, general use or benefit of the minor. However, the account may not be used to discharge the liabilities normally associated with raising the child, such as for payment of food, shelter, and so on.

There are few restrictions as to who can act as a custodian for a minor's account:

- For each account, there may be only one custodian and one minor or beneficial owner.
- One person may not be the custodian for two minors in a joint account, nor can there be two people sharing custodial duties for one minor.
- A minor can be the beneficiary of more than one account and a person may serve as custodian for more than one UGMA as long as each account benefits only one minor.
- The donor of the securities can act as custodian or can appoint someone else to the responsibility.
- Parents, unless acting as custodians for a minor's account, have no legal control over, or recourse to, the account or any of the securities in it.

The registered rep is not responsible for determining whether the appointment is valid or whether the custodian's activities are actually within his authority. However, the rep should determine whether securities being given are already owned by the minor.

Opening an UGMA Account

When opening an UGMA account for a customer, the rep must ensure that the account application contains the custodian's name, the minor's name and Social Security number, and the state in which the UGMA is registered.

Registration of UGMA Securities

Any securities in an UGMA account are registered in the name of the custodian for the benefit of the minor; they cannot be registered *in street name*. Typically, the securities will be registered to "Joan R. Smith as custodian for Brenda Lee Smith," or a variation of this form. When the minor reaches the age of majority, all of the securities in the account will be registered in her name.

The gift of the securities is considered to have been made when this registration has been completed.

Fiduciary Responsibility

The UGMA custodian is charged with fiduciary responsibilities in the management of the minor's account. Certain restrictions have been placed on what is deemed to be proper handling of the investments in an UGMA; the most important are:

- UGMAs may only be opened and managed as cash accounts.
- Securities in the account may not be purchased on margin or pledged by the custodian as collateral for a loan.
- All cash proceeds, dividends and interest must be reinvested by the custodian within a reasonable period of time. Cash proceeds from sales or dividends may be held in a noninterest-bearing custodial account for a reasonable period, but should not remain idle for long.
- Investment decisions must take into account the age of the minor and the custodial relationship; commodities futures, naked options and other high-risk securities are examples of inappropriate investments. Options may not be placed or purchased in a custodial account because no evidence of ownership is issued to an option buyer.
- Stock subscription rights or warrants must be either exercised or sold.
- A custodian for an UGMA may not grant trading authority to a third party.
- A custodian may loan money to the account, but may never borrow from it.

The custodian may be reimbursed for any reasonable expenses incurred in the management of the account (unless the custodian is also the donor).

Taxation

The minor's Social Security number appears on the account, and the minor must file an annual income tax return and pay taxes on any income produced by the UGMA at *the parent's top marginal tax rate*, regardless of the source of the gift, until the minor reaches the age of 14. Exclusions are available, and they are indexed for inflation. The law specifies that when the minor reaches age 14, any taxes incurred by the account will be charged at the minor's rate, rather than at the parent's rate.

In most states, although the minor is the beneficiary of the account and is responsible for any and all taxes on the account, it is the custodian's responsibility to see that the taxes are paid.

Death of the Minor, Custodian or Donor

If the minor beneficiary of an UGMA dies, the securities in the account pass to the minor's estate, not to the parents' or custodian's estates. In the event of the death or resignation of the custodian, a new custodian must be appointed by either a court of law or the donor. If the donor dies, additional gifts to a minor's UGMA may not be made by will (although, in some states, a gift under UGMA may be made through a will, trust or estate).

Review Questions

1. A customer wishes to open a new account but declines to provide all of the financial information requested by the member firm. In this case the member firm may

    I.   not open an account
    II. open the account if it determines by other means that the customer has the financial resources to carry the account and determines that trading is suitable
    III. enter unsuitable trades with the order ticket marked *unsolicited*

    A. I
    B. II
    C. II and III
    D. III

2. A change in which of the following should be indicated in a customer's file?

    I.   Name or address
    II. Marital status
    III. Objectives

    A. I only
    B. I and II only
    C. III only
    D. I, II and III

3. Tex Longhorn wants to open a cash account with you. In order to open this account you must do all of the following EXCEPT

    A. get his signature on the new account form
    B. ascertain his age
    C. get his Social Security number
    D. learn his occupation

4. By definition, "margin" is the

    A. minimum amount of cash that a customer is required to deposit when purchasing securities
    B. maximum amount that a broker is allowed to loan a customer for the purchase of securities
    C. maximum amount of cash that a customer is required to deposit when purchasing securities
    D. minimum amount that a broker is allowed to loan a customer for the purchase of securities

5. Under the act of 1934, the power to set margin requirements for securities transactions was granted to the

    A. SEC, which has established and currently enforces such rules
    B. SEC, which has delegated responsibility to the Federal Reserve Board for enforcing such rules
    C. Federal Reserve Board, which has delegated responsibility to the SEC for enforcing such rules
    D. Department of the Treasury, which has empowered the Federal Reserve Board to establish such rules

6. Which of the following is true when a customer gives limited power of attorney to his registered rep?

    A. The registered rep needs written permission from the customer for each trade.
    B. The customer must renew the power of attorney every year.
    C. The power of attorney must have the customer's signature.
    D. The branch manager must initial each order before it is entered.

7. Which Social Security number is used when opening a custodial account?

    A. Parent's or guardian's of the minor
    B. Minor's
    C. Custodian's
    D. Any of the above is acceptable.

8. Which of the following instructions can be described as a discretionary order?

    A. "Sell 300 shares of FLB whenever you think the time is right."
    B. "Buy $25,000 worth of MTN bank stock."
    C. "Sell 100 shares of ZOO at your discretion."
    D. "Buy 500 shares of a computer company's stock."

9. Which of the following statements about discretionary accounts are true?

    I.   The rules regarding churning do not apply to discretionary accounts.
    II. Discretionary orders must be approved by a registered principal either before or after they are executed.
    III. Discretionary orders must be approved by a principal prior to entry.
    IV. An order in which the investor designates the name of the security, the number of contracts and whether to buy or sell, but gives the rep discretion as to time and price, is not considered to be discretionary.

    A. I and III only
    B. II, III and IV only
    C. II and IV only
    D. I, II, III and IV

10. Under the Uniform Gifts to Minors Act, you can

    I.   give an unlimited amount of cash
    II. give securities
    III. give up to $10,000 cash
    IV. revoke a gift

    A. I
    B. I and II
    C. I, II and IV
    D. II and III

Answers & Rationale

1. **C.** If a customer refuses to provide financial information, the member firm must use whatever information it has available to decide whether to open the account. Any recommendation made to a customer must be suitable, taking into account the customer's investment objectives, financial situation and any other relevant information.   (Page 152)

2. **D.** All of the information that affects your recommendations or the financial situation of a customer must be noted immediately in the file.   (Page 152)

3. **A.** In opening a cash account, you do not need the signature of the customer. You do need to ascertain whether he is of legal age and to obtain other information, including his Social Security number and his occupation.   (Page 152)

4. **A.** "Margin" is the minimum amount of cash that a customer is required to deposit on the purchase or short sale of securities.   (Page 155)

5. **C.** The extension of credit in the securities industry came under regulation in the Securities Exchange Act of 1934, whereby the Federal Reserve Board was given power to set margin requirements; the FRB delegates the enforcement of these requirements to the SEC.   (Page 155)

6. **C.** The registered rep must have prior written authority from the customer and have received approval from a supervisory person before accepting discretionary authority. While a designated principal must frequently review the account, the branch manager need not initial each order before it is entered.   (Page 159)

7. **B.** The minor's Social Security number is used because the account will be fully owned by, and taxed to, the minor and not to either the custodian or the parent.
                                                                               (Page 162)

8. **D.** If a customer specifies three things—buy/sell, quantity and exact security—the order is considered nondiscretionary. A registered rep may decide other elements of the order, such as time and/or price, without specific customer authorization. Answers A, B and C orders specify what is necessary to label them nondis-

cretionary. The answer D order does not specify the exact security and is therefore discretionary.   (Page 159)

9.   **C.**   All discretionary trades must be approved by a branch manager or another registered principal by the end of the day. Choice IV correctly discriminates between order discretion and discretionary account business.   (Page 160)

10.   **B.**   There is no limit to the size of gift that may be transferred under an UGMA account. The $10,000 is the gift tax exclusion and relates only to the amount of the gift that may be subject to tax. Gifts under UGMA are irrevocable.   (Page 161)

Glossary

abandon The act of not exercising or selling an option before its expiration.

Accelerated Cost Recovery System (ACRS) *See* Modified Accelerated Cost Recovery System (MACRS).

accordion loan A broker's collateral loan that requires the brokerage firm to deposit additional securities into a single loan account and enables it to withdraw more money; only one loan need be maintained. *See also* broker's loan, call loan.

account executive *See* registered representative.

accredited investor As defined in Rule 502 of Regulation D, an accredited investor is any institution or individual meeting minimum net worth requirements for the purchase of securities qualifying under the Regulation D registration exemption.

An *accredited investor* is generally accepted to be one who:

- has a net worth of $1 million or more; or
- has had an annual income of $200,000 or more in each of the two most recent years (or $300,000 jointly with a spouse) and who has a reasonable expectation of reaching the same income level in the current year.

accretion of bond discount An accounting process whereby the initial cost of a bond purchased at a discount is increased to reflect its basis as the bond's maturity date approaches.

accrual accounting A method of reporting income when earned and expenses when incurred, as opposed to reporting income when received and expenses when paid. *See also* cash basis accounting.

accrued interest Interest that is added to the contract price of a bond transaction. This interest has accrued since the last interest payment up to but not including the settlement date. Exceptions are income bonds, bonds in default and zero-coupon bonds.

accumulation unit An accounting measure (net asset value) that represents a contract owner's proportionate unit of interest in a separate account (the portfolio) during the accumulations (deposit) period. *See also* separate account.

acid test ratio A more stringent test of liquidity than current ratio, calculated by adding the sum of cash, cash equivalents and accounts and notes receivable and dividing that sum by total current liabilities. *See also* current ratio.

acquisition fee The total of all fees and commissions paid by any party in connection with the selection or purchase of property by a program. Included in the computation of such fees or commissions shall be any real estate commission, acquisition fee, development fee, selection fee or construction fee of a similar nature. Acquisition expenses include such items as legal and appraisal expenses, settlement costs, title insurance and any development fee paid to a person not affiliated with a sponsor in connection with the actual development of a project after acquisition of the land by the program. The cost is added to the basis in the asset for the purpose of depreciation and calculating gain or loss on sale.

ACRS *See* Accelerated Cost Recovery System.

ACT *See* Automated Confirmation Transaction service.

active crowd That section of the NYSE that trades actively traded bonds. (*Syn.* free crowd)

actual The physical commodity being traded, as opposed to the futures contracts on that commodity.

adjacent acreage Producing or nonproducing oil or gas leases located within the area of an existing well site. Adjacent acreage may prove valuable for continued development of the original oil or gas prospect.

adjusted basis Basis adjusted by additions and subtractions to reflect deductions taken with respect to the property and capital improvements to the property. Adjusted basis is used to compute gain or loss on the sale or another disposition of property.

adjusted gross income (AGI) Gross income minus allowable deductions for trade and business expenses.

adjustment bond *See* income bond.

administrator A person authorized by a court of law to liquidate the estate of an intestate decedent. The official or agency administering the securities laws of a state.

ADR *See* American depositary receipt.

ad valorem tax A tax based on the value of real property or personal property. Property taxes are the major source of revenues for local governing units. *See also* assessed value, mill rate.

advance/decline line A technical analysis tool representing the total of differences between advances and declines of security prices. The advance/decline line is considered the best indicator of market movement as a whole.

advance refunding A new municipal bond is issued, the proceeds of which will be used to refinance an existing issue prior to the existing issue's maturity or call date. The proceeds of the new issue will be invested, and the principal and interest earned will be used to pay the principal and interest of the securities being refunded. *See also* defeasance. (*Syn.* prerefunding)

advertisement Any material designed for use by newspapers, magazines, radio, television, telephone recording or any other public medium to solicit business. The firm using advertising has little control over the type of individuals being exposed to the advertising. *See also* sales literature.

advisory board Under the Investment Company Act of 1940, an advisory board serves to advise an investment company on matters concerning its investments in securities, but does not have the power to make investment decisions or take action itself. An advisory board must be composed of persons who have no other connection with, and serve no other function for, the company.

affiliate Any person directly or indirectly owning, controlling or holding with power to vote 10% or more of the outstanding voting securities of another person; also, any officer, director or partner of another entity for which such person acts in such capacity.

When used with respect to a member or sponsor, *affiliate* shall mean any person who controls, is controlled by or is under control with such member or sponsor and includes:

A. any partner, officer or director (or any person performing similar functions) of:
- such member or sponsor; or
- a person who beneficially owns 50% or more of the equity interest in, or has the power to vote 50% or more of the voting interest in, such member or sponsor; or

B. any person who beneficially owns or has the right to acquire 10% or more of the equity interest in or has the power to vote 10% or more of the voting interest in (a) such member or sponsor or (b) a person who beneficially owns 50% or more of the voting interest in, or has the power to vote 50% or more of the voting interest in, such member or sponsor.

agency basis Securities sold through normal broker transactions and executed through a national dealer market. The broker is acting for the accounts of others.

agency issue A debt security issued by an authorized agency of the federal government. Such issues are backed by the issuing agencies themselves, not by the full faith and credit of the U.S. government (except GNMA and Federal Import Export Bank).

agency transaction A transaction in which the broker-dealer is acting for the accounts of others by buying or selling securities on behalf of customers; also, securities sold through normal broker transactions, executed through a national dealer market.

agent 1) An individual acting for the accounts of others; any person licensed by a state as a life insurance agent. (*Syn.* broker). 2) An agent is a securities salesperson who represents a broker-dealer or issuer when selling or trying to sell securities to the investing public. This individual is considered an agent whether he actually receives or simply solicits orders. In other words, an agent is a registered representative or anyone who receives an order while representing a broker-dealer.

The term "agent" is defined in the Uniform Securities Act so that it can be legally determined who must register in the state as an agent. If an individual does not fall into the classification of agent as defined by the law, then the registration process is not necessary. An individual is not considered an agent if he represents any of the following exempt *issuers* or exempt *securities:*

- U.S. government;
- municipality;
- Canadian government, Canadian province or municipality;
- any foreign government with which the U.S. maintains diplomatic relations;
- U.S. banks, savings institutions or trust companies;
- commercial paper with maturities of nine months or less; or
- investment contracts issued in connection with an employee's stock purchase, savings, pension, profit-sharing or similar benefit plan.

An individual is also not considered an agent if he represents an issuer in an exempt transaction. The following are considered exempt transactions:

- isolated nonissuer transactions;
- transactions between an issuer and its underwriters;
- transactions with savings institutions or trust companies; and
- transactions with an issuer's employees, partners or directors if no commission is paid directly or indirectly for the soliciting.

An individual is not considered an agent merely because he is a partner, officer or director of a brokerage firm. If the partner, officer or director of a brokerage firm limits his activities to managerial functions and does not attempt to effect purchases or sales, that person is not considered an agent.

aggregate indebtedness (AI) 1) An accounting of all money (liabilities) a broker-dealer is obligated to pay out to customers, other broker-dealers, banks and other lenders, business suppliers and vendors, and anyone who does business with or works for the firm. Liabilities that are excluded from aggregate indebtedness include those that are secured by fixed assets and other amounts payable that are secured by the firm's own securities (Rule 15c3-1). 2) Customer net margin debit balances.

aggressive investment strategy A method of investing a person uses when trying to get the maximum return on a portfolio by timing purchases and sales to coincide with expected market movements and by varying the structure of the portfolio in line with these expected market moves.

AGI *See* adjusted gross income.

agreement among underwriters If an underwriting syndicate is being formed to help with an issue, the syndicate manager's responsibilities include drawing up an agreement among underwriters. This agreement sets forth the terms under which each member of the syndicate will participate and states the duties and responsibilities of the manager of the underwriting.

AIR *See* assumed interest rate.

allied member A general partner of an NYSE member firm who is not an NYSE member, an owner of 5% or more of the outstanding voting stock of an NYSE member corporation or a principal executive director or officer of a member corporation. Allied members do not own seats on the NYSE.

all or none offering (AON) All-or-none underwriting is one form of best-efforts underwriting. The underwriter agrees to sell all the shares (or a prescribed minimum) or none of them. This type of agreement may be used when the issuer requires a minimum amount of capital to be raised. If the minimum is not reached, the securities sold and the money raised are returned. Commissions will not be paid unless the offering is completed.

all or none order (AON) An order in which the floor broker is instructed to execute an entire order in one transaction (no partial executions).

allowance A deduction from the invoiced amount allowed by the seller of goods to compensate the buyer for losses or damage. *See also* quality allowance.

alternative minimum tax (AMT) An alternate tax computation that includes certain tax preference items that are added back into adjusted gross income for determining the AMT. The AMT is paid if it is higher than the regular tax liability for the year. The tax is currently 28%, or 26% for amounts less than $175,000. The regular tax and the amount by which the AMT exceeds the regular tax are paid.

AMBAC The AMBAC Indemnity Corporation offers insurance on the timely payment of interest and principal obligations of municipal securities. Bonds insured by AMBAC usually receive an AAA rating from the rating services.

American depositary receipt (ADR) A negotiable receipt for a given number of shares of stock in a foreign corporation. An ADR is bought and sold in the American securities markets just as stock is traded.

American Stock Exchange AUTOAMOS The American Stock Exchange uses the Automatic AMEX Options Switch (AUTOAMOS) system for options orders. AUTOAMOS can be used to electronically route day, GTC and marketable limit orders from brokers to AMEX specialists and execution reports from the specialists back to the brokers. AUTOAMOS automatically executes trades for the four to six most active stocks of the *Standard & Poor's 100 Index* options. AUTOAMOS accepts options orders from brokers for up to 20 contracts.

American Stock Exchange AUTOPER The American Stock Exchange uses the Automatic Post Execution & Reporting (AUTOPER) system for equity orders. AUTOPER can be used to electronically route day, GTC and marketable limit orders from brokers to AMEX specialists and execution reports from the specialists back to the brokers. AUTOPER accepts both odd- and round-lot equity orders from brokers for up to 2,000 shares.

amortization Paying off debt (principal) over a period of time in periodic installments. *Amortization* is also defined as the ratable deduction of certain capitalized expenditures over a specified period of time.

amortization of bond premium An accounting process whereby the initial price of a bond purchased at a premium is decreased to reflect the basis of the bond as it approaches maturity.

AMT *See* alternative minimum tax.

annuitant A person who receives the distribution of an annuity contract.

annuitize To change an annuity contract from the accumulation period to the distribution of the funds.

annuity A contract between an insurance company and an individual, which generally guarantees lifetime income to the person on whose life the contract is based in return for either a lump sum or a periodic payment to the insurance company. *See also* deferred annuity, fixed annuity, immediate annuity, variable annuity.

annuity unit The accounting measure used to determine the amount of each payment to an annuitant during payout of the annuity.

AON *See* all or none offering, all or none order.

AP *See* associated person.

appraisal A written opinion of the value of a property prepared by an independent appraiser qualified to appraise that particular type of property.

appreciation The increase in value of an asset.

approved plan *See* qualified retirement plan.

arbitrage Effecting sales and purchases simultaneously in the same or related securities to take advantage of a market inefficiency; also, two assets improperly priced relative to one another. *See also* market arbitrage, security arbitrage.

arbitrageur One who engages in arbitrage.

ask The current price for which a security may be bought, as in the OTC market. For mutual funds, the asked price includes any sales charge that is added to the net asset value. *See also* public offering price. (*Syn.* bid, offer, quote)

assessed value The value of property as appraised by a taxing authority for the purpose of levying taxes. Assessed value may equal market value or a stipulated percentage of market value.

assessment An additional amount of capital that a participant may be called upon to furnish beyond the subscription amount. Assessments may be mandatory or optional, are limited to the original subscription amount and must be called within twelve months.

asset Anything that an individual or a corporation owns.

assignee A person who has acquired a beneficial interest in one or more units from a third party but who is neither a substituted limited partner nor an assignee of record.

assignee of record An assignee who has acquired a beneficial interest in one or more units, whose ownership of such units has been recorded on the books of the partnership and whose ownership is the subject of a written instrument of assignment, the effective date of which assignment has passed.

assignment 1) A document accompanying or part of a stock certificate that is signed by the person named on the certificate for the purpose of transferring the certificate's title to another person's name. 2) The act of identifying and notifying an account holder that an option held short in that account has been exercised by the option owner. *See also* stock power.

assistant representative/order processing *See* Series 11.

associated person of a member (AP) Any employee, manager, director, officer or partner of a member broker-dealer or another entity (issuer, bank, etc.) or any person controlling, controlled by or in common control with that member is considered an associated person of that member.

assumed interest rate (AIR) The rate of investment return that would be required to be credited to a variable life insurance policy—after deducting charges for taxes, investment expenses and mortality and expense guarantees—to maintain the variable death benefit equal at all times to the amount of death benefit. This does not include incidental insurance benefits, which would be payable under the plan of insurance if the death benefit did not vary according to the investment experience of the separate account.

A base for projecting payments from a variable annuity, the AIR is not a guarantee. AIRs offered by companies vary. Naturally, the higher the assumption, the higher the initial benefit and vice versa. The importance of the AIR as a base for projection rests with the fact that, once selected, the account must earn that rate to maintain the initial benefit level.

at-the-close A customer's order that specifies it is to be executed at the close of the market or of trading in that security. If the order is not executed at-the-close, it is canceled. The or-

der does not have to be executed at the closing price. *See also* at-the-open.

at-the-money An option in which the underlying stock is trading precisely at the exercise price of that option. *See also* in-the-money, out-of-the-money.

at-the-open A customer's order that specifies it is to be executed at the open of the market or of trading in that security. If the order is not executed at-the-open, it is canceled. The order does not have to be executed at the opening price. *See also* at-the-close.

auction market A market in which buyers enter competitive bids and sellers enter competitive offers simultaneously. The NYSE is an auction market. (*Syn.* double auction market)

audited financial statement A financial statement of a program, a corporation or an issuer (including the profit and loss statement, cash flow and source and application of revenues statement, and balance sheet) that has been audited by an independent certified public accountant.

authorized stock The number of shares of stock that a corporation is permitted to issue. This number is stipulated in the corporation's state-approved charter and may be changed by a vote of the corporation's stockholders.

authorizing resolution The document enabling a municipality or state government to issue municipal securities. The resolution provides for the establishment of a revenue fund in which receipts or income is deposited.

AUTOAMOS *See* American Stock Exchange AUTOAMOS.

Automated Confirmation Transaction (ACT) service The ACT service is a postexecution, online transaction reporting and comparison system developed by the NASD. ACT's primary purpose is to make reconciliation and matching telephone-negotiated trades easier for member firms, thereby increasing the efficiency of the firms' back office operations.

AUTOPER *See* American Stock Exchange AUTOPER.

back away The failure of an over-the-counter market maker to honor a firm bid and asked price.

backwardation *See* inverted market.

balanced fund A type of mutual fund whose stated investment policy is to have at all times some portion of its investment assets in bonds and preferred stock as well as in common stock. Therefore, there is a balance between the two classes, equity and debt. *See also* mutual fund.

balance of payments An international accounting record of all payments made from one nation to another; *balance* means that a particular country has taken in as much foreign currency as it has paid out in its own currency.

balance sheet A report of a company's financial condition at a specific time.

balloon maturity A maturity schedule for an issue of bonds wherein a large number of the bonds come due at a prescribed time (normally at the final maturity date). This kind of maturity schedule is a type of serial maturity. *See also* maturity date.

BAN *See* bond anticipation note.

banker's acceptance A money market instrument used to finance international and domestic trade. A banker's acceptance is a check drawn on a bank by an importer or exporter of goods and represents the bank's conditional promise to pay the face amount of the note at maturity (normally less than three months).

bank guarantee letter The document supplied by an approved bank in which the bank certifies that a put writer has sufficient funds on deposit at the bank to equal the aggregate exercise price of the put.

base grade The standard grade of a commodity on which a futures contract is based.

basis 1) The cost of property. 2) The difference between the spot or cash price of a commodity and a futures contract price of the same commodity. Basis is usually computed between the spot and the nearby futures contract.

basis point Equal to 1/100 of 1% of yield (e.g., 1/2% = 50 basis points).

basis quote The price of a security quoted in terms of the yield that the purchaser can expect to receive.

bearer bond *See* coupon bond.

bear market A market in which prices of securities are falling or are expected to fall.

bedbug letter *See* deficiency letter.

benefit base The amount to which the net investment return is applied.

best efforts offering Acting as an agent for the issuer, the underwriter puts forth its best efforts to sell as many shares as possible. The issuer pays the underwriter a commission for those shares sold. The underwriter has no liability for unsold shares, as in the case of a firm commitment agreement.

beta coefficient A means of measuring the volatility of a security or portfolio of securities in comparison with the market as a whole. A beta of 1 indicates that the security's price will move with the market. A beta higher than 1 indicates that the security's price will be more volatile than the market. A beta of less than 1 means that it will be less volatile than the market as a whole.

bid An indication by an investor, a trader or a dealer of a willingness to buy a security or commodity. *See also* offer. (*Syn.* quotation, quote)

bid form The form submitted by underwriters in a competitive bid on a new issue of municipal securities. The underwriter states the interest rate, price bid and net interest cost to the issuer.

bid price *See* net asset value.

blind pool A direct participation product that does not state in advance the specific properties in which the general partners will invest the partnership's money. (*Syn.* unspecified property program)

block trade A trade of 10,000 or more shares.

blue chip stock The issues of normally strong, well-established companies that have demonstrated their ability to pay dividends in good and bad times.

Blue List, The A daily trade publication for the secondary market that lists the current municipal bond offerings of banks and brokers nationwide.

blue-sky To qualify a securities offering in a particular state.

blue-sky laws The nickname for state regulations governing the securities industry.

board of directors A unit that governs the NYSE, composed of 20 members who are elected for a term of two years by the general membership of the NYSE; also, individuals elected by stockholders to establish corporate management policies. A board of directors decides, among other items, if and when dividends will be paid to stockholders.

Board of Governors The body that governs the NASD, composed of 27 members elected by both the general membership and the Board itself.

board order A customer's order that becomes a market order as soon as the market touches or breaks through the order price. Board orders to buy are placed below the current market. Board orders to sell are placed above the current market. (*Syn.* market-if-touched order)

bona fide quote A quote from a dealer in municipal securities that is willing to execute a trade under the terms and conditions stated at the time of the quote. *See also* firm quote.

bond An evidence of debt issued by corporations, municipalities and the federal government. Bonds represent the borrowing of money by a corporation or government. A bond is a legal obligation of the issuing company or government to repay principal at the maturity of the bond. Terms of the repayment and any interest to be paid are stated in the bond indenture. Bonds are issued with a par value ($1,000) representing the amount of money borrowed. The issuer promises to pay a percentage of the par value as interest on the borrowed funds. The interest payment is stated on the face of the bond at issue.

bond anticipation note (BAN) A short-term debt instrument issued by a municipality to be paid from the proceeds of long-term debt issued.

bond attorney An attorney retained by a municipal issuer to give opinions concerning the legality of a municipal issue. *See also* legal opinion of counsel. (*Syn.* bond counsel)

***Bond Buyer, The* indexes** Index, published by *The Bond Buyer,* of yield levels of municipal bonds. The indexes are indicators of yields that would be offered on AA and A general obligation bonds with 20-year maturities and revenue bonds with 30-year maturities.

bond counsel *See* bond attorney.

bond fund A type of mutual fund whose investment policy is to provide stable income with a minimum of capital risks. It invests in both bonds and preferred stock and may invest in corporate, government or municipal bonds. *See also* mutual fund.

bond quote A corporate bond that is quoted on a percentage of par with increments of 1/8, where a quote of 99 1/8 represents 99.125% of par ($1,000), or $991.25. Bonds may also be quoted on a yield to maturity basis.

bond ratio The percentage of a company's invested capital that is provided by long-term debt financing. It is found by dividing the face value of the outstanding bonds by the invested capital. (*Syn.* debt ratio)

bond swap A technique used by investors in municipal bonds that involves the sale of a bond or bonds at a loss and the simultaneous purchase of entirely different bonds in a like amount, with comparable coupons or maturities.

book-entry security A security sold without delivery of a certificate. Evidence of ownership is maintained on records kept by a central agency, such as the Treasury on the sale of Treasury bills. Transfer of ownership is recorded by entering the change on the books.

book value per bond *See* net tangible assets per bond.

book value per share A measure of the net worth of each share of common stock that is calculated by subtracting intangible assets and preferred stock from total net worth and then dividing by the number of shares of common outstanding. (*Syn.* net tangible assets per common share)

branch office A branch office is any location identified by any means to the public as a location in which the member conducts an investment banking or securities business. An office is considered a branch office if:

- the member firm pays all or a substantial portion of the operating expenses (especially rent) involved in maintaining the space, either in a commercial or residential setting;
- the location is identified to the general public as an office of the member through any kind of signage or listing in a directory;
- the location is advertised in any way; or
- it is listed in any publication (trade or otherwise, including telephone directories) as a designated office of the firm.

breadth-of-market theory A technical theory that forecasts the strength of the market based on the number of issues that advance or decline in a particular trading day. (*Syn.* advance/decline line)

breakeven call spread Breakeven is calculated by adding the net premium to the lower strike price.

breakeven long hedge Breakeven occurs when the market price of a stock equals the purchase price of the stock plus the premium paid for the put.

breakeven point The market price that a stock must reach for the option buyer to avoid a loss if he exercises. For a call, it is the strike price plus the premium paid. For a put, it is the strike price minus the premium paid.

breakeven point straddle Two breakeven points on straddles that are calculated by adding and subtracting the total premium from the exercise price on the straddle.

breakeven put spread Breakeven for a put spread is calculated by subtracting the net premium from the higher strike price.

breakeven short hedge The short sales price minus the premium paid to buy the call.

breakout The movement of a security's price through an established support or resistance level.

breakpoint The schedule of discounts offered by a mutual fund for lump-sum or cumulative investments.

breakpoint sale The sale of mutual fund shares in quantities just below the level at which the purchaser would qualify for reduced sales charges. This violates the NASD Rules of Fair Practice.

broad tape The news wires from which price and background information on securities and commodities markets can be gathered.

broker 1) An individual or firm that charges a fee or commission for executing buy and sell orders submitted by another individual or firm. 2) The role of a broker firm when it acts as an agent for a customer and charges the customer a commission for its services.

The term "broker-dealer" is defined in the Uniform Securities Act so that it can be determined who must register in the state as a broker-dealer. If the person does not fall under the definition of broker-dealer as defined by the law, then the registration process is not necessary.

The following persons would not be classified as broker-dealers:
- agents (registered representatives);
- issuers;
- banks, savings institutions or trust companies; or
- persons who have no place of business in the state and who: (a) effect securities transactions in the state exclusively through the issuers of the securities, other broker-dealers or financial institutions (banks, savings institutions, trust companies, insurance companies, and in-

vestment companies), or (b) do not during any period of 12 consecutive months direct more than 15 solicitations into the state to persons other than those specified above.

brokerage house *See* commission house.

broker fail *See* fail to deliver.

broker's broker A specialist handling orders for a commission house broker; also, a floor broker on an exchange or a broker-dealer in the over-the-counter market acting on behalf of (as an agent for) another broker in executing a trade. *See also* correspondent broker-dealer.

broker's loan A money loan made to a brokerage firm by a commercial bank or another lending institution for financing a margin account debit balance. *See also* call loan, loan for set amount.

bucketing The act of accepting customer orders and using firm or other customer positions or orders to offset them without executing them immediately through an exchange.

bulletin board *See* OTC bulletin board.

bullion Ingots or bars of gold assayed at .995 fine or higher.

bull market A market in which prices of securities are moving or are expected to move higher.

bunching orders The act of combining odd-lot orders from different clients into a round lot so as to save the clients the odd-lot differential.

business day A day on which the NYSE is open for business (trading).

buyer's option A settlement contract that calls for delivery and payment according to the number of days specified by the buyer. *See also* seller's option.

buy-in The procedure that occurs when the seller of a security fails to complete a contract to sell according to its terms. The buyer can close the contract by buying the securities in the open market and charging them to the account of the seller who failed to complete the contract.

buying a hedge The purchase of futures options as a means of protecting against an increase in commodities prices in the future. *See also* long hedge, short hedge, selling a hedge.

buying power The dollar amount of securities that a client can purchase using only the special memorandum account balance and without depositing additional equity.

cabinet crowd *See* inactive crowd.

calendar spread The spread between options with the same exercise price but different expiration dates. (*Syn.* horizontal spread)

call An option contract giving the owner the right to buy stock at a stated price within a specified period of time.

callable bond A type of bond issued with a provision allowing the issuer to redeem the bond prior to maturity at a predetermined price. *See also* call price.

callable preferred stock A type of preferred stock carrying the provision that the corporation retains the right to call in the stock at a certain price and retire it. *See also* call price, preferred stock.

call buyer An investor who pays a premium for an option contract and receives the right to buy, during a specified time, the underlying security at a specified price.

call date The date after which the issuer of a bond has the option to redeem the issue at par or at par plus a premium.

call loan A collateralized loan of a brokerage firm having no maturity date that may be called (terminated) at any time and having a fluctuating interest rate recomputed daily. Generally the loan is payable on demand the day after the loan has been contracted. If not called, the loan is automatically renewed for another day. *See also* broker's loan, loan for set amount.

call loan rate The rate of interest a brokerage firm charges its margin account clients on their debit balances.

call price The price paid (usually a premium over the par value of the issue) for preferred stocks or bonds redeemed prior to maturity of the issue.

call protection This provision limiting the right to call an issue is normally stated in terms of time (five years, ten years, etc.) from the original issue before the issuer may exercise the call provision. *See also* call provision.

call provision The written agreement between an issuing corporation and its bondholders or preferred stockholders, giving the corporation the option to redeem its senior securities at a specified price before maturity and under specified conditions.

call spread The result of an investor buying a call on a particular security and writing a call with a different expiration date, differ-

ent exercise price or both on the same security.

call writer An investor who receives a premium and takes on, for a specified time, the obligation to sell the underlying security at the specified price, at the call buyer's discretion.

cancel former order (CFO) An instruction by a customer to cancel a previously entered order.

can crowd *See* inactive crowd.

capital Accumulated money or goods used to produce income.

capital appreciation A rise in the market prices of assets owned.

capital asset Broadly defined to include all property held by a taxpayer, whether or not connected with her trade or business. However, there are a number of exceptions to this definition, the most important of which excludes a taxpayer's stock in trade, inventory or property held by the taxpayer primarily for sale to customers in the ordinary course of her trade or business.

capital contribution The gross amount of investment in a program by a participant or all participants, not including units purchased by the sponsors.

capital cost Any cost required to be capitalized for income tax purposes, such as the cost of acquiring leaseholds, geological and geophysical exploration costs, the cost of acquiring tangible property and equipment and the cost of real property.

capital gain The gain (selling price minus cost basis) on an asset. *See also* capital loss, long-term gain.

capitalization The sum of a company's long-term debt, capital stock and surpluses. *See also* capital structure. (*Syn.* invested capital)

capitalization ratio A ratio revealing the percentage of bonds, preferred stock or common stock to total capitalization.

capitalize An accounting procedure whereby the taxpayer records an expenditure as a capital asset on its books instead of charging it to expenses for the year.

capital loss The loss (cost basis minus selling price) on an asset. *See also* capital gain, long-term loss.

capital market That segment of the securities market that deals in instruments with more than one year to maturity—that is, long-term debt and equity securities.

capital stock The total stated value or par value of all outstanding preferred stock and common stock of a corporation.

capital structure The composition of long-term funds (equity and debt) a company has as a source for financing. *See also* capitalization, invested capital.

capital surplus The money a corporation receives in excess of the stated value of the stock at the time of sale. *See also* par value. (*Syn.* paid-in surplus)

carrying broker *See also* clearing broker.

carrying charge Any cost associated with holding or storing a commodity, including interest, insurance, rents and so on.

carrying charge market The situation that exists when the difference in price between delivery months of a commodity in the futures markets covers all interest, insurance and storage costs. (*Syn.* contango, normal market)

carryover Any part of the supply of a commodity (particularly crop production) carried over from one year to the next.

cash account An account in which a client is required to pay in full for securities purchased not later than the seventh business day from the trade date.

cash and carry market *See* cash market.

cash assets ratio The most stringent test of liquidity, this ratio is calculated by adding the sum of cash and cash equivalents and dividing that sum by total current liabilities.

cash basis accounting An accounting method whereby revenues and expenses are accounted for when received or paid, rather than earned or incurred. *See also* accrual accounting.

cash commodity The actual, physical good being traded, rather than a futures contract on that good.

cash dividend A cash payment to a company's stockholders out of the company's current earnings or accumulated profits. The dividend must be declared by the board of directors.

cash equivalent A security that is extremely liquid and can be readily converted into cash (e.g., Treasury bill, certificate of deposit and money-market fund).

cash flow The money received by a business minus the money paid out. Cash flow is also equal to net income plus depreciation or depletion.

cashiering department The department within a brokerage firm that delivers and receives securities and money to and from other firms and clients of the firm. (*Syn.* security cage)

cash market Transactions between buyers and sellers of commodities that entail immediate delivery of and payment for a physical commodity. *See also* futures market. (*Syn.* cash and carry market)

cash price The market price for goods to be delivered and paid for immediately.

cash securities equivalent Any Treasury bill, certificate of deposit, money market fund and so on that is extremely liquid and readily converted into cash.

cash transaction A securities settlement contract that calls for delivery and payment on the date of the trade, due by 2:30 pm EST (or within 30 minutes of the trade if made after 2:00 pm) in New York. (*Syn.* cash trade)

casing A heavy steel pipe cemented to the wall of the hole drilled to reinforce a well when it reaches a certain depth.

catastrophe call The redemption of a bond due to disaster (e.g., a power plant built with proceeds from an issue burns to the ground). *See also* mandatory call.

CBOE *See* Chicago Board Options Exchange.

CCC *See* Commodity Credit Corporation.

CD *See* negotiable certificate of deposit.

CEA *See* Commodity Exchange Authority.

certificate of deposit *See* negotiable certificate of deposit.

CFO *See* cancel former order.

CFTC *See* Commodities Futures Trading Commission.

change The change from the previous day's settlement price.

chartist A securities analyst who uses charts and graphs of the past price movements of a security to predict its future movements. *See also* technical analysis.

Chicago Board Options Exchange (CBOE) The first national securities exchange for the trading of listed options.

Chicago Board Options Exchange ORS The Chicago Board Options Exchange (CBOE) uses the Order Routing System (ORS) to collect, store, route and execute public customer (nonbroker-dealer) orders. ORS automatically routes option market and limit orders of up to 2,000 contracts to the CBOE member firm's floor booth, to the floor brokers in the trading crowd, to the order book official's electronic book or to RAES.

Chicago Board Options Exchange RAES Market orders and executable limit orders of ten or fewer contracts received by ORS are sent to the Retail Automatic Execution System (RAES). Customer orders sent through RAES receive instantaneous executions (fills) at the prevailing market quote and are confirmed almost immediately to the originating firm.

Chinese wall The wall through which insider information must not pass from corporate advisers to investment traders, who could make use of the information to reap large profits.

Christmas tree The assembly of valves, gauges and pipes at the wellhead of an oil or gas well.

churning Excessive trading in a customer's account. The term suggests that the registered representative ignores the objectives and interests of clients and seeks only to increase commissions. (*Syn.* overtrading)

class All options of the same type (e.g., all calls or all puts) on the same underlying security. *See also* series, type.

clearing agency The purpose of a clearing agency is to act as an intermediary between the sides in a securities transaction, receiving and delivering payments and securities. Any organization that fills this function, including a securities depository but not including a Federal Reserve Bank, is considered a clearing agency.

clearing broker A broker-dealer that clears its own trades, as well as trades of introducing brokers. A clearing broker-dealer can hold customers' securities and cash. (*Syn.* carrying broker)

Clearing Corporation Refers to the Clearing Corporation of the Chicago Board of Trade, through which transactions in futures and option contracts are settled, guaranteed, offset and filled. The Clearing Corporation positions itself between the buyer and the seller in a contract, becoming the buyer for all sellers and the seller for all buyers. It settles all transactions at the end of each business day and is the guarantor of all contracts.

clearinghouse 1) An agency of a futures exchange, through which transactions in futures and option contracts are settled, guaranteed, offset and filled. The clearing-house may be an independent corporation or exchange-owned. 2) A member firm of the Clearing Corporation. *See also* Clearing Corporation.

close The price of the last transaction for a particular security on a particular day. The mid-price of a closing trading range.

closed-end lien A provision of a bond issue preventing the issuer from issuing additional bonds having an equal claim to the same collateral or revenues.

closed-end management company A management investment company operated in much the same manner as a conventional corporation. The closed-end fund will issue a fixed number of shares for sale (fixed capitalization). The shares may be of several classes. Shares are bought and sold in the secondary marketplace; the fund does not offer to redeem shares. The market price of the shares is determined by supply and demand and not by their net asset value. The shares may be traded on an exchange or over-the-counter market.

closed-end pledge *See* junior lien debt.

closing date The date designated by the general partners when sales of units in a program cease. Typically the offering period is for one year.

closing purchase transaction The act of closing out an opening sale by buying options of the same series.

closing range The relatively narrow range of prices at which transactions take place in the closing minutes of the trading day.

closing sale transaction The transaction that takes place when an investor who owns an option closes out the position in that option by selling it.

CMV *See* current market value.

COD *See* collect on delivery.

Code of Arbitration The Code of Arbitration provides a method of handling securities-related disputes or clearing controversies between members, public customers, clearing corporations or clearing banks. Any claim, dispute or controversy subject to arbitration is required to be submitted to arbitration.

Code of Procedure The Code of Procedure is the NASD's procedure for handling trade practice complaints. The NASD District Business Conduct Committee (DBCC) is the first body to hear and judge complaints. Appeals and review of DBCC decisions are handled by the NASD Board of Governors.

collateral trust bond A form of debt backed by stocks or bonds of another issuer. The collateral is held by a trustee for safekeeping. (*Syn.* collateral trust certificate)

collateral trust certificate *See* collateral trust bond.

collection ratio A rough measure of the length of time accounts receivable have been outstanding. It is calculated by multiplying the receivables by 360 and dividing that amount by the net sales. For municipal bonds, the collection ratio is calculated by dividing taxes collected by taxes assessed.

collect on delivery (COD) *See* delivery vs. payment.

combination An option position that represents a put and a call on the same stock in which the investor has neither purchased a straddle nor sold a straddle.

combined account A customer account that has cash and long and short margin positions in different securities.

combined distribution *See* split offering.

commercial bank An institution that accepts deposits and makes business loans.

commercial paper An unsecured, short-term promissory note issued by well-known businesses chiefly for financing accounts receivable. It is usually issued at a discount reflecting prevailing market interest rates. Maturities range up to 270 days.

commingling The failure to clearly identify and segregate securities (carried for the account of any customer) that have been fully paid or that are excess margin securities.

commission broker A member eligible to execute orders for customers of her member firm on the floor of the Exchange. (*Syn.* floor broker)

commissioner The commissioner of insurance of the state.

commission house A registered member firm of a given commodity exchange that handles customer accounts and transactions on that exchange. (*Syn.* brokerage house, futures commission merchant, wire house)

Committee on Uniform Securities Identification Procedures (CUSIP) A committee that assigns identification numbers and codes to all securities, to be used when recording all buy and sell orders.

Commodities Futures Trading Commission (CFTC) The federal regulatory agency established by the Commodities Futures Trading Commission Act of 1974 to administer the Commodities Exchange Act. The five CFTC commissioners are appointed by the President (subject to Senate approval).

commodity Any bulk good traded on an exchange or in the cash (spot) market, such as metals, grains, meats, and so on.

Commodity Credit Corporation (CCC) A government-owned and -sponsored corporation that aids American agriculture through price support programs, controlling supplies and controlling foreign sales.

Commodity Exchange Authority (CEA) The predecessor of the Commodities Futures Trading Commission established by the U.S. Department of Agriculture to administer the Commodities Exchange Act of 1936.

commodity pool operator (CPO) An individual or organization involved in the solicitation of funds for the purpose of pooling them to invest in commodities futures contracts.

commodity trading adviser (CTA) An individual or organization that makes recommendations and issues reports on commodities futures or options trading for a fee.

common stock An equity security that represents ownership in a corporation. This is the first security a corporation issues to raise capital. *See also* equity, preferred stock.

competitive bidding The submission of sealed bids by rival underwriting syndicates that want the privilege of underwriting the issue of securities. Competitive bidding normally is used to determine the underwriters for issues of general obligation municipal bonds and is required by law in most states for general obligation bonds of more than $100,000. *See also* negotiated underwriting.

completion of the transaction The point at which a customer pays any part of the purchase price to the broker-dealer for a security he has purchased or delivers a security that he has sold. If the customer makes payment to the broker-dealer before the payment is due, the completion of the transaction occurs when the broker-dealer delivers the security.

compliance department The department within a brokerage firm that oversees the trading and market-making activities of the firm. It ensures that the employees and officers of the firm are in compliance with the rules and regulations of the SEC, exchanges and SROs.

concession The allowance (profit) that an underwriter allows a broker-dealer that is not a syndicate member. The broker-dealer will purchase the security at the public price minus the concession. (*Syn.* reallowance)

confidence theory A technical theory that analyzes the confidence of investors by comparing the yields on high-grade bonds to the yields on lower rated bonds.

confirmation A bill or comparison of trade that is sent or given to a customer on or before the settlement date. *See also* duplicate confirmation.

congestion A narrow price range within which a commodity's price trades for an extended period of time.

consent to lend agreement *See* loan consent agreement.

Consolidated Quotation System (CQS) The NASD offers a quotation and last-sale reporting service for NASD members that are active market makers of listed securities in the third market. As a quotations collection system, CQS is used by market makers willing to stand ready to buy and sell the securities for their own accounts on a continuous basis but that do not wish to do so through an exchange.

CQS is part of the Nasdaq market-making system. Quotation display service is available to all Nasdaq subscribers (at a fee), while quotation input service is available only to those members that are registered to do business in third market stocks. NASD members that are registered market makers may enter quotes into CQS through the Nasdaq system.

Consolidated Tape The Consolidated Tape system (also known as the Consolidated Ticker Tape) is a service of the NYSE designed to deliver real-time reports of securities transactions to subscribers as they occur on the various exchanges. Subscribers to the Tape can choose to receive transaction reports in either of two ways: over the high-speed electronic line (directly linked to their Quotrons® or other types of terminals); or through the low-speed ticker (visible report) line—the type of report commonly seen as quotes racing across a sign at a brokerage counter.

The Tape distributes reports over two different networks that subscribers can tap into through either the low-speed or the high-speed lines. *Network A* reports transactions in NYSE-listed securities (stocks, warrants, rights and so on) wherever they are traded. As an example, a transaction involving NYSE-listed IBM that occurs on the Pacific Stock Exchange will be reported on Network A. *Network B* carries reports of AMEX-listed securities transactions as well as reports of transactions in regional exchange issues that *substantially meet* AMEX listing requirements. Transactions in these securities must be reported within 90 seconds for inclusion on the Consolidated Tape.

consolidation The narrowing of the trading range for a commodity or security. Technical analysts consider consolidation an indication that a strong price move is imminent.

constant dollar plan An investment technique where a constant sum of money is invested regardless of the price fluctuation in a security. The objective is to average out the prices of securities purchased.

constant ratio plan A method of investment in which an investor tries to maintain a predetermined ratio of debt to equity and makes purchases and sales to maintain the desired ratio.

construction fee A fee for acting as general contractor to construct improvements on a program's property either initially or at a later date.

Consumer Price Index (CPI) A measure of inflation or deflation based on price changes in consumer goods and services.

contango *See* normal market.

contingent-deferred sales load A sales load that is charged upon redemption of mutual fund shares or variable contracts; also called a *back-end load*. The load is charged on a declining basis annually, usually reduced to zero after an extended holding period (up to eight years).

contra broker The broker on the other side of a transaction.

contract One unit of trading in futures.

contract grade The exchange-authorized grade of a commodity that can be delivered against a contract.

contractionary policy A fiscal policy that has as its end the decrease (contraction) of the money supply.

contract market A Commodities Futures Trading Commission–designated exchange on which a specified commodity can be traded.

contract month The designated month in which a particular futures contract may be satisfied by making delivery (the contract seller) or taking delivery (the contract buyer).

contractual plan For mutual funds, a type of accumulation plan in which the investor makes a firm commitment to invest a specific amount of money in the fund during a specific time. *See also* front-end load, mutual fund, spread-load option. (*Syn.* penalty plan, prepaid charge plan)

contract unit The unit of delivery specified in a futures contract.

control (controlling, controlled by, under common control with) The possession, direct or indirect, of the power to direct or cause the direction of the management and policies of a person, whether through the ownership of voting securities, by contract other than a commercial contract for goods or nonmanagement services, or otherwise, unless the power is the result of an official position with or corporate office held by the person. Control shall be presumed to exist if any person, directly or indirectly, owns, controls, holds with the power to vote, or holds proxies representing more than 10% of the voting securities of any other person. This presumption may be rebutted by a showing made to the satisfaction of the Commissioner that control does not exist in fact. The Commissioner may determine, after furnishing all persons in interest notice and the opportunity to be heard and after making specific findings of fact to support such determination, that control exists in fact, notwithstanding the absence of a presumption to that effect.

control (of securities) Securities are considered in the possession or under the control of a broker-dealer if they are in the broker-dealer's physical possession, are in an alternate location acceptable to the SEC, or are in transit for a period of time that does not exceed standards set by the SEC.

control person Includes: 1) a director, an officer or another affiliate of an issuer, or 2) a stockholder who owns at least 10% of any class of a company's outstanding securities.

control security Any security owned by a director, an officer or another affiliate of the issuer or by a stockholder who owns at least 10% of any class of a company's outstanding securities. Who owns the security is the factor that determines that specific securities are control securities, not the securities themselves. Public offerings of control securities must comply with SEC Rule 144.

conversion The conversion of income taxable at ordinary income rates into gain taxable at long-term gains rates.

conversion parity The state of having two securities (one of which can be converted into the other) of equal dollar value.

conversion price The amount of par value exchangeable for one share of common stock. This term really refers to the stock price and means the dollar amount of the bond's (or preferred stock's) par value that is exchangeable for one share of common stock.

conversion privilege *See* exchange privilege.

conversion rate *See* conversion ratio.

conversion ratio The number of shares per $1,000 debenture (or preferred stock) that the holder would receive if the debenture were converted into shares of common stock. *See also* debenture. (*Syn.* conversion rate)

conversion value The total market value of common stock into which a debenture (or preferred stock) is convertible. *See also* convertible bond, debenture.

convertible bond A type of debt security (usually in the form of a debenture) that can be converted into (exchanged for) equity securities of the issuing corporation, that is, common and preferred stock. *See also* debenture.

convertible preferred stock A type of preferred stock that offers the holder the privilege of exchanging (converting) the preferred stock for (into) common stock at specified prices or rates. Dividends may be cumulative or noncumulative. *See also* cumulative preferred stock, noncumulative preferred stock, preferred stock.

cooling-off period The period (a minimum of 20 days) between the filing date of a registration statement and the effective date of the registration. In practice, this period varies in length.

copartnership account An account in which the individual members of the partnership are empowered to act on behalf of the partnership as a whole.

Corporate Securities Limited Representative *See* Series 62.

corporation A form of business organization in which the organization's total worth is divided into shares of stock, each share representing a unit of ownership. By law, the corporation has certain rights and responsibilities. It is characterized by a continuous life span and by the limited liability of the owners.

correspondent broker-dealer A broker-dealer that performs services (transactions) for another broker-dealer in a market or locale in which the first broker-dealer has no office.

cost basis Money on which taxes have been paid. A return of cost basis is a return of capital and not subject to tax.

cost depletion A method of depletion whereby the capitalized cost of the producing property is written off over the property's life by an annual deduction. The annual deduction takes into account the number of known recoverable units to arrive at a cost-per-unit figure. The allowance is then determined by multiplying this figure by the number of units sold.

cost of carry All out-of-pocket costs incurred by an investor while holding an open position in a security, including margin costs, interest costs, opportunity costs and so on.

cost-push inflation A type of inflation caused by higher production costs (e.g., wages).

coterminous Municipal entities that share the same boundaries (e.g., a school district and a fire district), which can issue debt separately. *See also* overlapping debt.

country basis The local cash (or spot) market price in comparison to the nearby futures price at the Chicago Board of Trade. (*Syn.* local basis)

coupon bond A bond without the name of the owner printed on its face and with coupons representing semiannual interest payments attached. Coupons are submitted to the trustee by the holder to receive the interest payments. (*Syn.* bearer bond)

coupon yield *See* nominal yield.

covenant A promise or restriction of an issue made part of a trust indenture (bond contract). Examples include rate covenants that establish a minimum revenue coverage for a bond; insurance covenants that require insurance on a project; and maintenance covenants that require maintenance on a facility constructed by the proceeds of a bond issue.

cover 1) Futures purchased to offset a short position. 2) Being long actuals when shorting futures.

coverage For revenue bonds, a measure of safety for payment of principal and interest. Coverage is the multiple of earnings that exceed debt service plus operating and maintenance expenses payable for a time period.

covered call writer An investor who writes a call and owns some other asset that guarantees the ability to perform if the call is exercised.

covered put writer An investor who writes a put and owns some other asset that guarantees the ability to perform if the put is exercised.

CPI *See* Consumer Price Index.

CPO *See* commodity pool operator.

CQS *See* Consolidated Quotation System.

CR *See* credit balance.

cracking spread A spread established with long crude oil futures and short heating oil or gasoline futures. *Cracking* is the term used to describe the process by which crude oil is turned into distillates.

credit An amount applied against the amount of tax due. Every dollar of tax credit reduces the amount of tax due dollar for dollar.

credit agreement An agreement signed in conjunction with a margin agreement, outlining the conditions of the credit arrangement between broker and client.

credit balance (CR) The amount of money remaining in a client's account after all commitments have been paid in full. *See also* debit balance. (*Syn.* credit record, credit register)

credit record *See* credit balance.

credit register *See* credit balance.

credit risk Like financial risk, credit risk involves the safety of one's principal. The term is generally associated with bonds, and the risk is that the issuer will default in the payment of either principal or interest. (*Syn.* default risk)

credit spread The difference between the value of two options when the value of the option sold exceeds the value of the option bought; the opposite of a debit spread.

cross hedge The act of hedging a futures contract risk with a different but related commodity.

cross-reference sheet A compilation of the guideline sections, referenced to the page of the prospectus, partnership agreement or another exhibit, and a justification of any deviation from the guidelines.

cross trade A manipulative practice where customers' buy and sell orders are offset against each other off the floor of the Exchange and the resultant transaction is not recorded with the Exchange.

crush spread A spread established with long soybean futures and short soybean oil and meal futures (*crushing* is the term used to describe the process by which soybeans are turned into oil and meal).

CTA *See* commodity trading adviser.

cum rights Stock trading with rights. *See also* ex-rights.

cumulative preferred stock A type of preferred stock that offers the holder any unpaid dividends in arrears. These dividends accumulate and must be paid to the holder of cumulative preferred stock before any dividends can be paid to the common stockholders. *See also* noncumulative preferred stock, preferred stock.

cumulative voting rights A voting procedure that permits stockholders to cast all of their votes for any one director or to cast their total number of votes in any proportion they choose.

current assets Assets that are in the form of cash or are expected to be converted into cash within the next twelve months in the normal course of business.

current liabilities A corporation's debt obligations due for payment within the next twelve months.

current market value (CMV) The current market price of the securities in an account, based on the closing prices on the previous business day. (*Syn.* long market value)

current price *See* offering price.

current ratio A measure of liquidity that is calculated by dividing total current assets by total current liabilities. (*Syn.* working capital ratio)

current yield The annual dollar return on a security (interest or dividends) divided by the current market price of the security (bonds or stock).

CUSIP *See* Committee on Uniform Securities Identification Procedures.

custodian The institution or person responsible for protecting the property of another. Mutual funds have custodians responsible for safeguarding certificates and performing clerical duties. *See also* mutual fund custodian.

custodian of a minor One who manages a gift of securities to a minor under the Uniform Gifts to Minors Act; also, someone who takes charge of an incompetent's affairs.

customer Any person who is not a broker, dealer or municipal securities dealer is considered a customer.

customer protection rule *See* Rule 15c3-3.

customer statement A statement of a customer's account showing positions and entries. The SEC requires that a customer statement be sent quarterly, but customers generally receive them monthly.

cycle A particular set of months of maturities for listed options (e.g., January, April, July and October make up a cycle).

dated date The date on which interest on a bond issue begins to accrue.

day order An order that is canceled if it is not executed on the day it is entered.

day trader A trader in securities or commodities who opens all positions after the opening of the market and offsets or closes out all positions before the close of the market on the same day.

DBCC *See* NASD District Business Conduct Committee.

dealer The role of a brokerage firm when it acts as a principal in a particular trade. A firm is acting as a dealer when it buys or sells a security for its own account and at its own risk and then charges the customer a markup or markdown. Any person who is *engaged in the business* of buying and selling securities for her own account either directly or through a broker, and who is not a bank, is considered a dealer. (*Syn.* principal)

debenture A debt obligation backed by the general credit of the issuing corporation. *See also* convertible bond.

debit balance (DR) The amount of money a client owes a brokerage firm. *See also* credit balance.

debit record *See* debit balance.

debit register *See* debit balance.

debt ratio The percent of debt in relation to total capitalization of a corporation. *See also* capitalization ratio. (*Syn.* bond ratio)

debt security An evidence of debt issued by corporations, municipalities and the federal government.

debt service The annual amount needed to pay interest and principal (or the scheduled sinking fund contribution) on an outstanding debt.

debt-to-equity ratio The ratio of total debt to total stockholder's equity.

declaration date The date on which a company declares an upcoming dividend.

declining balance method of depreciation A uniform rate is applied each year to the unrecovered cost or another basis of the property. No salvage value is taken into account in determining the annual allowances under this method. Normally a switch to straight-line depreciation occurs in order to maximize the deduction available.

deduction An item or expenditure subtracted from gross income and adjusted gross income to arrive at taxable income, thus reducing the amount of income subject to tax.

deed of trust *See* trust indenture.

default 1) The failure to pay interest or principal promptly when due. 2) The failure to perform on a futures contract as required by an exchange.

default risk *See* credit risk.

defeasance A corporation or municipality removes debt from its balance sheet by issuing a new debt issue or creating a trust to be funded by assets, typically U.S. government securities that will generate enough cash flow to provide for the payment of interest and principal on the debt issue removed from the balance sheet (refunded). *See also* advance refunding, prerefunding.

defensive industry An industry that is relatively unaffected by business cycles, such as the food industry or the utility industry.

defensive issue An issue of an established company in an industry relatively unaffected by business cycles. (*Syn.* defensive stock)

defensive stock *See* defensive issue.

defensive strategy An investment method whereby an investor seeks to minimize the risk of losing principal (e.g., the policy of making purchases and sales according to predetermined objectives without regard for market changes).

deferred annuity An annuity contract that guarantees payment of income, installment payments or a lump-sum payment will be made at an agreed upon future time. *See also* annuity.

deficiency letter A list of additions or corrections that must be made to a registration statement before the SEC will release an offering to the public. The SEC sends a deficiency letter to the issuing corporation. (*Syn.* bedbug letter)

deflation A persistent fall in the general level of prices.

delivery The change in ownership or control of the actual commodity in exchange for cash in settlement of a futures contract.

delivery month The month specified for delivery in a futures contract.

delivery point The location or facility (storage, shipping, etc.) to which a commodity must be delivered in order to fulfill a commodities contract.

delivery vs. payment (DVP) A transaction settlement procedure in which the securities are delivered to the buying institution's bank in exchange for payment of the amount due. (*Syn.* collect on delivery)

delta A term used to describe the responsiveness of option premiums to a change in the price of the underlying asset. Deep in-the-money options have a delta near 1; these show the biggest response to futures price changes. Deep out-of-the-money options have very low deltas.

demand The consumers' desire and willingness to pay for a good or service.

demand-pull A type of inflation resulting from an excessive money supply that increases the demand for goods (i.e., too much money chasing too few goods).

depletion An allowance deducted as an expense to enable the recovery of the cost of a natural resource (coal, oil, gas, quarries, etc.). Two methods of depletion are allowed: cost depletion and percentage depletion.

depreciation An expense allowed for the recovery of the cost of qualifying property; with currency exchange rates, a decrease in the value of a particular currency relative to other currencies. *See also* Modified Accelerated Cost Recovery System.

depreciation expense A noncash expense charged against earnings to recover the cost of an asset over its useful life. Depreciation (recovery) is a bookkeeping entry that does not require the outlay of cash.

designated order An order of a specified minimum size to be executed by (and commissions paid to) a dealer designated by a client (generally in reference to municipal bond transactions). The size of the order establishes its priority for subscription to an issue. *See also* member order, presale order.

development fee A fee for the packaging of a program's property, including negotiating and approving plans, and undertaking to assist in obtaining zoning and necessary variances and financing for the specific property either initially or at a later date.

development well A well drilled within an area of proven oil or gas reserves.

DI *See* disposable income.

diagonal spread The simultaneous purchase and sale of options of the same class but with different exercise prices and expiration dates.

dilution A reduction in earnings per share of common stock. Dilution occurs through the issuance of additional shares of common stock and the conversion of convertible securities.

direct debt The percentage of an issuer's debt evidenced by outstanding bonds and notes.

direct participation program (DPP) A program that provides for flow-through tax consequences, regardless of the structure of the legal entity or the vehicle for distribution. These programs include but are not limited to oil and gas programs, real estate programs, agricultural programs, cattle programs, condominium securities, Subchapter S corporate offerings and all other programs of a similar nature, regardless of the industry represented by the program or any combination thereof.

Direct Participation Programs Limited Representative *See* Series 22.

discount The difference between the price paid for a security and the security's face amount at issue.

discount bond A bond selling below par. *See also* premium.

discount rate The interest rate charged to member banks that borrow from the nine Federal Reserve Banks.

discretionary account An account in which the principal (beneficial owner) has given a registered rep authority to make transactions in the account at the registered rep's discretion. The registered rep may use discretion about price (buy or sell), time and choice of securities (bought or sold). Orders must be marked "DE" (discretion exercised) or "DNE" (discretion not exercised).

disposable income (DI) The sum that people divide between spending and personal savings.

disproportionate sharing arrangement In a disproportionate sharing arrangement, the sponsor will share costs of the program but will receive a disproportionately higher percentage of the revenues. One arrangement would have the sponsor paying 10% of program costs and receiving 25% of revenues. The sponsor shares in dry hole costs, and investors share in both deductible and nondeductible costs.

distant contract Of two or more futures contracts, the contract with the longest time remaining to expiration. *See also* nearby contract. (*Syn.* distant delivery)

distant delivery *See* distant contract.

distributable cash from operations The funds provided by operations after debt service and less the partnership management fee (cash flow).

distribution Any cash or other property distributed to holders and general partners that arises from their interests in the partnership. It does not include any payments to the general partners or agent(s) for partnership expenses.

diversified common stock fund *See* growth fund.

diversified management company A management company that has at least 75% of its total assets in cash, receivables or securities invested, no more than 5% of its total assets invested in the voting securities of any company, and no single investment representing ownership of more than 10% of the outstanding voting securities of any one company.

divided account *See* Western account.

dividend A distribution of the earnings of a corporation. Dividends may be in the form of cash, stock or property (securities owned by a corporation). The board of directors must declare a dividend. *See also* dividend yield.

dividend exclusion An arrangement whereby a corporation may exclude from its taxable income 70% of dividends received from domestic preferred and common stocks. The Tax Reform Act of 1986 repealed the dividend exclusion for individual investors. Formerly the Internal Revenue Code allowed an investor to exclude up to $100 of dividend income from taxable income ($200 on a joint return).

dividend payout ratio A ratio used to analyze a company's policy of paying cash dividends, calculated by dividing the dividends paid on common stock by the net income available for common stockholders.

dividend yield The annual percentage of return that an investor receives on either common or preferred stock. The yield is based on the amount of the annual dividend divided by the market price (at the time of purchase) of the stock. *See also* current yield, dividend.

DJIA *See* Dow Jones Industrial Average.

DK *See* don't know.

DNR *See* do not reduce order.

dollar bonds A term used to describe municipal bonds that are quoted and traded on a basis of dollars rather than yield to maturity. Term bonds, tax-exempt notes and Public Housing Authority bonds are dollar bonds. Municipal serial bonds are quoted on a yield-to-maturity basis.

dollar cost averaging For mutual funds, a system of buying fixed dollar amounts of securities at regular fixed intervals, regardless of the price of the shares. This method may result in an average cost that is generally lower than the average price of all prices at which the securities were purchased.

do not reduce order (DNR) An order that stipulates that the price of limit or stop orders should not be reduced as a result of cash dividends.

don't know (DK) An acronym for "don't know," indicating a lack of information about a transaction or a record of transaction between broker-dealers.

double auction market *See* auction market.

double-barreled bond A municipal revenue bond backed by the full faith and credit of the issuing municipality, as well as by pledged revenues. *See also* general obligation bond, revenue bond.

double declining balance depreciation A form of accelerated depreciation in which a corporation writes off more of the value of an asset in its early years.

Dow Jones Industrial Average (DJIA) The most widely used market indicator, composed of 30 large, actively traded issues.

down tick *See* minus tick.

Dow theory A technical market theory that seeks to interpret long-term trends in the stock market by analyzing the movements of the Dow Jones Industrial Averages.

DPP *See* direct participation program.

DR *See* debit balance.

dry hole Any well that is plugged and abandoned without being completed or that is abandoned for any reason without having produced commercially for 60 days.

dual purpose fund A type of closed-end investment company that offers two classes of stock: income shares and capital shares. Income shares entitle the holder to all net dividends and interest paid to the fund on both income and capital shares but do not allow the holder to participate in any capital appreciation. Capital shares entitle the holder to profit from the growth of all the securities held by the fund. *See also* closed-end management company.

due bill A printed statement showing the transfer of a security's title or rights or showing the obligation of a seller to deliver the securities or rights to the purchaser. The due bill is used as a demand for dividends due a buyer when the transaction occurs before the ex-dividend date.

due diligence The careful investigation by the underwriters that is necessary to ensure that all material information pertinent to an issue has been disclosed to the public.

due diligence meeting A meeting between an issuing corporation's officials and representatives of the underwriting group held to discuss details of the pending issue of securities. These details include the registration statement and the preparation of prospectuses.

duplicate confirmation A copy of a client's confirmation that a brokerage firm sends to an agent or an attorney if the client requests it in writing. Clients must receive copies unless they specify in writing that they do not wish to receive them. *See also* confirmation.

DVP *See* delivery vs. payment.

early warning A broker-dealer is in early warning if its net capital falls to less than 120% of the required minimum or if the firm's ratio of aggregate indebtedness to net capital (AI:NC) exceeds 12:1. When a broker-dealer is in early warning, its FOCUS reporting requirements are stepped up until three months after it is out of early warning.

earned income Income that is derived from personal services, such as wages, salary, tips, commissions and bonuses. *See also* unearned income.

earned surplus *See* retained earnings.

earnings per share (EPS) The net income available for common stock divided by the number of shares of common stock outstanding.

earnings per share fully diluted The earnings per share calculated assuming that convertible securities (convertible preferred stock, convertible bonds) have been converted. (*Syn.* primary earnings per share)

Eastern account Liability for the distribution of an issue of securities is undivided, and each member of the underwriting syndicate is responsible for a proportionate share of any securities remaining unsold. *See also* Western account.

economic risk The risk related to international developments and domestic events.

EE savings bond A nonnegotiable government debt issued at a discount from face value. The difference between the purchase price and the value of the bond upon redemption determines the interest rate. Currently EE bonds pay a variable rate of interest linked to 85% of the rate paid on five-year treasury securities.

effective date The date the registration of an issue of securities becomes effective. The underwriter confirms sales of the newly issued securities after this date.

efficient market theory A theory based on the assumption that the stock market processes information efficiently. This theory postulates that new information, as it becomes known, is reflected immediately in the price of stock and, therefore, stock prices represent fair prices.

elasticity The responsiveness of consumers and producers to a change in prices. A large change in demand or production resulting from a small change in price for a good would be considered an indication of elasticity. A small or no change in production or demand following a change in price would be considered an indication of inelasticity.

Employee Retirement Income Security Act (ERISA) A 1974 law governing the operation of most private pension and benefit plans. The law eased pension eligibility rules, set up the Pension Benefit Guaranty Corporation and established guidelines for the management of pension funds.

endorsement The signature on the back of a certificate by the person named on the certificate as owner. Owners must endorse certificates when transferring them to another person's name.

EPS *See* earnings per share.

equipment note or bond *See* equipment trust certificate.

equipment trust *See* equipment trust equity.

equipment trust certificate A debt obligation backed by equipment. The title to the equipment is held by an independent trustee (usually a bank), not the company. Equipment trust certificates are generally issued by transportation companies such as railroads. *See also* New York plan. (*Syn.* equipment note or bond, equipment trust)

equity The ownership interest of common and preferred stockholders in a corporation; also, the client's net worth in a margin account; also, what is owned less what is owed. *See also* common stock, margin account, preferred stock.

equity financing When stock (common or preferred) is sold to individuals or institutions and, in return for the money paid, the individuals or institutions receive ownership interest in the corporation.

equity interest When used with respect to a corporation, *equity interest* means common stock and any security convertible into, exchangeable for or exercisable for common stock. When used with respect to a partnership, *equity interest* means an interest in the capital or profits or losses of the partnership.

equity security The SEC defines an equity security as any:

- stock or similar security;
- certificate of participation in any profit-sharing agreement;
- preorganization certificate, subscription, transferable share, voting trust certificate or certificate of deposit for an equity security;
- limited partnership interest, interest in a joint venture or certificate of interest in a business trust;
- convertible security, warrant or rights certificate that carries the right to subscribe to an equity security; or

• put, call or other option that offers the privilege of buying or selling an equity security.

If the market price of the security in question trends or tracks with the price of the common stock, it is an equity security.

ERISA *See* Employee Retirement Income Security Act.

escrow receipt The certificate provided by an approved bank that guarantees that the indicated securities are on deposit at that bank and will be delivered if the option is exercised.

Eurobond A bond issued by a government or corporation in a particular country and denominated in that country's currency but sold outside that country.

Eurodollar U.S. currency held in banks outside the United States.

excess equity The amount of money in a margin account that is in excess of the federal requirement. (*Syn.* margin excess, Regulation T excess)

exchange Any organization, association or group of persons that maintains or provides a marketplace in which securities can be bought and sold. An exchange does not have to be a physical place, and several strictly electronic exchanges do business around the world.

exchange distribution A block trading procedure in which a block of stock is crossed on the floor of the exchange with no prior announcement on the broad tape.

exchange-listed security In order for a security to be traded by exchange members on an exchange, it has to be listed on that exchange. Once it is accepted for listing, it is admitted to full trading privileges on that exchange. Listed securities can also be traded in the over-the-counter market (which is known as third-market trading).

exchange offer An offer to exchange one type of security for another.

exchange privilege The ability of an investor who has invested in one fund to transfer to another fund under the same sponsor without incurring an additional sales charge. (*Syn.* conversion privilege)

exchange rate The price at which one country's currency can be converted into that of another.

ex-date The first day buyers are not entitled to receive distributions previously declared.

The ex-date is usually four business days before the record date. (*Syn.* ex-dividend date)

ex-dividend date *See* ex-date.

executor A person authorized to manage a brokerage account for an estate. An executor's authority is established by the last will of the decedent.

exempt security A security exempt from the registration requirements (although not from the antifraud requirements) of the Securities Act of 1933 (e.g., U.S. government and municipal securities).

exempt transaction Exempt transactions are those transactions exempted from registration and advertising requirements under the Uniform Securities Act. Examples of exempt transactions include the following:

• isolated nonissuer transactions;
• nonissuer transactions in outstanding securities (normal market trading);
• transactions with financial institutions (banks, savings institutions, trust companies, insurance companies, pension or profit sharing plans, broker-dealers, etc.);
• unsolicited transactions;
• fiduciary transactions;
• private placement transactions;
• transactions between an issuer and its underwriters; and
• transactions with an issuer's employees, partners or directors if no commission is paid directly or indirectly for the soliciting.

Exemption from the act's registration and advertising requirements does not mean that a transaction is exempt from the act's antifraud provisions.

exercise To implement the rights of an option or a warrant (e.g., a call holder exercises a call by implementing the right to buy 100 shares of the underlying stock at the agreed-upon price).

exercise price The price per share at which the holder of a call, an option or a warrant may buy (or the holder of a put may sell) the underlying security. (*Syn.* strike price, striking price)

ex-legal trade A municipal issue trading without a legal opinion of counsel accompanying the bond. An ex-legal trade must be designated as such at the time of the trade.

expansionary policy A fiscal policy that has as its end the increase (expansion) of the money supply.

expense ratio A ratio used to compare the efficiency of a mutual fund. The ratio is calculated by dividing expenses of operation by the fund's net assets.

expiration date The specified date on which an option becomes worthless and the buyer no longer has the rights specified in the contract.

ex-pit transaction A trade executed outside the normal exchange trading ring or pit.

exploratory well A well drilled either 1) in search of a new and as yet undiscovered pool of oil or gas or 2) with the hope of substantially extending the limits of a pool already developed.

ex-rights Stock purchased without rights. *See also* cum rights.

ex-rights date The date on or after which stocks will be traded without subscription rights.

ex-warrants The date on or after which the buyer of a security is no longer entitled to warrants that will be distributed to the security's owners.

FAC *See* face-amount certificate company.

face-amount certificate company (FAC) The certificates (debt instruments) issued by an investment company that obligate it to pay an investor a stated amount of money (the face amount) at a specific time. The investor pays into the certificate in periodic payments or in a lump sum.

face value *See* par value, principal.

fail to deliver Any situation where the broker-dealer on the sell side of a transaction or contract has not delivered the securities specified in the trade to the broker-dealer on the buy side.

fail to receive Any situation where the broker-dealer on the buy side of a transaction or contract has not received the securities specified in the trade from the broker-dealer on the sell side.

Fannie Mae *See* Federal National Mortgage Association.

farm out An agreement whereby the owner of a leasehold or working interest agrees to assign his interest in certain specific acreage to the assignees, retaining such interest as an overriding royalty, offset acreage or another type of interest, subject to the drilling of one or more specific wells or another performance as a condition of the assignment.

FCM *See* futures commission merchant.

FDIC *See* Federal Deposit Insurance Corporation.

feasibility study A study to determine whether a proposed municipal project will generate sufficient funds to cover operation of the project and debt service. A feasibility study is generally required before the issuance of a municipal revenue bond.

Fed, the *See* Federal Reserve System.

Fed call *See* margin call.

federal call *See* margin call.

Federal Deposit Insurance Corporation (FDIC) The federal agency established in 1933 to provide deposit insurance for member banks and to conduct business activities to prevent bank and thrift failures.

federal funds The reserves of banks and certain other institutions greater than the reserve requirements or excess reserves. These funds are available immediately.

federal funds rate The interest rate charged by one institution lending federal funds to another.

federal margin *See* margin call.

Federal National Mortgage Association (FNMA) A publicly held corporation whose common stock is traded on the NYSE. FNMA purchases conventional mortgages and mortgages guaranteed by the Federal Housing Administration, Department of Veterans Affairs and Farmers Home Administration. (*Syn.* Fannie Mae)

Federal Open Market Committee (FOMC) A committee that makes decisions concerning the Fed's open market operations. *See also* open market operations.

Federal Reserve Board (FRB) A seven-member group appointed by the president (subject to approval by Congress) to oversee operations of the Federal Reserve System.

Federal Reserve System (Fed) The central bank system of the United States. Its chief responsibility is to regulate the flow of money and credit. (*Syn.* The Fed)

FGIC *See* Financial Guaranty Insurance Corporation.

fictitious quotation A bid or an offer of which the interdealer quotation system is unaware.

fidelity (surety) bond 1) A bond required by NYSE Rule 319 for all employees, officers and partners of member firms to protect clients against acts of misplacement, fraudulent trading and check forgery. 2) Every member firm required to join the Securities Investor Protection Corporation (that is, any firm doing business with the public) must purchase and maintain a blanket fidelity bond that indemnifies against losses due to acts such as check forgery, lost securities or fraudulent trading. The minimum coverage must not be less than $25,000, with substantially higher coverage amounts necessary based on the size of the firm and the scope of its business operations.

fiduciary A person legally appointed and authorized to represent another person and act on her behalf.

FIFO *See* first in, first out.

filing date The day on which a registration statement is filed with the SEC.

fill or kill order (FOK) An order that instructs the floor broker to fill the entire order immediately or kill (cancel) the entire order. A partial fill is not acceptable.

final prospectus The prospectus delivered by an issuing corporation that includes the price of the securities, the delivery date, the underwriting spread and other material information.

Financial and Operational Combined Uniform and Single Report *See* FOCUS Report

Financial Guaranty Insurance Corporation (FGIC) An insurance company that offers insurance on the timely payment of interest and principal on municipal issues and unit investment trusts.

financial risk The risk associated with the safety of one's principal related to the ability of an issuer of a security to meet principal, interest or dividend payments.

firm commitment underwriting When the underwriter offers to sell the entire issue of securities to be offered by the issuer. The underwriter is acting as a dealer and will pay the issuer as such in a lump sum for the securities. The underwriter assumes all financial responsibility for any unsold shares.

firm quote The actual price at which a trading unit (such as 100 shares of stock or five bonds) of the security may be bought or sold.

first in, first out (FIFO) An accounting method for assessing a company's inventory in which it is assumed that the first goods acquired are the first to be sold. Also used to designate the order in which sales or withdrawals from an investment are made to determine cost basis for tax purposes. *See also* last in, first out.

fiscal policy The federal tax and spending policies set by Congress or the White House.

Fitch Investors Service, Inc. A rating service for corporate bonds, municipal bonds, commercial paper and other debt obligations.

5% markup policy The NASD's general guideline for the percentage markup, markdown and commissions on securities transactions.

fixed annuity (annuity guaranteed) An annuity contract in which the insurance company makes fixed dollar payments to the annuitant for the term of the contract (usually until the annuitant dies). The insurance company guarantees both earnings and principal amount. *See also* annuity. (*Syn.* fixed dollar annuity, guaranteed dollar annuity)

fixed asset A tangible, physical property owned by a corporation that is used in the production of the corporation's income.

fixed dollar annuity *See* fixed annuity.

fixing The act of trading in a new security for the purpose of stabilizing its price above the established public offering price. (*Syn.* pegging)

flat A term used to describe bonds traded without accrued interest. The bonds are traded at the agreed upon market price only.

flexible premium policy Any variable life insurance policy other than a scheduled premium policy.

floating debt Any obligation payable on demand or having a very short maturity.

floor broker (*Syn.* commission broker)

floor trader An exchange member who enters transactions only for his own account from the floor of the exchange. (*Syn.* local)

flower bond A type of Treasury bond that can be used to settle estate taxes. Flower bonds tend to trade at discounts due to their low coupon rates.

flow of funds The priority for payment of revenues collected.

flow-through A term used to describe the way income, deductions and credits resulting from the activities of a business are applied to individual tax and expenses returns as though each incurred the income and deductions (expenses) directly. *See also* limited partnership.

FNMA *See* Federal National Mortgage Association.

FOCUS Report Broker-dealers are required to file periodic Financial and Operational Combined Uniform and Single (FOCUS) Reports with the SEC at both the Commission's Washington office and the broker-dealer's regional SEC office. General securities broker-dealers are required to file a FOCUS Report Part I monthly and a FOCUS Report Part II quarterly. Introducing broker-dealers are required to file a FOCUS Report Part IIA quarterly, but are not required to file a monthly report.

FOK *See* fill or kill order.

FOMC *See* Federal Open Market Committee.

forced conversion A process used by a corporation that strongly encourages a convertible bondholder to exercise the conversion option. Often conversion is forced by calling the bonds when the market value of the stock is higher than the redemption price offered by the corporation. *See also* redemption.

foreign associate A non-U.S. citizen employed by an NASD member firm, usually in a Canadian or an overseas branch office is not subject to registration and licensing with the Association. This does not include U.S. citizens living and working in overseas or Canadian branch offices, however.

Each exempted foreign associate must agree not to: 1) engage in the securities business in any country or territory under the jurisdiction of the United States, or 2) do business with any U.S. citizen, national or resident alien.

foreign currency The currency of a country other than the one in which the investor resides. Options and futures contracts trade on numerous foreign currencies.

foreign fund *See* specialized fund.

Form 3 A form used by officers, directors and principal stockholders to file an initial statement of beneficial ownership of equity securities. The form is filed with the exchange(s) on which those securities trade (although if there is more than one exchange listing the securities, the issuer can designate the one exchange with which it will file its reports).

Form 4 A form used to report changes in the beneficial ownership of a corporation.

Form 8K A form nicknamed "the current report" by the SEC and filed only when events (or transactions) of consequence occur. For example, Form 8K is used to report:
- changes in the control of a company
- changes in a company's name or address
- the commencement of bankruptcy
- a change of auditors
- resignations of members of the board
- mergers or acquisitions
- changes in assets

Form 10C A form used by issuers of securities that are quoted on Nasdaq. An issuer would use a 10C to report a change in its name and changes of more than 5% in the amount of securities it has outstanding (more than a 5% increase or decrease from the last report).

Form 10K An annual audited report that covers essentially all the information in the original registration statement. The report is due within 90 days of year end.

Form 10Q A quarterly report containing unaudited financial data. Certain types of non-recurring events that arise during the quarterly period, such as significant litigation, must be reported on Form 10Q. This report is due 45 days after the end of each of the first three fiscal quarters (i.e., May 15th, August 14th and November 14th of each year).

forward contract A cash market transaction in which a future delivery date is specified. Forward contracts differ from futures contracts in that the terms of forward contracts are not standardized and are not traded in contract markets.

forward market The nonexchange trading of commodities specifying delivery at some future date.

forward pricing When pricing mutual fund shares, the valuation of the portfolio occurs at least once per day, and orders to purchase or redeem shares are completed at the valuation following the order placement.

fourth market The trading of securities directly from one institutional investor to another without the services of a brokerage firm, primarily through the use of INSTINET. (*Syn.* INSTINET)

fractional share A portion of a whole share of stock. Fractional shares used to be generated when corporations declared stock dividends, merged or voted to split stock. These days it is more common for corporations to issue the cash equivalent of fractional shares to investors. Mutual fund shares are frequently issued in fractional amounts.

fraud The deliberate concealment, misrepresentation or omission of material information or the truth to deceive or manipulate another party for unlawful or unfair gain.

FRB *See* Federal Reserve Board.

free credit balance Cash balances (customer funds) in customer accounts. Broker-dealers are required to notify customers of their free credit balances at least quarterly. *See also* Rule 15c3-2.

free crowd *See* active crowd.

free-look letter (45-day letter) A letter to clients explaining the sales charge and operation of a contractual plan. The letter must be sent within 60 days of the sale. During the free-look period, the client may terminate the plan without paying a sales charge. *See also* contractual plan.

freeriding The illegal extension of credit for the purpose of trading securities.

freeriding and withholding A violation of the NASD Rules of Fair Practice, freeriding and withholding is the failure of a member participating in the distribution of a new issue to make a bona fide public offering at the public offering price for an issue that is hot. A hot issue is one that opens in the secondary market at a premium to the public offering price.

front-end load 1) The fees and expenses paid by any party for any service rendered during the program's organization or acquisition phase, including front-end organization and offering expenses, acquisition fees and expenses and any other similar fees designated by the sponsor. 2) A system of sales charge for contractual plans that permits up to 50% of the first year's payments to be deducted as a sales charge. Investors have a right to withdraw from the plan, but there are some restrictions if this occurs. *See also* contractual plan, sales charge.

frozen account An account requiring cash in advance to buy and securities in hand to sell.

Full Disclosure Act Another name for the Securities Act of 1933.

full faith and credit bonds *See* general obligation bond.

full trading authorization The authorization for someone other than the customer to have full trading privileges in her account, which includes making purchases, sales and withdrawals.

fully registered A bond registered as to both principal and interest.

functional allocation A sharing arrangement formulated around the types of costs that exist in an oil and gas program. Investors are responsible for intangible costs, and the sponsor is responsible for tangible (capitalized) costs. The revenue-sharing arrangement reflects the percentage of the costs in the program.

fund With mutual funds, the entity responsible for the general administration and supervision of the investment portfolio.

fundamental analysis A method of securities analysis that tries to evaluate the intrinsic value of a particular stock. It is a study of the overall economy, industry conditions and the financial condition and management of a particular company.

funded debt All long-term financing of a corporation or municipality, that is, all outstanding bonds maturing in five years or longer.

funding The conversion of floating debt into bonded debt. *See also* floating debt, funded debt.

fund manager With mutual funds, the entity responsible for investment advisory services. *See also* mutual fund.

funds statement A financial statement that analyzes why a company's working capital increases or decreases.

fungibility Having the same value or quality. A security that is freely transferable with another security and can be used in place of the security traded is considered a fungible security.

futures Exchange-standardized contracts for the purchase or sale of a commodity at a future date.

futures commission merchant (FCM) An individual or organization engaged in the solicitation or acceptance of orders and the extension of credit for the purchase or sale of commodities futures.

futures contract A standardized, exchange-traded contract to make or take delivery of a particular type and grade of commodity at an agreed upon place and point in the future. Futures contracts are transferable between parties.

futures exchange A centralized facility for the trading of futures contracts.

futures market A continuous auction market in which participants buy and sell commodities contracts for delivery at a specified point in the future. Trading is carried on through open outcry and hand signals in a trading pit or ring. *See also* cash market.

general account All assets of an insurer other than assets in separate accounts whether or not established for variable life insurance.

general obligation bond (GO) A type of municipal bond backed by the full faith, credit and taxing power of the issuer for payment of interest and principal. (*Syn.* full faith and credit bond)

general partner (GP) A partner in a partnership who is personally liable for all debts of the partnership and who partakes in the management and control of the partnership.

general partnership (GP) An association of two or more entities forming to conduct a trade or partnership business. The partnership does not require documents for formation, and the general partners are joint and severally liable for the partnership's liabilities.

General Securities Representative *See* Series 7.

Ginnie Mae *See* Government National Mortgage Association.

GNMA *See* Government National Mortgage Association.

GNP *See* gross national product.

GO *See* general obligation bond.

good delivery A security that is negotiable in compliance with the contract of the sale and ready to be transferred from seller to purchaser.

good faith deposit A deposit by underwriters bidding for a municipal issue required to ensure performance by the low bidder. This requirement is stipulated in the official notice of sale sent to prospective underwriters; the amount required is usually 2% to 5% of the bid.

good till canceled order (GTC) An order that is left in force until it is executed or canceled. (*Syn.* open order)

Government National Mortgage Association (GNMA) A wholly owned government corporation that issues several types of securities backed by the full faith and credit of the U.S. government. (*Syn.* Ginnie Mae)

government security An obligation of the U.S. government, backed by the full faith and credit of the government, and regarded as the highest grade or safest issue (i.e., default risk-free). The U.S. government issues short-term Treasury bills, medium-term Treasury notes and long-term Treasury bonds.

GP *See* general partner, general partnership.

GPM *See* gross processing margin.

grade The specified quality of a commodity.

grantor The writer or seller of an option or a contract.

gross income All income of a taxpayer, from whatever source derived.

gross national product (GNP) The total value of goods and services produced in a society during one year. This includes consumption, government purchases, investment and exports minus imports.

gross proceeds The aggregate total of the original invested capital of the original and all of the additional limited partners.

gross processing margin (GPM) The difference between the cost of soybeans and the revenue from the resultant meal and oil after processing.

gross revenue pledge The pledge that debt service is the first payment to be made from revenues received from a municipal project. *See also* net revenue pledge.

gross revenues All revenues from the operation of properties owned by a partnership. The term "gross revenues" typically does not include revenues from interest income or from the sale, refinancing or another disposition of partnership properties.

group net order An order received by an underwriting syndicate for the benefit of the syndicate. Commissions (takedowns) are paid to members according to their participation in the syndicate.

growth fund A type of diversified common stock fund that has capital appreciation as its primary goal. It invests in companies that reinvest most of their earnings for expansion, research or development. The term also refers to growth income funds that invest in common stocks for both current income and long-term growth of both capital and income. *See also* diversified common stock fund, mutual fund.

growth stock A relatively speculative issue, often paying low dividends and selling at high price-earnings ratios.

GTC *See* good till canceled order.

guaranteed Securities that have a guarantee, usually from a source other than the issuer, as to the payment of principal, interest or dividends.

guaranteed bond A debt obligation in which a company other than the issuing corporation guarantees payment of interest and principal on the bond.

guaranteed dollar annuity *See* fixed annuity.

guaranteed stock Generally a preferred stock that has divided payments guaranteed by a corporation other than the issuing corporation but that remains the stock of the issuing corporation. Guaranteed stock is considered a dual security.

guarantor *See* writer.

guardian A person who manages a gift of securities to a minor under the Uniform Gifts to Minors Act; also, a person who takes charge of an incompetent's affairs.

haircut The formula used to calculate the discounted value of securities in a broker-dealer's possession in the computation of net capital.

head and shoulders A technical trading pattern that has three peaks resembling a head and two shoulders. The stock moves up to its first peak (the left shoulder), drops back, then moves to a higher peak (the top of the head), drops again but recovers to another, lower peak (the right shoulder). A head and shoulder formation after a substantial rise would indicate a market reversal. An inverted head and shoulders would indicate an advance.

heating oil #2 fuel oil.

hedge 1) The act of investing to reduce the risk of a position in a security (typically the risk of adverse price movements), normally by taking a protecting position in a related security. 2) The protective position taken.

high The highest price a security or commodity reaches during a specified period of time.

holder *See* long.

holding company A company organized to invest in and manage other corporations.

holding period A time period that starts the day after a purchase and ends on the day of the sale.

horizontal spread *See* calendar spread.

hot issue An issue that sells at a premium over the public offering price. *See also* freeriding and withholding.

house maintenance call *See* maintenance call.

house requirement The minimum amount of equity that a client must maintain in a margin account according to the particular firm's rules (most firms have a higher maintenance requirement than that set by the NYSE).

Housing Authority bond A type of municipal bond issued by local public housing authorities to redevelop and improve certain areas. (*Syn.* Public Housing Authority bond)

HR-10 plan *See* Keogh plan.

hypothecation The pledging of clients' securities as collateral for loans. Brokerage firms hypothecate clients' securities to finance their margin loans to customers.

IDB *See* industrial development bond.

identified share The particular share from a multiple position of the same security that a client identifies as being the share that he wants delivered for sale.

immediate annuity An annuity contract purchased for a lump sum (single premium) that starts to pay immediately following its purchase. *See also* annuity.

immediate family Includes a parent, a mother-in-law or father-in-law, husband or wife, children or any relative to whose support the sponsor, member or person associated with the member contributes directly or indirectly.

immediate or cancel order (IOC) An order instructing the floor broker to execute immediately. Any portion of the order that remains unexecuted is canceled.

inactive crowd That section of the NYSE that trades inactive, infrequently traded bonds. (*Syn.* cabinet crowd, can crowd)

incidental insurance benefit Any insurance benefit in a variable life insurance policy, other than the variable death benefit and the minimum death benefit, and including but not limited to any accidental death and dismemberment benefit, disability income benefit, guaranteed insurability option, family income benefit or fixed-benefit term rider.

income bond A debt obligation that promises to repay bond principal in full at maturity. Interest on these bonds is paid only if the corporation's earnings are sufficient to meet the interest payment and if the interest payment is declared by the board of directors. These bonds are usually traded flat. *See also* flat. (*Syn.* adjustment bond)

income fund A type of mutual fund that seeks to provide a stable current income from investments by investing in securities that pay interest. *See also* mutual fund.

income statement A financial statement that summarizes a corporation's revenues and expenses for a specific fiscal period.

indication of interest (IOI) An investor's expression of conditional interest in buying an upcoming securities issue after the investor has reviewed a preliminary prospectus. An indication of interest is not a commitment to buy.

individual retirement account (IRA) A qualified tax-deferred retirement plan for employed individuals that allows a contribution of 100% of earned income up to a maximum of $2,000 per year. Some or all of the contribution may be tax deductible, depending on the individual's compensation level and coverage by other qualified retirement plans. *See also* qualified retirement plan.

industrial development bond (IDB) A municipal security issue, the proceeds from which a state or municipal authority uses to finance construction or the purchase of facilities to be leased or purchased by a private company. The bonds are backed by the credit of the private company and often are not considered an obligation of the issuing municipality.

industrial revenue bond *See* industrial development bond.

industry fund *See* specialized fund.

inflation An increase in the general level of prices.

inflation risk *See* purchasing power risk.

initial margin requirement The amount of equity a customer must deposit when making a new purchase in a margin account. The Regulation T requirement is currently 50% for equity securities. The NYSE and NASD initial requirement is an equity of $2,000 but not more than 100% of the purchase cost. *See also* margin.

initial public offering (IPO) A company's initial public offering, sometimes referred to as "going public," is the first sale of stock by the company to the public.

inside information Material and nonpublic information obtained or used by a person for the purpose of trading in securities.

inside market For any given over-the-counter stock at any given point during trading hours, the inside market is the best bid (highest) price at which stock can be sold in the interdealer market and the best ask (lowest) price at which the same stock can be bought.

insider Any person who has nonpublic knowledge (material information) about a corporation. Insiders include directors, officers and stockholders who own more than 10% of any class of equity security of a corporation.

INSTINET An electronic system owned by Reuters Holdings PLC that offers its subscribers a means of trading over 10,000 American and European securities without using a broker-dealer or going through an exchange. INSTINET collects price quotations from exchange-based market makers and Nasdaq and displays the best bid and asked for each security. INSTINET is registered as a broker-dealer with the SEC. (*Syn.* fourth market)

institutional account An institutional account is an account held for the benefit of others. Examples of institutional accounts include banks, trusts, pension and profit-sharing plans, mutual funds and insurance companies. An institutional order can be of any size.

institutional investor A person or organization that trades securities in large enough share quantities or dollar amounts that it qualifies for preferential treatment and lower trade costs (commissions). Institutional investors are covered by fewer protective regulations because it is assumed that they are more knowledgeable and better able to protect themselves.

in-street-name account An account in which the customer's securities are held in the name of the brokerage firm. *See also* street name.

intangible asset An asset that is not physical, such as a copyright or good will.

intangible drilling development expense An expense in the drilling operations for oil and gas, such as labor, fuel or other nontangible costs. These costs may be expensed in the year incurred or capitalized and depleted at a later date.

interest coverage ratio A ratio describing the safety of a corporate bond. The ratio is calculated by dividing operating income by interest expense. The ratio reveals the multiple of income-to-interest expense; the higher the multiple, the less risk there is of default on interest payment.

interest rate risk The risk associated with investments relating to the sensitivity of price or value to fluctuation in the current level of interest rates; also, the risk that involves the competitive cost of money. This term is generally associated with bond prices, but it applies to all investments. In bonds, the price carries an interest risk because if bond prices rise, outstanding bonds will not remain competitive unless their yields and prices are adjusted to reflect the current market.

interlocking directorate Two (or more) corporate boards of directors that have individual directors who serve simultaneously on both. The Investment Company Act of 1940 requires that at least 40% of the board remain independent from the operations of the investment company. The law states that no more than 60% of the directors may also hold an affiliated position within the fund (an affiliated position would be a director who is also the fund's investment adviser, custodian, etc.).

internal rate of return (IRR) That rate of discount at which the present value of future cash flows is exactly equal to the initial capital investment.

international arbitrage A purchase or sale of a security on a securities exchange effected for the purpose of profiting from the difference between the price of the security on that exchange and the price of the security on a securities market not within or subject to the jurisdiction of the U.S. government.

in-the-money An option that has intrinsic value (e.g., a call option in which the stock is selling above the exercise price or a put option in which the stock is selling below the exercise price). *See also* at-the-money, intrinsic value, out-of-the-money.

intrastate offering A conditional offering of unregistered securities limited to companies that do business in one state and sell their securities only to residents of that same state (SEC Rule 147).

intrinsic value The mathematical value of an option (e.g., a call option is said to have intrinsic value when the stock is trading above the exercise price).

introducing broker A broker-dealer that does not hold investors' money or securities. Instead, it introduces those accounts to a clearing broker-dealer, which then handles all cash and securities for those accounts.

inventory turnover ratio A ratio that measures the efficiency with which a company can sell and replace its inventory, calculated by dividing net sales by inventory.

inverted market A futures market in which nearby contracts are selling at higher prices than distant contracts. (*Syn.* backwardation)

inverted yield curve A chart that shows long-term debt instruments having lower yields than short-term debt instruments. *See also* normal yield curve.

invested capital *See* capitalization, capital structure.

investment adviser Any person who, for compensation (a flat fee or percent of assets managed), offers investment advice. For investment companies, the adviser has the day-to-day responsibility of investing the cash and securities held in a mutual fund's portfolio. The adviser must adhere to the objectives as stated in the fund's prospectus. This definition includes persons who issue written reports or analyses for compensation.

The term "investment adviser" does not include:

- institutions such as banks, saving institutions or trust companies;
- professionals such as lawyers, accountants or teachers whose performance of these services is solely incidental to the practice of their profession;
- broker-dealers who offer investment portfolio advice as part of their business of being a broker-dealer and receive no special compensation for that service;
- publishers of any financial publication of general, regular and paid circulation. However, a person who sells subscriptions to investment advisory publications (market letters) is considered an investment adviser under the Uniform Securities Act;
- person whose investment advice relates only to U.S. government securities and certain municipal securities; or
- person having no place of business within the state and whose activities are limited to: (a) professional clients (institutions), (b) a very few solicitations or sales to clients other than those above. For instance, some states limit this activ-

ity to no more than five clients in any 12 consecutive months.

The term "investment adviser" also excludes any person that the state administrator of the Uniform Securities Act decides not to include.

investment adviser representative Any partner, officer, director or other individual employed by or associated with an investment adviser who: 1) gives investment advice or makes recommendations, 2) manages client accounts or portfolios, 3) determines which investment recommendations or advice should be given, 4) offers or sells investment advisory services, or 5) supervises employees involved in any of these activities.

investment banker A financial professional who raises capital for corporations and municipalities.

investment banking (securities) business The business carried on by a broker, dealer or municipal or government securities dealer of underwriting or distributing new issues of securities as a dealer or of buying and selling securities on the order and for the benefit of others as a broker.

investment company A company engaged primarily in the business of investing and trading in securities, including face-amount certificate companies, unit investment trusts and management companies.

Investment Company Act Amendments of 1970 Amendments to the Investment Company Act of 1940 requires a registered investment company issuing periodic payment plan certificates (contractual plans) to offer all purchasers withdrawal rights and purchasers of front-end load plans surrender rights.

Investment Company Act Amendments of 1975 Amendments to the Investment Company Act of 1940; in particular, that sales charges must relate to the services a fund provides shareholders.

Investment Company Act of 1940 Congressional legislation enacted to regulate investment companies; it requires any investment company in interstate commerce to register with the SEC.

Investment Company/Variable Contract Products Limited Representative *See* Series 6.

investment grade security A security with a rating (S&P, Moody's, etc.) of BBB/Baa or above.

investment in properties The amount of capital contributions actually paid or allocated to the purchase, development, construction or improvement of properties acquired by the program. The amount available for investment equals the gross proceeds raised less front-end fees.

investment objective Any goal a client hopes to achieve through investing.

investment value The market price at which a convertible security (usually a debenture) would sell if it were not converted into common stock. *See also* convertible bond, debenture.

investor The purchaser of a unit or security, including the sponsor to the extent it purchases units.

invitation for bids The "advertising" for bids to be submitted for the underwriting of a bond issue. Invitations are published in *The Bond Buyer*, newspapers, journals and *Munifacts*.

in-whole-call The call of a bond issue in its entirety by the issuer, as opposed to the redemption of issues based on a lottery held by an independent trustee.

IOC *See* immediate or cancel order.

IOI *See* indication of interest.

IPO *See* initial public offering.

IRA *See* individual retirement account.

IRA rollover The reinvestment of assets that an individual receives as a distribution from a qualified tax-deferred retirement plan into another qualified plan. The individual may reinvest either the entire lump sum or a portion of that sum, and typically does so in an account designated as an IRA rollover account. IRA rollovers differ from IRA transfers in that the account owner takes possession of the cash or securities received from the account rather than directing that the cash and securities be transferred directly from the existing plan custodian to the new plan custodian. *See also* individual retirement account.

IRA transfer The direct movement and reinvestment of assets that an individual receives as a distribution from the custodian of one qualified tax-deferred retirement plan to the custodian of another qualified plan. IRA transfers differ from IRA rollovers in that the account owner never takes possession of the cash or securities received from the account, directing that the cash and securities be transferred directly from the existing plan custodian to the new plan custodian. *See also* individual retirement account.

IRR *See* internal rate of return.

issued stock Stock that has been sold to the public.

issuer 1) The corporation or municipality that offers its securities for sale; also, the creator of an option (the issuer of an over-the-counter option is the option writer, and the issuer of a listed option is the Options Clearing Corporation). 2) According to the Uniform Securities Act, any person who issues or proposes to issue any security.

When a corporation or municipality raises additional capital through an offering of securities, that corporation or municipality is the "issuer" of those securities. An issuer transaction is also called a "primary" transaction.

There are two exceptions to the basic definition of issuer. In the case of voting-trust certificates or collateral-trust certificates, "issuer" refers to the person who assumes the duties of depositor or manager. There is considered to be no issuer for certificates of interest or participation in oil, gas, or mining titles or leases where payments are made out of production.

joint account An account in which two or more individuals act as co-tenants or co-owners of the account. The account may be joint tenants in common or joint tenants with right of survivorship. *See also* joint tenants with right of survivorship, joint tenants in common.

joint tenants in common (JTIC) A form of ownership directing that upon the death of one tenant, the decedent's fractional interest in the joint account must be retained by the estate. This form of ownership may be used by any two or more individuals.

joint tenants with right of survivorship (JTWROS) A form of ownership that requires that a deceased tenant's fractional interest in an account be retained by the surviving tenant(s). It is used almost exclusively by husbands and wives. *See also* joint tenants in common.

joint venture The joining of two or more persons in a specific business enterprise, rather than in a continuing relationship, as in a partnership.

JTIC *See* joint tenants in common.

JTWROS *See* joint tenants with right of survivorship.

junior lien debt A bond backed by the same collateral backing a previous issue and having a junior claim to the collateral in the event of default. *See also* open-end pledge. (*Syn.* closed-end pledge)

Keogh plan A qualified tax-deferred retirement plan for persons who are self-employed and unincorporated or who earn extra income through personal services aside from their regular employment. *See also* qualified retirement plan. (*Syn.* HR-10 plan)

L L is a measure of the money supply that includes all of the components of M1, M2 and M3 as well as Treasury bills, savings bonds, commercial paper, bankers' acceptances and Eurodollar holdings of U.S. residents.

last in, first out (LIFO) A method of assessing a company's inventory in which it is assumed that the goods acquired last are the first to be sold. Also used to designate the order in which sales or withdrawals from an investment are made to determine cost basis for tax purposes. *See also* first in, first out.

lease A full or partial interest in the use of an asset; for mineral properties, the interest in the property that authorizes the lessee to drill for, produce and sell oil and gas, other minerals or any combination thereof.

legal investment (legal list) The limited list of securities selected by a state agency (such as a state banking or insurance commission) that can be used in fiduciary accounts (mutual savings banks, pension funds, insurance companies) or in an insurer's general account.

legal opinion of counsel Regardless of the type of municipal bond issued, the bond must be accompanied by a legal opinion of counsel. The opinion of counsel affirms that the issue is a municipal issue and that interest is exempt from federal taxation, among other items.

legislative risk The risk associated with the impact of changes in law on investment.

lending at a premium The act of charging the borrower of securities (the short seller) for the loan of the securities. The charge is stated in terms of dollars per 100 shares per business day.

lending at a rate The act of paying interest on the money received in connection with securities loaned to short sellers.

letter of intent (LOI) A signed purchase agreement under which a fund can sell shares to an investor at a lower overall sales charge, based on the total dollar amount of the intended investment. An LOI is valid only if the investor completes the terms of the purchase agreement within 13 months of the time this agreement is signed. An LOI may be backdated 90 days. (*Syn.* statement of intention)

level debt service Where principal and interest payments remain essentially constant from year to year over the life of the issue.

Level One The basic level of Nasdaq service. It provides registered representatives with the up-to-the-minute inside bid and asked quotations on hundreds of over-the-counter stocks through a desktop quotation machine. *See also* Nasdaq.

Level Two The second level of Nasdaq service. It provides up-to-the-minute inside bid and asked quotations and the bids and askeds of each marker maker for a security through a desktop quotation machine. *See also* Nasdaq.

Level Three The highest level of Nasdaq service. It provides up-to-the-minute inside bid and asked quotations, supplies the bids and askeds of each market maker for a security and allows each market maker to enter changes in those quotes through a desktop quotation machine. *See also* Nasdaq.

leverage The use of borrowed capital to increase earnings. (*Syn.* trading on the equity)

leverage transaction merchant (LTM) An individual or organization registered with the Commodities Futures Trading Commission and permitted to engage in the off-exchange trading of selected futures instruments.

liability A debt owed by an entity; a legal obligation to pay. Current liabilities are debts payable within twelve months. Long-term liabilities are debts payable over a period of more than twelve months.

LIFO *See* last in, first out.

lifting cost An expenditure made and a cost incurred in producing and marketing oil and gas from completed wells. Such costs include, in addition to labor, fuel, repairs, hauling, materials, supplies, utilities and other costs incident to or therefrom, ad valorem and severance taxes, insurance and casualty losses and compensation to well operators or others for services rendered in conducting such operations.

limited partner (LP) A partner who does not participate in the management or control of a partnership and whose liability for partnership debts is limited to the amount invested in the partnership. *See also* participant, passive investor.

limited partnership A form of business organization in which one or more of the partners is liable only to the extent of the amount of dollars they have invested. Limited partners are not involved in management decisions but enjoy direct flow-through of income and expenses. *See also* flow-through.

limited partnership agreement The articles of limited partnership of each limited partnership. The agreement forms the contract between the limited and general partners and states the rights and responsibilities of each.

limited principal A person who has passed a qualifications examination attesting to her knowledge and qualifications to supervise the business of a member in one or more limited areas of expertise. If a limited principal expects to function in one or more of the general fields of expertise reserved for a General Securities Principal, she must also be registered as a General Securities Principal.

limited tax bond A general obligation bond where the security of the bond provided by the issuer's taxing power is limited to a specified maximum rate.

limited trading authorization The authorization for someone other than the customer to have trading privileges in his account. These privileges are limited to purchases and sales; withdrawal of assets is not allowed.

limit order A customer's order with instructions to buy a specified security below a certain price or sell a specified security above a certain price. (*Syn.* or better order)

liquidity The ease with which something can be bought or sold (converted to cash) in the marketplace. A large number of buyers and sellers and a high volume of trading activity are important components of liquidity.

liquidity ratio With a corporation, a measure of the company's ability to meet its current obligations; for investments, the ability to convert the asset into cash without an appreciable loss on the investment. The ratio compares current assets to current liabilities. *See also* current ratio.

listed option An option that can be bought and sold on a national securities exchange in a continuous secondary market. *See also* OTC option. (*Syn.* standardized option)

listed security A security that is traded on a regional or national securities exchange such as the NYSE.

LMV *See* long market value.

loan consent agreement A lending agreement between a brokerage firm and a client that permits the brokerage firm to lend the client's securities. This is part of the margin agreement. (*Syn.* consent to lend agreement)

loaned flat Securities loaned to short sellers without an interest charge.

loans for set amount A type of broker's collateral loan that requires a brokerage firm to deposit new collateral before it can obtain a new loan when additional funds are needed. *See also* broker's loan, call loan.

loan value *See* maximum loan value.

local basis *See* country basis.

local *See* floor trader.

LOI *See* letter of intent.

long The state of owning a security, contract or commodity. A purchase of 5 May wheat contracts would be referred to as *going long May wheat*. The speculator would have a *long* position.

long hedge A long securities or actuals position protected by a long put position. *See also* hedge, short hedge.

long market value (LMV) The current market price of the securities a customer owns, based on the closing prices of the previous day. (*Syn.* current market value)

long straddle Buying a call and a put on the same stock with the same strike price and expiration month.

long-term gain The taxable gain on a capital asset that an investor has owned for more than twelve months. *See also* capital gain, long-term loss.

long-term loss The taxable loss on a capital asset that an investor has owned for more than twelve months. *See also* long-term gain.

loss carryover The capital loss that is carried over to later years for use as a capital loss deduction. *See also* capital loss.

low The lowest price a security or commodity reaches during a given period of time.

LP *See* limited partner.

LTM *See* leverage transaction merchant.

M1 A narrow definition of money supply that includes all coins, currency, demand deposits (checking accounts) and NOW accounts.

M2 A broader definition of money supply that includes all coins, currency, checking deposits, time deposits, savings deposits and non-institutional money-market funds.

M3 Those currencies included in the M2 definition of money supply plus large time deposits, institutional money-market funds, short-term repurchase agreements and certain other large liquid assets.

maintenance call A brokerage firm's demand that a client deposit money or securities when the client's equity falls below the brokerage firm's minimum maintenance requirement, or the higher maintenance call set by the NYSE. *See also* house maintenance call, NYSE maintenance call.

maintenance excess The difference between the equity in an account and the NYSE minimum margin (25% long and 30% short). *See also* equity, NYSE maintenance requirement.

maintenance requirement *See* NYSE maintenance requirement.

majority vote The vote of limited partners who own more than 50% of the total outstanding units.

Major Market Index (MMI) A 20-stock index designed to track the Dow Jones 30 industrials. The MMI is composed of 15 of the Dow Jones 30 and 5 other large NYSE-listed stocks.

make a market The action of a broker-dealer firm when, on a regular basis, it holds itself out to other firms as ready to buy or sell a particular over-the-counter stock for its own account. Such a firm accepts the risk of holding the position in the security. *See also* market maker.

Maloney Act Section 15 of the Securities Exchange Act of 1934 is known as the Maloney Act, named for its sponsor, the late Sen. Francis Maloney of Connecticut. This legislation provided for the creation of a securities industry association for the specific purpose of supervising the over-the-counter securities market.

managed offering The offering for a sale of securities in which the sponsor uses a dealer-manager to hire soliciting dealers.

management company An investment company that manages a portfolio of various types of securities. *See also* closed-end management company, diversified management company, nondiversified management company, open-end management company.

management fee A fee paid to a sponsor of a program for managing and administering the program.

manager *See* underwriting manager.

manager of the syndicate *See* underwriting manager.

managing partner The sponsor when acting in its capacity as managing partner under the articles of partnership establishing the partnership.

managing underwriter *See* underwriting manager.

mandatory call The redemption of bonds by an issuer based on a predetermined schedule or event. *See also* catastrophe call.

margin The amount of equity as a percentage of current market value in a margin account. *See also* equity, margin call, Regulation T.

margin account An account in which a brokerage firm lends a client part of the purchase price of securities. *See also* Regulation T, special arbitrage account.

margin call A demand for a client to deposit money or securities when a purchase is made in a margin account. *See also* initial margin requirement, margin. (*Syn.* call, fed call, federal call, federal margin, Reg T call, T call)

margin deficiency The amount by which the required margin exceeds the equity in a margin account. (*Syn.* margin requirement)

margin department The department within a brokerage firm that computes the amount of money a client must deposit in both margin and cash accounts.

margin excess The amount by which the equity in a margin account exceeds the required margin. (*Syn.* excess equity)

margin of profit A ratio used to determine the operating efficiency of a business, calculated by dividing the operating profit by the net sales. (*Syn.* profit margin)

margin requirement *See* margin deficiency.

margin risk The risk that an investor will be required to deposit additional cash if her security positions are subject to adverse price movements.

markdown The difference between the best (highest) current bid price among dealers and the actual price that a dealer pays to a customer.

marketability The ease with which a security can be bought or sold; having a readily available market for trading.

market arbitrage The simultaneous purchase and sale of the same security in different markets to take advantage of a price disparity between the two markets. *See also* arbitrage.

market if touched order (MIT) An order that becomes a market order only if the market touches (or hits) the specified price. A buy MIT order is placed below the current market, and a sell MIT is placed above the current market.

market letter A publication that comments on securities and is distributed to an organization's clients or to the public.

market maker (principal) A dealer willing to accept the risk of holding securities to facilitate trading in a particular security or securities. *See also* make a market.

market NH *See* market not held order.

market not held order A market order for a sizable amount of stock that gives the floor broker discretion about the price or timing of the order's execution. *See also* market NH.

market order An order that is to be executed at the best available price.

market-out clause The standard clause in a firm commitment underwriting agreement that relieves the underwriter of its obligation to underwrite the issue under certain unusual circumstances (e.g., unexpected bad news just before or after the offering date).

market risk That risk due to day-to-day fluctuations in prices at which securities can be bought or sold. *See also* systematic risk.

market value The price at which an investor will buy or sell each share of common stock or each bond at a given time. Market value is determined by the interaction between buyers and sellers in the market. *See also* current market value.

market value on the trade date The gross amount of a long purchase (including commissions) or the net proceeds of a short sale.

market value per share The current price at which a stock is trading in the open market.

mark to the market The act of adjusting the value of an account to the current market value of the security positions in the account; the current valuation of market value and equity.

markup The difference between the best (lowest) current offering price among dealers and the actual price a dealer charges its customer.

markup policy *See* NASD 5% markup policy.

married put When an investor buys a stock and on the same day buys a put on that stock and specifically identifies that position as a hedge. The holding period starts on the day of the purchase and does not end until the stock is sold, through the exercise of the put or otherwise.

matching orders The act of simultaneously entering identical (or nearly identical) orders for the purchase or sale of a security to create the appearance of active trading in the security.

material information Any fact that could affect an investor's decision to buy a certain security.

maturity date The date on which the principal is repaid to the investor. *See also* par value, principal.

maximum loan value The maximum amount a broker-dealer can loan a customer for the purchase of securities, based on the complement of Reg T (e.g., if Reg T were 65%, the maximum loan would be 35%). (*Syn.* loan value)

MBIA *See* Municipal Bond Investors Assurance Corp.

member 1) Of the New York Stock Exchange (NYSE): One of the 1,366 individuals owning a seat on the NYSE. 2) Of the National Association of Securities Dealers (NASD): Any broker or dealer admitted to membership in the NASD.

member firm A firm in which at least one of the principal officers is a member of the New York Stock Exchange, another organized exchange, a self-regulatory organization, or a clearing corporation.

member order An order by a syndicate member for a retail or an institutional client. Each syndicate member receives the commission on orders filled by the syndicate manager. Member orders generally have the lowest priority during the order period. *See also* designated order, presale order.

membership The members of the New York Stock Exchange, another exchange, a self-regulatory organization or a clearing corporation.

mill rate The tax per dollar of assessed value of property ($.001).

minimum death benefit The amount of the guaranteed death benefit, other than any incidental insurance benefit, payable under a variable life insurance policy, regardless of the investment performance of the separate account.

minimum subscription amount The minimum amount to which a person must initially subscribe in a new offering of a direct participation program.

minus tick An execution price below the previous sale. A short sale may not be executed on a minus tick. *See also* plus tick, plus tick rule. (*Syn.* down tick)

MIT *See* market if touched order.

mixed account A margin account having both long and short positions in different securities. *See also* margin account.

MMI *See* Major Market Index.

Modified Accelerated Cost Recovery System (MACRS) An accounting method used to recover the cost of qualifying depreciable property. The MACRS system eliminated the acceleration of deductions for real property. Deductions are based on percentages prescribed in the Internal Revenue Code.

monetary policy The policies and actions of the Federal Reserve Board that determine the rate of growth and size of the money supply, which in turn affect interest rates.

money market The securities market that deals in short-term (less than one year) debt. Money market instruments are forms of debt that mature in less than a year and are very liquid. Treasury bills make up the bulk of trading in the money markets.

money-market fund An open-end investment company investing in money market instruments. Generally sold with no load, the fund offers draft-writing privileges and low opening investments.

money spread *See* price spread.

moral obligation bond A revenue bond issued with nonbinding legislative authority to apportion monies for shortfalls in revenues backing the bond.

mortgage bond A debt obligation secured by a property pledge. Mortgage bonds are liens or mortgages against the issuing corporation's properties and real estate assets.

municipal bond fund A type of mutual fund that invests in municipal bonds, operating either as a unit investment trust (units of interest in an existing portfolio of tax-exempt bonds) or as an open-end fund. *See also* mutual fund, open-end management company, unit investment trust.

Municipal Bond Investors Assurance Corp. (MBIA) A public corporation offering insurance as to timely payment of principal and interest when due on qualified municipal issues. Issues with MBIA insurance are generally rated AAA by Standard & Poor's.

municipal broker's broker A broker acting for another broker in the municipal market. The broker's broker does not take positions in the issue, nor does the broker transact orders for the public. *See also* broker's broker.

Municipal Securities Representative *See* Series 52.

municipal security A debt security issued by a state, a municipality or another subdivision (such as a school, a park, or a sanitary or some other local taxing district) to raise money to finance its capital expenditures. Such expenditures might include the construction of highways, public works or school buildings.

Munifacts A news wire service for the municipal bond industry; a product of *The Bond Buyer*.

mutual exclusion doctrine The doctrine that established the federal tax exemption status of municipal bond interest. This doctrine says that states and municipalities must not tax government-owned properties. The federal government reciprocates by excluding local government properties from federal taxation. (*Syn.* mutual reciprocity, reciprocal immunity)

mutual fund A type of investment company that offers for sale or has outstanding securities that it has issued that are redeemable on demand by the fund at current net asset value. All owners in the fund share in the gains or losses of the fund. (*Syn.* open-end management company)

mutual fund custodian Usually a national bank, a trust company or another qualified institution that physically safeguards securities. It does not manage investments; its function is solely clerical.

mutual reciprocity *See* mutual exclusion doctrine.

naked call (put) writer Any investor who writes a call (put) without owning the underlying stock or other related assets that would enable the writer to deliver the stock (or purchase the stock) should the option be exercised. (*Syn.* uncovered call [put] writer)

NASD *See* National Association of Securities Dealers.

Nasdaq *See* National Association of Securities Dealers Automated Quotation System.

Nasdaq National Market (NNM) Two hundred of the most actively traded over-the-counter stocks within the 4,000 stocks quoted on Nasdaq. Trades are reported as they occur.

Nasdaq 100 An index of the largest 100 non-financial stocks on Nasdaq, weighted by capitalization.

NASD Automated Quotation System *See* National Association of Securities Dealers Automated Quotation System.

NASD Bylaws The body of laws that describes how the NASD functions, defines its powers and determines the qualifications and registration requirements for brokers.

NASD District Business Conduct Committee (DBCC) A committee composed of up to twelve NASD members from within a district who serve as administrators for the district. The NASD is divided into 13 local districts to maximize the degree of local administration. The DBCC has original jurisdiction for hearings and judging complaints.

NASD 5% markup policy A guideline for reasonable markups, markdowns and commissions for secondary over-the-counter transactions. (*Syn.* markup policy)

NASD Rules of Fair Practice In general, these rules complement and serve as extensions of the 1934 act rules and also the rules under the 1933 act and the Investment Company Act of 1940.

NASD Small Order Execution System (SOES) An automatic order execution system designed to facilitate the trading of small public market and executable limit orders (500 or fewer shares). Any Nasdaq or NNM security with at least one active SOES market maker is eligible for trading through SOES. All NNM market makers (but not firms that make a market in Nasdaq securities not on the NNM list) are required also to participate in SOES. NNM market makers cannot voluntarily withdraw from SOES participation.

SOES electronically matches and executes orders, locks in a price and sends confirms directly to the broker-dealers on both sides of the trade. Small orders may be aggregated if the total is less than the maximum 500-share limit, but broker-dealers may not split up large orders for the purpose of avoiding the 500-share limitation.

Institutions and broker-dealers may not employ the system to trade for their own accounts. Only public market and executable limit orders are accepted by SOES.

National Association of Securities Dealers (NASD) The self-regulatory organization (SRO) for the over-the-counter (OTC) market. The NASD was recognized as the SRO for the OTC market by the Maloney Act of 1938.

National Association of Securities Dealers Automated Quotation System (Nasdaq) The nationwide electronic quotation system for up-to-the-minute bid and asked quotations on approximately 4,000 over-the-counter stocks.

National Futures Association NFA The self-regulatory organization of the commodities futures industry to which all futures exchange members, commodity-trading advisers (CTAs) and commodity pool operators (CPOs) must belong. The NFA is responsible to the Commodities Futures Trading Commission.

NAV *See* net asset value.

nearby contract Of two or more futures contracts, the contract with the shortest time remaining to expiration. (*Syn.* nearby delivery [month])

nearby delivery (month) *See* nearby contract.

negotiable certificate of deposit (CD) A negotiable certificate that evidences a time deposit of funds with a bank. It is an unsecured promissory note normally issued in $100,000 denominations.

negotiated underwriting An underwriting in which a brokerage firm consults with the issuer and arrives at a consensus about the most suitable price and timing of a forthcoming securities offering. *See also* competitive bidding.

net asset value (NAV) The value of a mutual fund share, calculated by deducting the fund's liabilities from the total assets of the portfolio and dividing this amount by the number of shares outstanding. This is calculated once a day, based on the closing market price for each security in the fund's portfolio. *See also* mutual fund. (*Syn.* bid price)

net capital Liquid capital (cash and assets readily convertible into cash) maintained by a broker-dealer. The uniform net capital rules are the SEC's primary means of regulating broker-dealers and making sure that firms have enough money (capitalization) to deal responsibly with the investing public. Net capital rules include:
- minimum dollar requirements for net capital;
- definition of and how to compute net capital;
- allowable aggregate indebtedness of broker-dealers;
- maximum aggregate indebtedness to net capital ratios;
- subordinated loan capital contribution rules; and
- maximum debt to equity ratios.

net change The difference between the closing price on the trading day reported and the previous day's closing price. In over-the-counter transactions, the term refers to the difference between the closing bids.

net current asset value per share The calculation of book value per share that excludes all fixed assets. *See also* book value per share.

net income to net sales A ratio that measures the after-tax profitability of a company, calculated by dividing net income by net sales. (*Syn.* net profit margin, net profits to sales, profits after taxes, profit ratio, return on sales)

net investment income The sum of dividends, interest, rents, royalties and short-term gains minus investment expenses. For mutual funds, net investment income represents the source for dividend payments.

net investment return The rate of investment return in a separate account to be applied to the benefit base.

net proceeds The total gross proceeds less expenses incurred, to be paid by the partnership in organizing the partnership and in offering units to the public.

net profit margin *See* net income to net sales.

net profits interest In a net profits interest arrangement, the sponsor shares in revenues after payments for royalties and operating expenses have been made. This payment is made to the sponsor, who has no other interest in the program (such as an overriding royalty) for packaging the deal. Net profits interest is limited to private placement.

net profits to sales *See* net income to net sales.

net revenue pledge A pledge of revenues funding a bond after payment of operating and maintenance expenses. The pledge is contained in the trust indenture. *See also* gross revenue pledge.

net tangible assets per bond A measure of the amount of producing assets behind each corporate bond, calculated by dividing net tangible assets by funded debt. (*Syn.* book value per bond)

net tangible assets per share *See* book value per share.

net worth The amount by which assets exceed liabilities. (*Syn.* shareholders' equity)

New Housing Authority bond (NHA) A municipal bond issued by local public housing authorities to redevelop and improve certain areas. (*Syn.* Public Housing Authority bond)

New Issues Act Another name for the Securities Act of 1933.

New York plan A financing method for the purchase of equipment similar to a conditional sale: a company purchases equipment by issuing bonds, and as the bonds are paid off, the company acquires full title to the equipment. *See also* equipment trust certificate.

New York Stock Exchange (NYSE) A corporation operated by a board of directors responsible for setting policy, supervising Exchange and member activities, listing securities, overseeing the transfer of members' seats on the Exchange and judging whether an applicant is qualified to be a specialist.

New York Stock Exchange maintenance call *See* NYSE maintenance call.

New York Stock Exchange maintenance requirement *See* NYSE maintenance requirement.

New York Stock Exchange Super Designated Order Turnaround system (SuperDot) The NYSE's computerized trading and execution system. Broker-dealers use this order routing system to choose the destination of an order and the route that order will take. An order can be routed directly to the appropriate specialist at his trading post on the floor of the Exchange, or it can be sent to the brokerage firm's house booth for handling by the Exchange member (commission broker) who represents the broker-dealer. Once the order is received by the specialist or commis-sion broker, the order is presented in the auction market. If the order is executed, the specialist or commission broker uses the same automated routing system to send an execution report back to the firm that submitted the order. The broker-dealer then notifies the registered representative, who notifies the customer that the order was executed. Orders executed through the SuperDot routing system are often confirmed back to the broker in less than 60 seconds.

NFA *See* National Futures Association.

NH *See* not held order.

NHA *See* New Housing Authority bond.

nine bond rule The NYSE rule that requires orders for listed bonds in quantities of nine bonds or fewer to be sent to the floor of the NYSE before being traded in the over-the-counter market.

NNM *See* Nasdaq National Market.

no-load fund A mutual fund whose shares are sold without a sales charge added to the net asset value. *See also* mutual fund, net asset value, sales charge.

nominal quote A quotation given for informational purposes only. (*Syn.* subject quote)

nominal yield The interest rate that is stated on the face of a bond representing the amount of interest paid by the issuer on the principal of the issue. (*Syn.* coupon rate, stated yield, yield)

nominee The person in whose name securities are registered if that person is other than the beneficial owner. This is the role of the brokerage firm when customer securities purchased on margin are registered in street name.

nonaccredited investor An investor not meeting the net worth requirements of Regulation D. Nonaccredited investors are counted for purposes of the 35-investor limitation under Rules 505 and 506 of Regulation D.

noncumulative preferred stock A type of preferred stock that does not have to pay any dividends in arrears to the holders. *See also* cumulative preferred stock, preferred stock.

nondiversified management company A management company that is not restricted in its choice of securities or by the concentration of interest it has in those securities. *See also* diversified management company, management company, mutual fund.

nonissuer The term "nonissuer" refers to a person other than the issuer of a security. In a nonissuer securities transaction, for example, the issuer is not one of the parties in the transaction, and the transaction is therefore not, according to the law, directly or indirectly for the benefit of the issuer.

When the Uniform Securities Act refers to a nonissuer transaction, it is referring to a transaction in which the proceeds of the sale go to the selling stockholder. For example, a trade of 100 shares of RCA on the New York Stock Exchange is a typical nonissuer transaction. Most nonissuer transactions are also called secondary transactions.

nonmanaged offering A method of distributing direct participation program interests. Rather than organizing a syndicate to distribute the interest, the program sponsor will contract with individual broker-dealers to offer the interests to the public. A wholesaler (broker-dealer) is often hired by the sponsor to arrange selling agreements with each firm.

nonrecourse financing Financing in which the property is made security for the debt, but there is no personal liability on the part of the borrower.

nonspecified property program A program where, at the time a securities registration is ordered effective, less than 75% of the net proceeds from the sale of program interests are allocated to the purchase, construction or improvement of identified properties or are allocated to a program in which the proceeds from any sale or refinancing of properties may be reinvested. Reserves shall be included in the nonspecified 25%. (*Syn.* blind pool, unspecified property program)

no-par value Stock issued without a stated value. *See also* par value.

normal market A futures market in which nearby contracts are selling at lower prices than distant contracts. (*Syn.* carrying charge market, contango)

normal yield curve A chart that shows long-term debt instruments having higher yields than short-term debt instruments. *See also* inverted yield curve.

not held order (NH) A market order for a sizable amount of stock that gives the floor broker discretion as to the price and timing of execution of the order. (*Syn.* market not held order)

numbered account An account titled with something other than a client's name, such as a number, symbol or special title. The client must sign a form designating ownership of the account.

NYSE *See* New York Stock Exchange.

NYSE maintenance call A demand for a client to deposit money or securities if the client's equity falls below the NYSE minimum maintenance level. *See also* equity.

NYSE maintenance requirement The minimum amount of equity that must be maintained in a margin account at all times according to NYSE rules. The minimum maintenance for corporate securities is 25% of the current market value for a long position.

OB *See* limit order.

OCC *See* Office of the Comptroller of the Currency, Options Clearing Corporation.

OCC Disclosure Document The disclosure document published by the Options Clearing Corporation that must be provided to every investor at the time the investor is approved for standardized options trading.

OCO *See* one cancels other.

odd lot Less than the normal unit of trading, which is less than 100 shares of stock or five bonds.

odd-lot differential The price differential that is often charged when an odd-lot order is executed on an exchange (usually the charge is 12.5 cents [1/8th of a point] per share).

odd-lot order An order for less than the normal unit of trading (normally 100 shares of stock).

odd-lot theory A technical theory based on the assumption that the public is always wrong. According to the theory, if odd-lot sales are up—that is, the public is selling stock—it is probably a good time to buy.

offer 1) An indication by an investor, a trader or a dealer of a willingness to sell a security or com-modity. 2) Under the Uniform Securities Act, every attempt to solicit a purchase or sale in a security for value. *See also* bid. (*Syn.* ask, quotation, quote)

offering circular A document that contains information about a corporation's issue of securities. The information included is similar to that made available in the prospectus but abbreviated. Its use is restricted to Regulation A offerings. *See also* Regulation A.

offering price With mutual funds, the price an investor will pay per share. The offering price is the net asset value plus a sales charge (for funds that have a sales charge).

See also mutual fund, net asset value. (*Syn.* current price)

office of supervisory jurisdiction (OSJ) Any office at which one or more of the following occur:

- order execution and/or market making;
- formation or structuring of public offerings or private placements;
- maintenance of custody of customer funds and/or securities;
- final approval of new accounts on behalf of the member;
- review and endorsement of customer orders;
- final approval of advertising or sales literature for use by persons associated with the member; and
- supervision of activities of persons at one or more of the member's branch offices.

Office of the Comptroller of the Currency (OCC) The bureau of the U.S. Treasury Department that regulates the corporate structure and banking practices of national banks. The Comptroller is appointed by the president, with Senate approval.

Office of Thrift Supervision (OTS) A bureau of the U.S. Treasury Department, authorized by Congress under the Financial Institution Reform, Recovery and Enforcement Act of 1989 to charter, regulate, examine and supervise thrift institutions.

official notice of sale The notification of bidding sent to prospective underwriters specifying such bid procedures as date, time and place of sale, description of the issue, maturities, call provisions and amount of good faith deposit required.

official statement (OS) A statement concerning the municipal issue offered (disclosing the underwriting spread, fees received by brokers for acting as agents of the issuer and initial offering price of each maturity), prepared by the underwriter from information provided by the issuer.

offset To enter an equivalent but opposite closing transaction. To offset an initial purchase, a sale would be made. To offset an initial sale, a purchase would be made.

OID *See* original issue discount.

oil and gas program A direct participation program that has as its primary purpose oil and gas exploration, development or purchase of production.

oil depletion allowance A percentage of revenue from oil production allowed as a deduction from gross revenues generated from the sale of oil and gas. The percentage allowable is 15% (subject to certain limits).

one cancels other (OCO) A dual order submitted with two sets of instructions. At the moment either order is executed, the other order is canceled.

open-end investment company *See* open-end management company.

open-end management company A management company that continually issues new shares. Its shares are redeemable on any business day at the net asset value. Open-end management companies may sell only common stock. (*Syn.* mutual fund, open-end investment company)

open-end pledge A provision in the trust indenture allowing the issuer to use collateral backing a bond for future borrowing. New creditors have the same claim on the collateral as existing creditors.

opening purchase transaction The act of entering the options market by buying calls or puts.

opening range *See* range.

opening sale transaction The act of entering the options market by selling calls or puts.

open market operations The buying and selling of securities (primarily government or agency debt) by the Federal Open Market Committee for increasing or decreasing the level of bank reserves to effect control of the money supply.

open order *See* good till canceled order.

operating expense Any production or leasehold expense of an oil and gas program incurred in the operation of a producing lease, including district expense; direct out-of-pocket expenses for labor, materials and supplies; shares of taxes and transportation charges not borne by overriding royalty interests; and, for other programs, the day-to-day expenses involved in operating the business for a profit.

operating ratio The ratio of operating expenses to net sales, the complement to the profit margin.

operator A person designated to supervise and manage the exploration, drilling, mining, production and leasehold operations of an oil and gas or mining program or a portion of such a program.

option The right to buy (or sell) a specified amount of a security (stocks, bonds, futures contracts, etc.) at a specified price within a specified time. An option represents a right acquired by the purchaser, but it is an obligation only on the part of the option seller.

option agreement The agreement a customer must sign within 15 days of being approved for options trading. In it the client agrees to abide by the rules of the listed options exchanges and not to exceed the exchanges' position or exercise limits.

Options Clearing Corporation (OCC) The organization through which the various options exchanges clear their trades. The OCC supervises the listing of new options and is considered the issuer of standardized options.

option term adjustment An automatic adjustment that is made to the terms of an option on the ex-dividend date when a stock pays a cash dividend (if over the counter) or a stock dividend or if there is a stock split.

order department The department within a brokerage firm responsible for transmitting an order to the proper market for execution. (*Syn.* order room, wire room)

order memorandum The paper form completed by a registered rep that contains the customer's instructions regarding the placement of an order. The order memorandum contains such information as the customer's name and account number, a description of the security, the type of transaction (buy, sell, sell short, etc.) and any special instructions (such as time or price limits). (*Syn.* order memo, order ticket)

order room *See* order department.

order ticket *See* order memorandum.

ordinary income Any income or gain that is not capital gain.

organization and offering expense Any expense that is incurred in preparing a direct participation program for registration and subsequently offering and distributing it to the public, including sales commissions paid to broker-dealers in connection with the distribution of the program.

original issue discount (OID) A bond issued at a discount from face value at maturity. The bond may or may not pay interest, and the discount is taxed as if accrued annually as ordinary income. (*Syn.* stripped bonds)

ORS *See* Chicago Board Options Exchange ORS.

OS *See* official statement.

OSJ *See* office of supervisory jurisdiction.

OTC *See* over the counter.

OTC Bulletin Board An electronic quotation system for non-Nasdaq securities; a computerized *Pink Sheet* for non-Nasdaq stock.

OTC option A put or call option that is not listed on an options exchange. All terms of the contract are negotiated between buyer and seller. *See also* listed option.

OTS *See* Office of Thrift Supervision.

out-of-the-money A term referring to an option that has no intrinsic value (e.g., a put option in which the stock is selling above the exercise price or a call option in which the stock is selling below the exercise price). *See also* at-the-money, in-the-money, intrinsic value.

outstanding stock Issued stock minus treasury stock (stock reacquired by the issuing corporation); stock that is in the hands of the public.

overbought A technical analyst's opinion that more and stronger buying has occurred in a market than the market fundamentals would justify.

overlapping debt A condition resulting when property in a municipality is subject to multiple taxing authorities or tax districts, each having tax collection powers and recourse to the residents of that municipality.

overriding royalty interest An interest in the production of an oil and gas well, carved out of the working interest without liability for any costs of extraction; a form of sharing arrangement in an oil and gas direct participation program paid to someone (generally the sponsor) other than the mineral rights owner.

oversold A technical analyst's opinion that more and stronger selling has occurred in a market than the market fundamentals would justify.

over the counter (OTC) 1) A security that is not listed or traded on a recognized exchange. 2) The non-exchange market for securities.

Both listed and unlisted (OTC) securities as well as municipal and U.S. government securities are traded in the OTC market. OTC trading takes place over computer and telephone networks that link brokers and dealers around the world.

overtrading *See* churning.

owners' equity (*Syn.* shareholders' equity)

PACE *See* Philadelphia Stock Exchange PACE.

Pacific Stock Exchange (PSE) SCOREX The PSE uses the Securities Communication, Order Routing and Execution (SCOREX) system to automatically route and execute orders. SCOREX serves the PSE as an automatic link between the national and regional stock exchanges, and quotes on SCOREX are based on quotes from each exchange trading that particular stock or option.

SCOREX accepts all types of orders, including market, good till canceled and limit orders in both odd and round lots. The specialists at the SCOREX terminals will execute orders up to the 10,099-share SCOREX limit and have the ability to waive that limit for larger orders.

paid-in capital That portion of shareholders' equity that has been generated through issuing stock above its stated value or through assets that have been received as gifts. (*Syn.* paid-in surplus)

paid-in surplus *See* paid-in capital.

parallel shift An up or down movement in a yield curve approximately the same percentage for all maturities.

parity In an auction, *parity* refers to all brokers that have an equal standing in terms of the bidding procedure. The term also refers to the intrinsic value of a convertible security in terms of the common stock into which it can be converted.

partial call The call by an issuer of a portion of a bond issue outstanding prior to the maturity date.

participant Any person who represents stockholders for or against management in a proxy contest; the purchaser or holder of an interest in a direct participation program. *See also* limited partner.

participating preferred stock A type of preferred stock that offers the holder a share of the earnings remaining after all senior securities have been paid. This payment is made in addition to the fixed dividend received. Dividends may be cumulative or noncumulative. *See also* convertible preferred stock, cumulative preferred stock, noncumulative preferred stock, preferred stock.

partnership A form of business organization in which two or more individuals manage the business and are equally and personally liable for its debts.

partnership management fee The fee payable to the general partners for operating the partnership function.

par value An arbitrary dollar value assigned to each share of stock at the time of issuance; the principal amount (face value) of a bond on which interest is calculated. *See also* maturity date. (*Syn.* principal, stated value)

passive income The income from a business in which the individual does not regularly and materially participate, as with a limited partnership income.

passive investor *See* limited partner.

passive loss Any loss from a business in which the individual does not regularly and materially participate, as with limited partnership losses. Passive losses can be used to offset only passive income and not wage or portfolio income.

pass-through certificate A security backed by a pool of conventional (or Department of Veterans Affairs and Farmers Home Administration) mortgages, the principal and interest payment of which are received by the pool and passed through to the certificate holder. Payments may or may not be guaranteed. *See also* Federal National Mortgage Association, Government National Mortgage Association.

pattern A repetitive series of price movements on a chart used by a technical analyst to predict future movements of the market.

payment date The day on which a declared dividend is paid.

PE *See* price-earnings ratio.

pegging The act of effecting transactions in a security for fixing or stabilizing the price of the security above the established offering price. (*Syn.* fixing)

penalty plan *See* contractual plan.

PE ratio *See* price-earnings ratio.

percentage depletion A method of depletion whereby a statutory percentage of gross income from the sale of a mineral resource is a deductible expense. Percentage depletion is available to small producers only and not to purchasers of producing interests.

periodic payment plan A mutual fund sales contract in which the customer commits to buying shares in the fund on a monthly basis over a long term (10 or 20 years).

person An individual, a corporation, a partnership, an association, a fund, a joint stock company, an unincorporated organization, a trust in which the interests of the beneficiaries are evidenced by a security, a government or a political subdivision of a government.

PHA *See* Public Housing Authority bond.

Philadelphia plan A type of financing for railroad equipment trust obligations that involves a vendor delivering equipment to a trustee. The vendor receives equipment trust certificates that are sold to investors. The railroad leases the equipment and pays a periodic rental fee, which covers interest installments and principal when due. When all rental payments are made, the title is transferred to the railroad.

Philadelphia Stock Exchange (PHLX) PACE The PHLX developed the PHLX Automated Communication and Execution (PACE) system in 1975 to automatically route and execute orders. PACE is designed to handle market and limit orders of up to 3,099 shares for over 1,100 actively traded stocks. The PACE system can provide electronic executions within approximately 15 seconds of order receipt and can get confirmations back to the originating broker-dealer in only a few seconds more.

PHLX An acronym for the Philadelphia Stock Exchange.

Pink Sheets The daily quotation sheets that publish the interdealer wholesale quotes for over-the-counter stocks.

placement ratio A ratio compiled by *The Bond Buyer* indicating the number of new municipal issues that have sold within the last week.

plus tick An execution price above the previous sale. *See also* minus tick, plus tick rule. (*Syn.* up tick)

plus tick rule The Securities and Exchange Commission regulation governing the market price at which a short sale may be made. No short sale may be executed at a price below the price of the last sale. *See also* minus tick, zero-plus tick. (*Syn.* up tick rule)

point *See* basis point.

policy processing day The day on which charges authorized in the policy are deducted from the policy's cash value.

POP An acronym for public offering price. *See also* offering price.

portfolio income The income from interest, dividends and other nonbusiness investments.

possession (of securities) *See* control (of securities).

position The amount of a security (shares, contracts, bonds, etc.) either owned (a long position) or owed (a short position) by an individual. A dealer will also take positions in specific securities to maintain an inventory to facilitate trading.

position limit The limitation established by the listed options exchanges that prohibits an investor from having a position of more than a specific number of contracts on the same side of the market.

position trading 1) Occurs when a dealer acquires or sells an inventory in a security. *See also* dealer, principal, make a market. 2) Occurs when a commodities speculator buys or sells positions in the futures markets as a means of speculating on long-term price movements. *See also* scalper, spreader.

precedence In an auction, the ranking of bids and offers according to size (the number of shares in a bid or an offer).

preemptive right The legal right of stockholders to purchase new stock in proportion to their holdings before the new stock is offered to the public.

preferred dividend coverage A financial ratio used to determine the margin of safety with which the fixed dividend requirements are covered for a preferred stockholder, computed by dividing preferred dividends by net income.

preferred stock An equity security that represents ownership in a corporation. Preferred stock has a fixed dividend, with dividend and asset preference over common stock, and it generally carries no voting rights.

preliminary prospectus Any prospectus that is distributed during the cooling-off period and includes the essential facts about the forthcoming offering except for the underwriting spread, final public offering price and date the shares will be delivered. (*Syn.* red herring)

premium The market price of an option; the cash price that the option buyer pays to the option writer; the price paid for a security over and above its face amount. Also, the selling price of an option.

premium bond A bond that sells above par (above 100% of $1,000); that is, the purchase price of the bond is greater than the par value (principal amount). *See also* par value; principal.

prepaid charge plan *See* contractual plan.

prerefunding *See* advance refunding.

presale order An order communicated to the syndicate manager prior to formulation of the bid. If the syndicate wins the bid, the order is already considered sold. A presale order normally has the highest priority in a municipal underwriting.

price-earnings ratio (PE) The ratio of the current market value of the stock divided by the annual earnings per share.

price spread A spread involving the purchase and sale of two options on the same stock with the same expiration date but with different exercise prices. (*Syn.* money spread, vertical spread)

primary distribution *See* primary offering.

primary earnings per share The earnings per share if all rights, stock options and warrants have been converted (if their total conversion will cause at least a 3% increase in the number of shares outstanding). (*Syn.* earnings per share fully diluted)

primary offering An offering in which the proceeds of the underwriting (either equity or debt) go to the issuing corporation or municipality. A corporation increases its capitalization by selling stock (either a new issue or a previously authorized but unissued stock). It may do this at any time and in any amount, provided the total stock outstanding never exceeds the amount authorized in the corporation's bylaws. A municipality raises money by issuing debt. (*Syn.* primary distribution)

prime rate The interest rate that commercial banks charge their prime or most creditworthy customers (generally large corporations).

principal 1) A person who positions trades in the secondary or primary market, including sole proprietors, officers, directors or partners of a company and managers of offices of supervision; also, an investment banker who assumes risk by actually buying securities from the issuer and reselling them. (*Syn.* dealer). 2) An arbitrary dollar value assigned to each share of stock at the time of issuance; the principal amount (face value) of a bond on which interest is calculated. *See also* maturity date. (*Syn.* par value, stated value)

principal transaction A transaction in which a broker-dealer or bank dealer buys stocks or bonds from customers and takes them into its own inventory. It then sells stocks or bonds to customers from its inventory.

priority In an auction, the first person to bid or offer at a given price establishes priority. Only one person can have priority.

prior preferred stock A class of preferred stock that has prior claim over other preferred stock in receipt of dividends, as well as in distribution of assets in the event of liquidation. *See also* preferred stock.

private placement An offering that complies with Regulation D (Rule 505 and Rule 506); generally speaking, the offer of an unregistered security to no more than 35 nonaccredited investors or to an unlimited number of accredited investors. *See also* Regulation D.

productive well Any well that is not a dry hole. As used here, *production* refers to the commercial marketing of oil or gas produced as a result of the recovery of a mineral resource.

profitability The ability of a company to generate a level of income and gain in excess of expense.

profitability ratio A ratio describing profit or income as a percent or multiple of sales.

profit after taxes *See* net income to net sales.

profit margin *See* margin of profit.

profit ratio *See* net income to net sales.

program A limited or general partnership, a joint venture, an unincorporated association or a similar organization other than a corporation formed and operated for the primary purpose of investment in, operation of, or gain from an interest in real property, oil and gas property, or another suitable property.

program interest The limited partnership unit or some other indication of ownership in a direct participation program.

program management fee A fee paid to the sponsor or some other person(s) for managing and administering the program.

progressive tax A tax that takes a larger percentage of the income of high-income people (e.g., the graduated income tax). *See also* regressive tax.

project note A short-term debt instrument issued in anticipation of a later issuance of Public Housing Authority bonds.

property management fee The fee paid to a sponsor or some other person for day-to-day property management services in connection with a real estate program's real property project.

proprietorship A business organization in which a single owner has total control over the business and makes all management decisions.

prospect An area in which a partnership intends to acquire an oil or gas interest or property.

prospectus The legal document that must be given to every investor who purchases registered securities in an offering. It describes the details of the company and the particular offering. (*Syn.* final prospectus)

Prospectus Act Another name for the Securities Act of 1933.

proxy In order to vote on corporate matters, a stockholder must attend the annual meeting. If the stockholder is unable to attend, the stockholder may still vote by proxy. A proxy is given in writing, authorizing another to vote for the stockholder according to the stockholder's instructions.

prudent man rule A legal maxim that restricts discretion in a client's account to investments in only those securities that a reasonably prudent person seeking reasonable income and preservation of capital might buy.

PSE An acronym for the Pacific Stock Exchange.

Public Housing Authority bond (PHA) A bond issued by the Public Housing Authority. (*Syn.* Housing Authority bond)

public offering *See* initial public offering.

public offering price (POP) The price of new shares that is established in the issuing corporation's prospectus; also, the price to investors for mutual fund shares.

purchase and sales department The department within a brokerage firm that computes commissions and taxes and sends confirmations to clients. *See also* trade confirmation.

purchasing power risk The risk that due to inflation a certain amount of money will not purchase as much in the future as it does today. (*Syn.* inflation risk)

put 1) An option contract that gives the owner the right to sell a specified number of shares of stock at a specified price within a specified time. 2) The act of exercising a put option.

put bond A bond requiring the issuer to purchase the bond at the bondholder's discretion, normally at a prescribed time. (*Syn.* tender bond)

put buyer An investor who pays a premium for an option contract and has, for a specified time, the right to sell the underlying security at a specified price.

put spread An investment in which an investor purchases one put on a particular stock and sells another put on the same stock but with a different expiration date, exercise price or both.

put writer An investor who receives a premium and takes on, for a specified time, the obligation to buy the underlying security at a specified price at the put buyer's discretion.

qualified block positioner A dealer that enters into block purchases or sales with customers and that meets all of its minimum net capital requirements.

qualified independent appraiser A person, including a qualified independent petroleum engineer and a qualified independent real estate appraiser, who holds himself out as an appraiser of a particular type of property and who:

  A. is licensed or registered to practice his profession with the appropriate professional or regulatory body, if any, within the state of his business activity, if such is required, and who can demonstrate himself to be qualified to appraise the type of property in respect to which he holds himself out; and

  B. is totally independent in that:

- he is informed of the purpose for which the appraisal is to be used and that it is to be relied upon for the public program;
- he has relied upon sufficient competent evidence of value and has based the appraisal on his own experience and judgment;
- he has no present interest or contemplated future interest, either legal or beneficial, in the property appraised;
- he has no interest in any proposed transaction involving the property or in the parties to such transaction;
- his employment and compensation are not contingent on any value found by him or on anything other than the delivery of his report for a predetermined fee; and
- he is not an affiliate of a sponsor.

qualified legal opinion A conditional opinion of the legality or tax-exempt status of a municipal bond. *See also* legal opinion of counsel.

qualified OTC market maker A dealer that makes a market in an over-the-counter

(OTC) margin security and that meets minimum net capital requirements.

qualified retirement plan A retirement plan that qualifies under sections 401 and 501 of the Internal Revenue Code. *See also* individual retirement account, Keogh plan. (*Syn.* approved plan)

qualified third-market maker A dealer that makes a market in an exchange-listed stock and that meets minimum net capital requirements.

quality adjustment The amount a settlement price is adjusted on a futures transaction when the delivered commodity differs from that specified in the original contract.

quality allowance *See* allowance.

quarterly securities count Every broker-dealer must conduct a count of securities in its control, verify securities in transit, compare counts with its securities records and record all unresolved securities differences at least quarterly.

quick ratio A test of a company's liquidity, computed by dividing current assets (cash, cash equivalents and receivables) by current liabilities.

quotation The bid and ask of a particular security.

quote (bond) Like stock quotes, bond prices are quoted in the financial press and most daily newspapers. Corporate bonds are quoted in 1/8ths. Government bonds are quoted in 1/32nds. The quotes for corporate and government bonds are percentages of the bonds' face value ($1,000). Municipal bonds may be quoted on a dollar basis or on a yield to maturity.

quote (stock) Many stocks traded are quoted in the financial press and most daily newspapers. A stock is quoted in points, with each point equal to $1. The price of the stock is further broken down into 1/8ths of a point, where 1/8th equals 12.5 cents.

RAES *See* Chicago Board Options Exchange RAES.

RAN *See* revenue anticipation note.

range A security's low price and high price for a particular trading period (e.g., close of the day's trading, opening of the day's trading, day, month, year). (*Syn.* opening range)

rate covenant A revenue coverage minimum set in a trust indenture for payment of main-tenance, debt service and reserve requirements to establish safety margins on the issue.

rating Bonds are rated for safety by various organizations such as Standard & Poor's and Moody's. These firms rate the companies and municipalities issuing bonds according to their ability to repay and make interest payments. Ratings range from AAA or Aaa (the highest) to C or D (representing a company in default).

rating service A company such as Moody's or Standard & Poor's that rates various debt and preferred stock issues for safety of payment of principal, interest or dividends. The issuing company or municipality pays a fee for the rating. *See also* rating.

ratio writing An option position in which the investor writes more than one call option for every 100 shares of underlying stock (or for every call option) that she owns.

R coefficient A statistical measure of how closely the movements of a security's price track with the movements of the market.

real estate investment trust (REIT) An investment trust that operates through the pooled capital of many investors who buy its shares. Investments are in direct ownership of either income property or mortgage loans.

real estate program A direct participation program that has as its primary purpose the investment in or operation of real property for a gain.

realized gain The amount of gain the taxpayer actually has on the sale or other disposition of property.

reallowance *See* concession.

recapitalization The act of converting a short-term liability into a long-term liability.

recapture The treatment as ordinary income of gain that should otherwise be treated as capital gain on the sale or other disposition of a capital asset because of previous deductions from ordinary income that are now treated as being excessive or otherwise not allowed.

reciprocal immunity *See* mutual exclusion doctrine.

reclamation The right of a party to a securities transaction to recover any loss incurred due to bad delivery or another irregularity in the settlement process.

record date The date established by the issuing corporation that determines which stockholders are entitled to receive dividends or rights distributions.

recourse financing Financing in which the taxpayer is personally liable for the debt.

redemption The return of an investor's interest (net asset value) in a mutual fund. By law, redemption must occur within seven days of receiving instruction from the investor to sell shares in the fund.

redemption notice A notice that a company or municipality is redeeming (or calling) a certain issue of bonds.

red herring *See* preliminary prospectus.

refinancing Issuing equity, the proceeds of which are used to retire debt.

refunding A method of retiring an outstanding bond issue using the money from the sale of a new offering. This may occur before maturity (advance refunding) or at maturity (refunding).

regional fund *See* specialized fund.

registered as to principal only A bond on which the name of the owner is printed but that has unregistered coupons payable to the bearer.

registered bond A bond on which the name of the owner appears on the certificate.

registered options principal (ROP) The officer or partner of a brokerage firm who approves in writing certain accounts for certain types of options transactions.

registered principal Anyone associated with a member who manages or supervises the member's investment banking or securities business must be registered as a principal with the NASD. This includes those people involved in training associated persons and in soliciting business. Unless the member firm is a sole proprietorship, there must be at least two registered principals per firm, one of whom must be registered as a General Securities Principal (Series 24).

In addition to having at least one general principal, each member must have at least one Financial and Operations Principal (FinOp—Series 27). If the member does options business with the public, there must be at least one Registered Options Principal (ROP—Series 4).

registered representative (RR) For NASD registration and exam and licensing purposes, the category of *registered representative* includes all associated persons engaged in the invest-

ment banking and securities business. This includes:

- assistant officers (who are not principals);
- individuals who supervise, solicit or conduct business in securities; and
- individuals who train people to supervise, solicit or conduct business in securities.

Anyone who is not a principal and not engaged in clerical or brokerage administration is subject to registration and exam licensing as a registered representative—except for foreign associates. (*Syn.* account executive, stockbroker)

registered secondary distribution *See* secondary distribution.

registered trader A member of an exchange who trades primarily for a personal account and at personal risk.

registrar An independent organization or part of a corporation charged with the responsibility of seeing that the corporation does not have more stock outstanding than is accounted for on the corporation's books.

registration by coordination A security is eligible for blue sky registration by coordination in a state if the issuer has filed for registration of that security under the Securities Act of 1933 and files duplicates of the registration documents with the state administrator. The state registration becomes effective at the same time the federal registration statement becomes effective.

registration by notification (filing) A security is eligible for blue sky registration by notification (also known as registration by filing) in a state if the issuer has filed for registration of that security under the Securities Act of 1933, meets minimum net worth and other requirements, and notifies the state of this eligibility by filing certain documents with the state administrator. The state registration becomes effective at the same time the federal registration statement becomes effective.

registration by qualification Any security is eligible for blue sky registration by qualification in a state if the issuer files registration documents for that security with the state administrator, meeting minimum net worth, disclosure and other requirements, and filing appropriate registration fees. The state registration becomes effective when the administrator so orders.

registration statement Before nonexempt securities can be offered to the public, they require registration under the Securities Act of 1933. The registration statement must disclose all pertinent information concerning the issuer and the offering. This statement is submitted to the SEC in accordance with the requirements of the 1933 act.

regressive tax A tax that takes a larger percentage of the income of low-income people (e.g., gasoline and cigarette taxes). *See also* progressive tax.

Reg T call *See* margin call.

regular way A settlement contract that calls for delivery and payment on the fifth business day following the date of trade. This is the usual type of settlement. For government securities, regular way is the next business day.

regulated investment company An investment company granted special status by Subchapter M of the Internal Revenue Code allowing the flow-through of tax consequences on a distribution to shareholders. If 90% of income is passed through to shareholders, the company is not subject to tax on the earnings.

Regulation A The securities regulation that exempts small public offerings from registration (those valued at no more than $5 million worth of securities offered during a twelve-month period).

Regulation D The securities regulation that exempts from registration certain small offerings and sales to specified individuals during a twelve-month period. *See also* private placement.

Regulation G The Federal Reserve Board regulation governing the extension of credit by persons other than banks, brokers or dealers. *See also* Regulation T, Regulation U.

Regulation Q The Federal Reserve Board regulation that establishes how much interest banks may pay on savings accounts. Reg Q was phased out in 1986.

Regulation T The Federal Reserve Board regulation governing the credit that brokerage firms and dealers may extend to clients for the purchase of securities. Regulation T also governs cash accounts.

Regulation T excess *See* excess equity.

Regulation U The Federal Reserve Board regulation governing loans by banks for the purchase of securities. Call loans are exempt from Reg U. *See also* broker's loan, call loan, time loan.

reinstatement privilege A term referring to the fund allowing an investor the privilege of withdrawing the money from the account and redepositing the money without paying a second sales charge.

reinvested earnings *See* retained earnings.

reinvestment For mutual funds, distributions (dividends and gains) are reinvested in the fund to purchase additional shares instead of receiving distributions in cash.

REIT *See* real estate investment trust.

rejection The right of a broker-dealer to refuse to accept securities delivered in completion of a trade because they do not meet the requirements of good delivery (e.g., missing signature, missing the coupons, mutilated, etc.).

reoffering scale The prices or yields at which municipal securities are sold to the public by the underwriters of a municipal offering.

repo *See* repurchase agreement.

repurchase agreement A sale and an attendant agreement to repurchase the securities sold at a higher price on an agreed upon future date. The difference between the sale price and the repurchase price represents the interest earned by the investor. In a repurchase agreement, the seller initiates the deal. Repos are commonly used by government securities dealers as a means of raising capital, typically to finance an inventory of securities. Repos are considered money-market instruments. *See also* reverse repurchase agreement. (*Syn.* repo)

reserves The money that a bank has in its vault or on deposit with the Federal Reserve Bank. A bank is required to maintain a certain percentage of reserves as set by the Fed.

resistance A term used in technical analysis to describe the top of a stock's trading range.

restricted account A margin account in which the equity is less than the Regulation T initial requirement. *See also* equity, initial margin requirements, margin account.

restricted security An unregistered nonexempt security acquired either directly or indirectly from the issuer or an affiliate of the issuer in a transaction that does not involve a public offering. *See also* holding period.

retail transaction A trade in which a client buys an over-the-counter stock from or through a broker-dealer or sells one to or through a broker-dealer. *See also* wholesale transaction.

retained earnings The amount of net income that remains after all dividends have been paid to preferred and common stockholders. (*Syn.* earned surplus, reinvested earnings)

retained earnings ratio The ratio of retained earnings to net income available for common stock. It is the complement of the dividend payout ratio. *See also* dividend payout ratio.

retention The securities that an underwriter sells directly to its own clients. The securities that it underwrites but does not retain are turned back to the manager to be sold by another firm.

retention requirement The proportion of sale proceeds that must be retained to reduce the debit balance if securities are sold from a restricted margin account. The retention requirement is 50%. *See also* restricted account.

retiring bonds The act of calling bonds by a notice in the newspaper, by purchasing bonds in the open market or by repaying bondholders the principal amount at maturity.

return on sales *See* net income to net sales.

revenue anticipation note (RAN) A municipal note issued in anticipation of revenue to be received.

revenue bond A bond whose interest and principal are payable only from specific earnings of an income-producing (revenue-producing) enterprise. *See also* municipal bond.

reverse repurchase agreement A purchase and an attendant agreement to resell the securities sold at a higher price on an agreed-upon future date. The difference between the purchase price and the sale price represents the interest earned by the investor. In a reverse repurchase agreement, the purchaser initiates the deal. *See also* repurchase agreement. (*Syn.* repo)

reversionary interest An interest in a program the benefits of which accrue in the future upon the occurrence of some event.

right A security representing a stockholder's right to purchase new securities in proportion to the number of shares already owned. Rights, also known as stock rights, are stock purchase options issued to existing stockholders only. The right is an option to purchase a company's new issue of stock at a predetermined price (normally for less than the stock's current market price). The right is issued for a short period of time, normally for

30 days, with the option expiring after that time. *See also* preemptive right, subscription right. (*Syn.* subscription right certificate)

right of accumulation The right to apply reduced sales loads (breakpoints) based on the dollar position held by the investor in a mutual fund.

rights offering An offering that gives each stockholder an opportunity to maintain a proportionate ownership in the company before the shares are offered to the public.

riskless and simultaneous transaction *See* riskless transaction.

riskless transaction An over-the-counter transaction in which a brokerage firm buys or sells a security to fill an order previously received from a client for the same security. Although the firm is technically acting as a principal in this trade, the transaction is relatively riskless because the purchase and sale are consummated almost simultaneously. (*Syn.* riskless and simultaneous transaction)

rolling forward (*Syn.* switching)

ROP *See* registered options principal.

royalty interest The right of a mineral rights owner to receive a share in the production of the resource, if and when production begins. The royalty interest retained is free from costs of production.

RR *See* registered representative.

Rule 144 A rule that covers the sale of two kinds of securities: control securities and restricted securities. Under Rule 144, persons who hold control or restricted securities can sell them only in limited quantities. All sales of restricted stock by control persons must be reported to the SEC by the filing of Form 144—Notice of Proposed Sale of Securities. *See also* control security, restricted security.

Rule 145 Rule 145 requires that whenever an offer is made to the stockholders of a publicly owned corporation, soliciting their vote or consent to a plan for reorganizing the company, full disclosure of all material facts must be made in a prospectus, which must be in the hands of the stockholders before the announced voting date.

Rule 147 Rule 147 provides exemption from the registration statement and prospectus requirements of the 1933 act for securities offered and sold exclusively intrastate.

Rule 15c2-1 SEC 15c2-1 governs the safekeeping of securities in customer margin accounts. Broker-dealers are prohibited from using customer securities in excess of customer aggregate indebtedness as collateral to secure loans (rehypothecation) without the express written permission of the customer. Broker-dealers are also prohibited from commingling customer securities without the customers' written permission.

Rule 15c3-1 SEC 15c3-1 governs the net capital requirements of broker-dealers. Net capital requirements differ for different types of broker-dealers and for different amounts of aggregate indebtedness.

Rule 15c3-2 SEC 15c3-2 requires broker-dealers to inform customers of their free credit balances at least quarterly.

Rule 15c3-3 SEC 15c3-3 is known as the *customer protection rule* and regulates the location, segregation and handling of customer funds and securities. Under 15c3-3, broker-dealers must segregate all customer fully paid and excess margin securities in a special reserve bank account for the exclusive benefit of customers.

Rule 405 The NYSE rule stating that each member organization must exercise due diligence to learn the essential facts about every customer; also known as the *know your customer rule.*

Rule 406 The NYSE rule stating that no member organization may carry an account designated by a number or symbol unless the customer has signed a written statement attesting to ownership of the account and the statement is on file with the member organization.

Rule 407 The NYSE rule stating that an employee of the NYSE or any of its members and certain nonmember organizations must have written permission from their employers before opening either cash or margin accounts but that employee banks, trust companies and insurance companies need their employers' permission only when opening margin accounts.

Rule 409 The NYSE rule stating that a customer's written instructions and the written approval of a member or an allied member are necessary before a customer's mail can be held.

Rule 504 A private placement offering of less than $1,000,000 during any twelve-month period may qualify for registration under Rule 504. Rule 504 does not restrict the number of accredited or nonaccredited purchasers.

Rule 505 A private placement offering of $1,000,000 to $5,000,000 during any twelve-month period may qualify for registration under Rule 505. Rule 505 restricts the number of non-accredited purchasers to 35; there is no restriction on accredited purchasers.

Rule 506 A private placement offering of more than $5,000,000 may qualify for registration under Rule 506. Rule 506 restricts the number of non-accredited purchasers to 35; there is no restriction on accredited purchasers.

Rules of Fair Practice The NASD rules that detail how member firms deal with the public.

sale leaseback A method of raising cash whereby a person sells property to a buyer and leases it back from him.

sales charge With mutual funds, the amount added to the net asset value (NAV) of mutual fund shares. The investor will pay the NAV and the sales charge, which equal the offering price. *See also* mutual fund, net asset value, offering price. (*Syn.* sales load)

sales literature Any written material used to help sell a product and that is distributed by the firm in a controlled manner. *See also* advertising, market letter.

sales load *See* sales charge.

satellite office A member location not identified as either an office of supervisory jurisdiction or a branch office is considered a satellite office (in general, a location not held out to the public as a place of business for the member).

scale Important data concerning each of the scheduled maturities in a new serial bond issue, including the number of bonds, date, maturity, coupon rate and offering price.

scalper A commodities trader who buys and sells many commodities contracts during a single day in the anticipation of profiting from small price fluctuations. Scalpers rarely carry positions from one day to the next, and their buying and selling activity contributes greatly to the liquidity of the commodities markets. *See also* position trading, spreader.

scheduled premium policy Any variable life insurance policy under which both the amount and the timing of premium payments are fixed by the insurer.

Schedule 13D A form that must be filed by an individual (or individuals acting in concert) after acquiring beneficial ownership of 5% or more of any nonexempt equity security. It must be sent within ten business days to the: issuing company, exchange where the stock is trading and the SEC.

Schedule 13e-3 A form that must be filed by a public company whenever it engages in a strategy to take the company private (e.g., when a transaction would decrease the number of stockholders to such a point that the company would no longer be required to file reports with the SEC [under 300 stockholders], a schedule 13e-3 would need to be filed). The transaction could also be a merger, tender offer or reverse stock split. The results of such a transaction must be reported promptly, but no later than ten days after the transaction. The schedule would seek disclosure of all the terms and the fairness of the transaction to unaffiliated stockholders.

Schedule 13e-4 A form also known as an issuer tender offer statement that must be filed by public companies when they make tender offers for their own securities. Schedule 13e-4 reporting must occur no later than ten days after the termination of the tender.

Schedule 13g An abbreviated 13D form that is used principally by broker-dealers, banks and insurance companies only if they acquire a 5% position in the normal course of business and not for the purpose of changing or influencing control of the companies. This schedule must be filed 45 days after the first calendar year end when the broker-dealer or bank becomes subject to the requirement.

SCOREX *See* Pacific Stock Exchange SCOREX.

SEC *See* Securities and Exchange Commission.

secondary distribution A distribution with a prospectus that involves securities owned by major stockholders (typically founders or principal owners of a corporation). In a secondary distribution, sale proceeds go to the sellers of the stock, not to the issuer. (*Syn.* registered secondary distributor)

secondary offering An offering in which one or more major stockholders in a company are selling all or a major portion of their holdings. The underwriting proceeds are paid to the stockholders, rather than to the corporation itself. Typically secondary offerings occur in situations where the founder of a business and perhaps some of the original financial backers determine that there is more to be gained by going public than by staying private. This offering does not increase the number of shares of stock outstanding. Also, a secondary offering is a block trading procedure for very large blocks that is executed off the floor of an exchange after the market closes. *See also* secondary distribution.

secured bond A bond backed by some form of collateral. In the event the company defaults on payment, the bondholders may attach the collateral backing the bond.

Securities Act of 1933 The federal legislation requiring the full and fair disclosure of all material information about the issuance of new securities.

Securities and Exchange Commission (SEC) The commission created by Congress to protect investors. The Commission enforces the Securities Act of 1933, the Securities Exchange Act of 1934, the Trust Indenture Act of 1939, the Investment Company Act of 1940, the Investment Advisers Act of 1940 and others.

Securities Exchange Act of 1934 The federal legislation establishing the Securities and Exchange Commission. Its purpose is to provide regulation of securities exchanges and over-the-counter markets and to protect investors from unfair and inequitable practices.

Securities Industry Association (SIA) The nonprofit organization that represents the collective business interests of its over 600 leading securities firm members headquartered throughout North America. SIA activities include government relations, industry research and educational and informational services for its members.

Securities Investor Protection Corporation (SIPC) A nonprofit membership corporation created by an act of Congress to protect clients of brokerage firms that are forced into bankruptcy. Membership is composed of all brokers and dealers registered under the Securities Exchange Act of 1934, all members of national securities exchanges and most NASD members. SIPC provides customers of these firms up to $500,000 coverage for their cash and securities held by the firms (although coverage of cash is limited to $100,000).

security Under the act of 1934, any note, stock, bond, investment contract, debenture, certificate of interest in profit-sharing or partnership agreement, certificate of deposit, collateral trust certificate, preorganization certificate, option on a security or other instrument of investment commonly known as a security.

Also categorized as "securities" are interests in the following: oil and gas drilling programs, real estate condominiums and cooperatives, farmland or animals, commodity option contracts, whiskey warehouse receipts, multilevel distributorship arrangements, and merchandising marketing programs.

The accurate determination of what is a security is crucial to registered representatives conducting their activities in compliance with state securities laws. In general, a security can be defined as any piece of securitized paper that can be traded for value, except an insurance policy or a fixed annuity. As established by the federal courts, the basic test for determining whether a specific investment comes within the definition of a "security" is whether the person invests his money in a common enterprise and is led to expect profits from the managerial efforts of the promoter or a third party.

security arbitrage The simultaneous purchase and sale of related or convertible securities to take advantage of a price disparity between the two securities. *See also* arbitrage.

security cage *See* cashiering department.

segregation The separation of client-owned securities and those securities owned by the brokerage firm. *See also* commingling.

self-regulatory organization (SRO) Each SRO is accountable to the SEC for the enforcement of federal securities laws, as well as the supervision of securities practices, within an assigned field of jurisdiction. Eight SROs function under the oversight of the Commission. Selected jurisdictions include:

- New York Stock Exchange (NYSE). All matters related to trading in NYSE-listed securities and the conduct of NYSE member firms and associated persons.
- National Association of Securities Dealers (NASD). All matters related to investment banking (securities underwriting) and trading in the over-the-counter market and the conduct of NASD member firms and associated persons.
- Municipal Securities Rulemaking Board (MSRB). All matters related to the underwriting and trading of state and municipal securities.
- Chicago Board Options Exchange (CBOE). All matters related to the writing and trading of standardized options and related contracts listed on that exchange.

sell The term "sale" or "sell" refers to every contract to sell a security or interest in a security. This definition is broad and specifically includes the following:

- Any security given or delivered with or as a bonus for any purchase of securities is considered to have been offered and sold for value.
- A gift of assessable stock is considered to involve an offer and sale.
- Every sale or offer of a warrant or right to purchase or subscribe to another security is considered to include an offer of the other security.

The term "sale" or "sell" does not include a bona fide pledge or loan, or a stock dividend if nothing of value is given by the stockholders for the dividend.

seller *See* writer.

seller's option A settlement contract that calls for delivery and payment according to the number of days specified by the seller. Settlement occurs from six business days to the expiration of the option.

selling a hedge The sale of futures options as a means of protecting against a decrease in commodities prices in the future. *See also* buying a hedge, long hedge, short hedge.

selling concession The portion of an underwriting spread that is paid to a selling group member on the securities it sells to the public during an offering.

selling dividends The illegal practice of inducing clients to buy mutual fund shares by implying that a pending distribution will benefit them; also, the act of combining dividend and gains distributions in the calculation of current yield.

selling group Brokerage firms that sell securities in an offering but that are not members of the underwriting syndicate.

sell-out A procedure that occurs when a buyer fails to accept delivery of securities as stipulated in a contract. The seller can close the contract by selling the securities at the best available price and holding the buyer liable for the price of the securities and the resulting transaction costs.

senior lien debt A bond issue sharing the same collateral backing as other issues but having a prior claim to the collateral in the event of default.

separate account With a variable annuity contract, the account in which the insurance company invests funds paid by contract holders. The funds are kept separate from the company's general investment account. *See also* accumulation unit, annuity.

separately identifiable department or division Under Municipal Securities Rulemaking Board (MSRB) rules, a department or division under the direct supervision of an officer of the bank. If a bank has such a department or division that engages in the business of buying or selling municipal securities, it is classified as a municipal securities dealer and must comply with MSRB regulations.

serial bond A bond issued under a type of maturity schedule in which parts of an outstanding issue of bonds mature at intervals until the issue's final maturity date. Most municipal bonds are serial bonds. *See also* series bond. (*Syn.* serial bond)

series Options of the same class that have the same exercise price and the same expiration date. *See also* class, type.

Series 6 The Series 6 is the Investment Company/Variable Contract Products Limited Representative license. This license entitles the representative to sell mutual funds and variable annuities and is used by many firms selling primarily insurance-related products. It can serve as the prerequisite for the Series 26.

Series 7 A Series 7 General Securities Registered Representative license allows a registered rep to sell all types of securities products, with the exception of commodities futures (which requires a Series 3). This is the most comprehensive of the NASD representative licenses available and serves as a prerequisite for most of the NASD's principals examinations.

Series 11 The Series 11 registration (Assistant Representative—Order Processing) allows a registered sales assistant to take unsolicited orders, enter order tickets, update client information, fill out client new account forms

and provide to customers quotes and other pro forma information relating to securities. This registration does not permit the assistant rep to determine suitability, make recommendations of transactions or provide advice to customers.

A broker-dealer may only compensate assistant representatives—order processing on a salary or hourly wage basis. Compensation, including bonuses and commissions, may not be related to the number or size of the transactions effected for customers.

Series 22 The Series 22 Direct Participation Programs Limited Representative license entitles the representative to sell oil and gas, real estate, motion picture and other types of limited partnerships and is used by many firms selling tax-advantaged limited partnership products. It can serve as a prerequisite for the Series 39.

Series 52 The Series 52 Municipal Securities Representative license entitles the representative to sell municipal and government securities and is used by many firms selling primarily municipal debt products. It can serve as a prerequisite for the Series 53.

Series 62 The Series 62 Corporate Securities Limited Representative license entitles the representative to sell all types of corporate securities but not municipal securities, options, direct participation programs or a limited number of other products. It is used by many firms selling general securities products that want to limit their representatives to corporate securities. The Series 62 can serve as a prerequisite for the Series 24.

series bond A bond issued in a scheduled series of public offerings. Series bonds have the same priority claim against corporate assets. *See also* serial bond.

Series EE bond A nonmarketable U.S. government savings bond issued at a discount from par.

Series HH bond A nonmarketable interest-bearing U.S. government savings bond issued at par.

settlement The completion of a securities trade through the delivery of the security (or commodity) for cash or another consideration.

settlement date The date on which a transaction must be settled (exchange of cash for securities).

shareholders' equity This is calculated by subtracting total liabilities from total assets. (*Syn.* net worth; owners' equity)

share identification An accounting method whereby the shares selected for liquidation are identified in any order.

sharing arrangement A method of determining responsibility for expenses and the right to share in revenues between the sponsor and limited partners.

shelf offering An offering that allows an issuer to register a new issue security without selling the entire issue at once. The issuer can sell limited portions of a registered shelf offering over a two-year period without having to reregister the security or incurring penalties. Shelf offerings provide issuers and their investment bankers with flexibility—money can be raised and expenses incurred only as needed.

short The state of having sold a security, contract or commodity. A sale of 10 September silver contracts would be referred to as *going short,* or shorting, September silver. The speculator would have a *short* position.

short against the box The sale of a security that the seller owns but prefers not to deliver; frequently done in an arbitrage account.

short exempt transaction A short sale in an arbitrage transaction that is exempt from the SEC plus tick rule.

short hedge A short securities or actuals position protected by a long call position. *See also* hedge, long hedge.

short interest theory A technical theory that measures the ratio of short sales to volume in a stock. A high ratio of short interest is considered bullish.

short sale The sale of a security that the seller does not own or any sale consummated by the delivery of a security borrowed by or for the account of the seller.

short straddle The position established by writing a call and a put on the same stock with the same strike price and expiration month. *See also* long straddle, spread.

short-term capital gain The taxable gain on a capital asset that is owned for twelve months or less. *See also* capital gain, capital loss, short-term capital loss.

short-term capital loss The taxable loss on a capital asset that is owned for twelve months or less. *See also* short-term capital gain, capital gain, capital loss.

simplified arbitration Disputes not involving customers can be submitted for resolution under simplified industry arbitration proceedings provided the dollar amount of the claim does not exceed $5,000. Under simplified industry arbitration, an arbitration panel consisting of at least one arbitrator (but not more than three) will review evidence and pleadings from both sides of the dispute and render a decision, usually without need for a hearing. All awards under simplified industry arbitration are made within 30 business days from the date the arbitration panel declares the disputed matter closed.

sinking fund A fund established by a corporation or municipality into which money is regularly deposited so that the corporation or municipality has the funds to redeem its bonds, debentures or preferred stock.

sinking fund call The early redemption of bonds from the proceeds of the sinking fund set up for this purpose. *See also* sinking fund.

SIPC *See* Securities Investor Protection Corporation.

SMA *See* special memorandum account.

Small Order Execution System *See* NASD Small Order Execution System.

SOES *See* NASD Small Order Execution System.

sole proprietorship A form of business organization in which a single owner has total control over her own business and makes all managerial decisions.

solvency The measure of a company's ability both to meet its long-term fixed charges and to have adequate money for long-term expansion and growth.

special arbitrage account A type of margin account for arbitrage transactions. *See also* market arbitrage, security arbitrage.

special assessment bond A revenue bond payable only from assessments on property owners who benefit from the services or improvements provided by the proceeds from the bond issue.

special bid *See* special offering.

special cash account *See* cash account.

specialist block purchase (sale) A block trading procedure for smaller blocks in which the specialist purchases (or sells) the block in a private transaction.

specialized fund A type of mutual fund that tries to achieve its investment objectives by concentrating its investments within a single industry or group of related industries.

special memorandum account (SMA) A notation on a customer's general or margin account. Funds are credited to the SMA on a memo basis, and the SMA is used much like a line of credit with a bank. The SMA preserves the customer's right to use excess equity. (*Syn.* special miscellaneous account)

special miscellaneous account *See* special memorandum account.

special offering A block trading procedure in which a block of stock is offered for sale after a prior announcement on the broad tape. (*Syn.* special bid)

special reserve bank account An account maintained by a broker-dealer for the exclusive use of customers and for the required deposits of customer funds.

special situation fund A type of mutual fund that invests in companies in special situations, such as firms undergoing reorganization or firms considered to be takeover candidates.

special tax bond A type of municipal bond that is payable only from the proceeds of a special tax, other than an ad valorem tax. *See also* municipal bond.

speculation The buying and selling of goods or securities solely for the purpose of profiting from those trades and not as a means of hedging or protecting other positions.

split offering An offering combining aspects of both a primary and a secondary offering. A portion of the securities is newly issued, and the proceeds of the sale go to the corporation itself. The remainder of the issue is a secondary offering, the proceeds of which go to the selling stockholders.

sponsor Any person directly or indirectly instrumental in organizing, wholly or in part, a partnership or any person who will manage or participate in the management of a partnership.

spot commodity The actual good as it is being traded, as opposed to futures or options on that good.

spot market A market in which goods are traded for immediate delivery and immediate payment.

spot price The actual price a particular good can be bought or sold for at a specified time and place.

spot secondary distribution A block trading procedure in which a secondary distribution is not registered and is announced suddenly. (*Syn.* unregistered secondary distribution)

spread In a quotation, the difference between the bid and offer; with options, simultaneously having a long and a short option position within the same class but not the same series.

spreader A commodities trader who attempts to profit from the price differences between commodities, markets or delivery months; a commodities arbitrageur. *See also* position trading, scalper.

spread-load option With mutual funds, a system of sales charges for contractual plans. It permits a decreasing scale of sales charges, with no more than 20% of the cost deducted in any one year and no more than an average of 16% of the cost deducted in a consecutive 48-month period. The maximum that may be deducted over the life of the plan is still 9%. Rights of withdrawal exist for 45 days, during which time the client may receive a return of all sales charges deducted plus the current value of the account. After 45 days, the client is entitled to the current net asset value only.

SRO *See* self-regulatory organization.

stabilizing The condition that occurs when a dealer appointed by the managing underwriter buys a security at or below the public offering price to prevent the price from dropping sharply.

stagflation Stagnation in the economy accompanied by a rise in prices.

Standard & Poor's 500 A market indicator composed of 400 industrial stocks, 20 transportation stocks, 40 financial stocks and 40 public utility stocks.

standardized option *See* listed option.

standby underwriter A brokerage firm that agrees to purchase any part of an issue that has not been subscribed to through a rights offering.

stated value *See* par value.

stated yield. *See* nominal yield.

statement of intention *See* letter of intent.

statutory disqualification A person is statutorily disqualified from association with a member organization if that person has been expelled, barred or suspended from association with a member of a self-regulatory organization; has had his registration suspended, denied or revoked by the SEC; has been the cause of someone else's suspension, barment or revocation; has been convicted of certain specified crimes; or has falsified any application or report that he is required to file with or on behalf of a membership organization.

statutory voting rights A voting procedure that permits a stockholder to cast one vote per share owned for each director.

steer averaging The act of investing fixed amounts of capital in cattle over a period of time in staged amounts, with the proceeds from the sale of the cattle automatically reinvested.

step-out well A well or prospect adjacent to a field of proven reserves.

stock ahead A limit order at a specific price that is not filled because other orders at that same price were entered before that order.

stockbroker *See* registered representative.

stock certificate Written evidence of ownership in a corporation.

stock dividend *See* dividend.

stockholders' equity *See* shareholders' equity.

stock power A standard form that duplicates the back of a stock certificate. It is used if the registered owner of a security does not have the certificate available for signature endorsement. *See also* assignment.

stock split A reduction in the par value of stock caused by the issuance of additional stock. A reverse split increases the stock's par value by reducing the number of shares outstanding.

stop limit order A stop order that becomes a limit order once the market price reaches or passes the specific price stated in the stop order. *See also* stop order.

stop order 1) An order by the SEC that suspends the sale of securities to the public. 2) An order that becomes a market order when the market price of the security reaches or exceeds the specific price stated in the stop order.

stopping stock When a specialist guarantees execution at a specific price for a public order submitted by a floor broker.

straddle Either a long or short position in a call and a put on the same security with the same expiration date and exercise price.

straddle—long The act of buying a call and a put on a stock with the same strike price and expiration.

straddle—short The act of writing a call and a put on a stock with the same strike price and expiration.

straight-line depreciation A method of depreciation by which a corporation writes off the cost of an asset in equal amounts each year over the asset's useful life.

strangle A combination of a put and a call where both options are out-of-the-money. A strangle can be profitable only if the market is highly volatile and makes a major move in either direction.

strap The purchase of two calls and one put on the same security with the same terms.

street name Securities held by a brokerage firm in its own name but owned by a client are referred to as being held in street name. *See also* in-street-name account.

strengthening basis A narrowing of the spread between the cash (spot) price and the futures price of a commodity.

strike price The price at which the underlying security will be sold if the option buyer exercises her rights in the contract. (*Syn.* exercise price)

striking price *See* strike price.

strip The purchase of two puts and one call on the same security with the same terms.

strip bond A bond stripped of its coupons, repackaged and sold at a deep discount and maturing at full face value.

stripper bond *See* original issue discount.

stripper well A well producing fewer than ten barrels of oil per day. Stripping a field means pumping the field occasionally and letting it rest between the pumping periods.

subject quote A quote that does not represent actual offers to buy or sell when prices are quoted. It represents an indication of how the market stands. (*Syn.* nominal quote)

subordinated debenture A debt obligation that has unsecured junior claims to interest and principal subordinated to ordinary debentures and all other liabilities of the issuing corporation. *See also* debenture.

subordinated debt A form of long-term capitalization used by broker-dealers, in which the claims of lenders are subordinated to the claims of other creditors. Subordinated financing is considered part of the broker-dealer's capital structure and is added to net worth (shareholders' equity) to compute total available capital when computing net capital.

subordinated interest An interest that is junior to the rights of participants until such time as the participants have received cumulative distributed cash or net revenues in an amount at least equal to their capital contributions.

subordinated reversionary working interest In this type of sharing arrangement, the sponsor bears no drilling cost and does not share in revenues until investors achieve payout. Payout occurs when an investor receives all monies invested plus a predetermined rate of return (normally 6% compounded annually). At payout, the program sponsor will receive a percentage of the revenues generated and share in additional expenses.

subscription agreement An agreement whereby an investor agrees to purchase securities and in addition agrees to become a limited partner and abide by the limited partnership agreement.

subscription amount The total dollar amount for which a participant in a direct participation program has subscribed for her participation in the program.

subscription right A stockholder's privilege of having the first opportunity to purchase new stock issued by the corporation so that the stockholder may retain his proportionate ownership in the corporation. Generally the price for subscription stock is lower than the current market value. *See also* preemptive right, right.

subscription right certificate *See* right.

sum-of-the-years-digits (SOYD) A method of depreciation in which a corporation writes off more of the value of an asset during its early years of use than during its later years of use.

SuperDot *See* New York Stock Exchange Super Designated Order Turnaround system.

supervision The act of ensuring that the employees and associated persons of a broker dealer comply with the applicable securities rules and regulations of the SEC, exchanges and SROs.

support A term used in technical analysis to describe the bottom of a stock's trading range.

switching The act of closing or offsetting a position that specifies one delivery (futures) or expiration (options) month and opening a po-

sition for the same commodity or security in another, more distant month. (*Syn.* rolling forward)

syndicate A group of broker-dealers formed to handle the distribution and sale of an issuer's security. The typical syndicate has several firms managing the underwriting effort. Each member of the syndicate is then assigned responsibility for the sale and distribution of a portion of the issue. *See also* Eastern account, Western account.

systematic risk The risk inherent in all securities of the same type (commodities, stocks, bonds, etc.) that cannot be eliminated through diversification or similar strategies. *See also* market risk.

takedown The discount at which a syndicate member buys securities from the syndicate. *See also* concession.

TAN *See* tax anticipation note.

Tape *See* Consolidated Tape.

taxability The risk of the erosion of investment income through taxation.

tax and revenue anticipation note (TRAN) A short-term municipal debt security.

tax anticipation note (TAN) A short-term municipal debt security to be paid off from tax revenues.

tax swap *See* bond swap.

T call *See* margin call.

technical analysis A method of securities analysis that analyzes statistics generated by market activity, such as past prices and volume. Technical analysis does not attempt to measure a security's intrinsic value.

tenants in common *See* joint tenants in common (JTIC).

tender bond *See* put bond.

tender offer An offer to buy securities for cash or for cash and securities.

term bond *See* term maturity.

term maturity A type of maturity in which the entire bond issue matures on a single date. *See also* maturity date. (*Syn.* term bond)

testamentary trustee A person authorized to administer a trust, including brokerage accounts, created by a decedent. The authority of the testamentary trustee is created by the last will of the decedent who created the trust.

third market The trading of listed securities in the over-the-counter market. Institutional investors are the primary users of the third market.

time loan A collateral loan of a brokerage firm that matures on a date agreed upon by the lender and the borrower and has a constant interest rate for the duration of the contract. *See also* broker's loan.

time spread A spread that involves different expiration dates but the same exercise price. (*Syn.* calendar spread, horizontal spread)

time value A term that refers to any current market value of an option above and beyond its intrinsic value. *See also* intrinsic value.

tombstone An advertisement that announces a securities offering and identifies the name of the issuer, the type of security, the underwriters and where additional information is available.

total outstanding units All units issued at or before the closing date.

trade comparison The memorandum or ticket exchanged by the two broker-dealers engaged in a trade. It is used to compare and confirm the details of the transaction.

trade confirmation A bill or comparison of a trade that is sent to a customer on or before the first day of business following the trade date.

trade date The date on which a transaction occurs.

trading authorization *See* full trading authorization, limited trading authorization.

TRAN *See* tax and revenue anticipation note.

transfer agent A person or an organization responsible for recording the names of registered stockholders and the number of shares owned, seeing that the certificates are signed by the appropriate corporate officers, affixing the corporate seal and delivering the securities to the transferee.

Treasury bill A marketable, short-term (90 days to one year) U.S. government debt security issued through a competitive bidding process at a discount from par value. There is no fixed interest rate.

Treasury bond A marketable, long-term (10 to 30 years), fixed-interest U.S. government debt security.

Treasury note A marketable, medium-term (one to ten years), fixed-interest U.S. government debt security.

treasury stock Common stock that has been issued and reacquired (purchased) by the cor-

poration from the public at the current market price.

trendline The line that traces a stock's movement by connecting the reaction lows in an upward trend or the rally highs in a downward trend.

triangle A pattern on a chart that shows a narrowing of the price range in which a security is trading. The left side of the triangle typically shows the widest range, and the right side narrows to a point.

trust agreement *See* trust indenture.

trustee of a living trust A person who administers a trust, including brokerage accounts, created by a living person. The authority is created by a trust agreement, not a will.

trust indenture The written agreement between a corporation and its creditors that details the terms of the debt issue. These terms include such things as the rate of interest, the maturity date, the means of payment and the collateral. (*Syn.* deed of trust, trust agreement)

Trust Indenture, Act of 1939 The legislation requiring that all publicly offered, nonexempt debt securities be registered under the Securities Act of 1933 and issued under a trust indenture.

Trust in Securities Act Another name for the Securities Act of 1933.

12b-1 asset-based fees Under Section 12b-1 of the Investment Company Act of 1940, a company may collect a fee for the promotion, sale or other activity connected with the distribution of its shares, determined annually as a flat dollar amount or as a percentage of the company's average total net asset value during the year. There are certain requirements:

- The percentage of net assets charged must be reasonable (typically 1/2 to 1% of net assets managed), and the annual fee cannot exceed 8.5% of the offering price on a per-share basis.
- The fee must reflect the anticipated level of distribution services.
- The payments must represent charges that would have been paid to a third party (an underwriter) had sales charges been negotiated for services involving sales promotion, services and related activities.

two-dollar broker A member of an exchange who freelances by executing orders for various member firms when their own floor brokers are especially busy. The broker charges a commission for her services. The amount of the commission is negotiated.

type A term that refers to whether an option is a put or a call option. *See also* class, series.

UGMA *See* Uniform Gifts to Minors Act.

UIT *See* unit investment trust.

uncovered call (put) writer An investor who writes a call (or put) without owning the underlying security or some equivalent security. (*Syn.* naked call, put, writer)

underlying securities The futures or securities that are bought or sold when an option is exercised or those on which an option is based.

underwriter The entity responsible for marketing stocks, bonds, mutual fund shares and so on.

underwriting The procedure by which investment bankers channel investment capital from investors to corporations and municipalities.

underwriting compensation The sales charge paid to a broker-dealer firm for its involvement in selling and offering securities.

underwriting discount *See* underwriting spread.

underwriting manager The brokerage firm responsible for organizing a syndicate, preparing the issue, negotiating with the issuer and underwriters and allocating stock to the selling group. (*Syn.* manager, manager of the syndicate, managing underwriter)

underwriting spread The difference between the public offering price and the price the underwriter pays to the issuing corporation. (*Syn.* underwriting discount)

underwriting syndicate A group of brokerage firms that agree in writing to cooperate in a joint venture to distribute a particular offering of securities. (*Syn.* syndicate)

undivided account *See* Eastern account.

unearned income The income that is derived from investments and other sources not related to personal services (e.g., interest from a savings account, bond interest and dividends from stock). *See also* earned income. (*Syn.* passive income)

Uniform Gifts to Minors Act (UGMA) The act that permits gifts of money and securities to be given to minors and allows adults to act as custodians for minors.

Uniform Practice Code The NASD code that governs and makes uniform a firm's dealings with other brokerage firms.

Unit A capital contribution to a partnership entitling the holder of the unit to an interests in the net income, net loss and distributions of the partnership, without regard to capital accounts.

unit investment trust (UIT) An investment company that has its own portfolio of securities in which it invests. It sells interests in this portfolio in the form of redeemable securities. UITs can be of two types: fixed (no portfolio changes are made) and nonfixed (portfolio changes are permissible). Unit investment trusts are organized under a trust indenture, not a corporate charter.

unqualified legal opinion A legal opinion of a security given without condition.

unregistered secondary distribution *See* spot secondary distribution.

unsecured bond *See* debenture.

unspecified property program *See* blind pool.

up tick rule *See* plus tick rule.

variable annuity A variable annuity is one form of annuity issued by life insurance companies. Like fixed annuities, variable annuities guarantee payment for life once the contract is annuitized, and the issuing insurance company accepts the mortality risk for the client. However, unlike fixed annuities, the variable annuity contract does not guarantee the amount of the annuity payment or performance of the account. The annuitant accepts the investment risk, not the company. *See also* annuity.

variable death benefit The amount of the death benefit (other than incidental insurance benefits, payable under a variable life insurance policy) dependent on the investment performance of the separate account, which the insurer would have to pay in the absence of the minimum death benefit.

variable life insurance policy Any individual policy that provides for life insurance, the amount or duration of which varies according to the investment experience of any separate account established and maintained by the insurer as to such policy.

variable ratio plan A defensive policy plan in which the investor makes purchases and sales on the theory that the higher the stock prices are, the riskier they are, whereas bond prices tend to be more stable. Therefore, the ratio of stocks to bonds decreases as the market rises and increases as the market falls.

vertical spread *See* price spread.

visible supply 1) The disclosure of all municipal securities known to be coming to market within the next 30 days that is published in *The Bond Buyer*. 2) All supplies of a commodity in licensed warehouses.

volatility The speed with which and extent to which the price of a security or commodity rises and falls within a given period of time.

volume of trading theory A technical theory that tries to confirm a strong or weak market by measuring the volume of trading.

voluntary accumulation plan A plan under which the client opens an account and voluntarily commits to additional periodic investments.

voting trust The transfer of common stock voting power to a trustee.

voting trust certificate A certificate evidencing the transfer of shares into a voting trust. The certificate does not carry the right to vote the shares.

warrant A security giving the holder the right to purchase securities at a stipulated price. This is usually a long-term instrument, affording the investor the option of buying shares at a later date at the subscription price, subject to the warrant's exercise.

wash sale The purchase of the same (or a substantially identical) security within 30 days before or after the sale establishing the loss. The claimed loss will be disallowed.

weakening basis A widening of the spread between the cash (spot) price and the futures price of a commodity.

Western account An arrangement under which syndicate members and dealers are liable only for the sale of securities allocated to them. *See also* Eastern account. (*Syn.* divided account)

when issued contract A settlement contract that calls for delivery on a day set by the NYSE (for securities listed on the NYSE), based on when the issuing corporation will have the physical certificates available for distribution. For unlisted securities, the NASD sets the delivery date.

when issued security (WI) A security offered for sale in advance of the issuance of the security by the issuer.

White's Tax-Exempt Bond Rating Service A rating service that is no longer in existence; it rated tax-exempt (municipal) debt based on the issue's marketability rather than the creditworthiness of the issuer.

wholesale transaction A trade in which a broker-dealer buys an over-the-counter stock from another broker-dealer. *See also* retail transaction.

WI *See* when issued security.

wire house *See* commission house.

withdrawal plan A plan allowing a client to request the systematic withdrawal of her account periodically. Withdrawals may be based on a fixed dollar amount, fixed number of shares, fixed percentage or fixed period of time. The plan is normally a free service offered by a mutual fund.

working capital ratio *See* current ratio.

working interest An operating interest entitling the holder to a share of production under an oil and gas lease and carrying with it the obligation to bear a corresponding share of all costs associated with the production of income.

workout quote A type of subject quotation in which a brokerage firm estimates the price that it thinks it can get if given reasonable time to enter the market and to find the stock to buy or sell.

writer The seller of an option. (*Syn.* guarantor, seller)

Yellow Sheets Pages that the National Quotation Bureau publishes daily and that contain wholesale quotations of dealers for corporate bonds.

yield The rate of return on an investment, generally expressed as a percentage of the current price. *See also* coupon yield, yield to maturity. (*Syn.* current yield, dividend yield)

yield curve The graphic representation of actual or projected yields of fixed-income securities.

yield to call (YTC) The rate of return on an investment that accounts for the cash difference between a bond's acquisition cost and its proceeds, as well as interest income calculated to the earliest date that the bonds may be called in by the issuing corporation.

yield to maturity (YTM) The rate of return on an investment that accounts for the cash difference between a bond's acquisition cost and its maturity proceeds, as well as interest received from owning the bond.

YTC *See* yield to call.

YTM *See* yield to maturity.

zero-coupon bond *See* original issue discount, strip bond.

zero-minus tick A sale made at a price equal to the price of the last sale but lower than the last different price.

zero-plus tick A sale made at a price equal to the price of the last sale but higher than the last different price.

Index

Notes

Notes